RELIGIOUS TOURISM AND PILGRIMAGE FESTIVALS MANAGEMENT

An International Perspective

RELIGIOUS TOURISM AND PILGRIMAGE FESTIVALS MANAGEMENT

An International Perspective

Edited by

Razaq Raj

and

Nigel D. Morpeth

Leeds Metropolitan University

www.cabi.org

CABI is a trading name of CAB International

CABI Head Office
Nosworthy Way
Wallingford
Oxfordshire OX10 8DE
UK

Tel: +44 (0)1491 832111
Fax: +44 (0)1491 833508
E-mail: cabi@cabi.org
Website: www.cabi.org

CABI North American Office
875 Massachusetts Avenue
7th Floor
Cambridge, MA 02139
USA

Tel: +1 617 395 4056
Fax: +1 617 354 6875
E-mail: cabi-nao@cabi.org

Library of Congress Cataloging-in-Publication Data
Religious tourism and pilgrimage festivals management : an international perspective / [edited by] Razaq Raj and Nigel D. Morpeth.
    p. cm.
  Includes bibliographical references and index.
  ISBN-13: 978-1-84593-225-1 (alk. paper)
  ISBN-10: 1-84593-225-0 (alk. paper)
1. Pilgrims and pilgrimages.   2. Tourism--Religious aspects.   3. Tourism--Management.   I. Raj, Razaq.   II. Morpeth, Nigel D.   III. Title.
  BL619.P5R45 2007
  203'.51--dc22

2006032416

ISBN: 978 1 84593 225 1

Typeset by Columns Design Ltd, Reading, UK
Printed and bound in the UK by Biddles Ltd, King's Lynn

Contents

Contributors   vii

**1   Introduction: Establishing Linkages between Religious Travel
       and Tourism**   1
       Razaq Raj and Nigel D. Morpeth

**2   The Globalization of Pilgrimage Tourism? Some Thoughts
       from Ireland**   15
       Kevin A. Griffin

**3   Motivations for Religious Tourism, Pilgrimage, Festivals and
       Events**   35
       Ruth Blackwell

**4   The Management and Marketing of Religious Sites,
       Pilgrimage and Religious Events: Challenges for Roman
       Catholic Pilgrimages in Croatia**   48
       Jurica Pavicic, Nikisa Alfirevic and Vincent John Batarelo

**5   Sustaining Tourism Infrastructures for Religious Tourists and
       Pilgrims within the UK**   64
       Ian D. Rotherham

6   Sacred Pilgrimage and Tourism as Secular Pilgrimage   78
       Vitor Ambrósio

7   Religion, Pilgrimage, Mobility and Immobility   89
       Alexandra Arellano

8   **Religious Tourism and Cultural Pilgrimage: a Chinese
     Perspective**   98
     Zhang Mu, Huang Li, Wang Jian-hong, Liu Ji, Jie Yan-geng and Lai Xiting

9   **Centring the Visitor: Promoting a Sense of Spirituality in the
     Caribbean**   113
     Jacqueline Mulligan

10   **Case Study 1: The Festival of Sacrifice and Travellers to the
     City of Heaven (Makkah)**   127
     Razaq Raj

11   **Case Study 2: Christian/Catholic Pilgrimage – Studies and
     Analyses**   140
     Vitor Ambrósio and Margarida Pereira

12   **Case Study 3: Ancient and Modern Pilgrimage: El Camino
     Frances**   153
     Nigel D. Morpeth

13   **Case Study 4: The Symbolic Representation of Religion,
     Culture and Heritage and their Implications on the Tourism
     Experience. The Example of the 'Ciudad de Cultura' in
     Santiago de Compostela**   161
     Martin Scheer

14   **Case Study 5: The Importance and the Role of Faith (Religious)
     Tourism in the Alternative Tourism Resources in Turkey**   170
     Ahmet Aktas and Yakin Ekin

15   **Case Study 6: Visiting Sacred Sites in India: Religious Tourism
     or Pilgrimage?**   184
     Kiran A. Shinde

16   **Case Study 7: Islamic Pilgrimage and the Market Need for
     Travel Insurance**   198
     Tahir Rashid

17   **Case Study 8: Fátima – the Religious Tourism Altar**   211
     Maria I.R.B. de Pinho and Isabel M.R.T. de Pinho

Index   222

Contributors

Nikisa Alfirevic, *Assistant Professor, Department of Management, Faculty of Economics, University of Split, Matice hrvatske 31, 21000 Split, Croatia; telephone: +385 21 430 657; fax: +385 21 430 700; e-mails: nalf@efst.hr or nalf@nalf.net*

Ahmed Aktas, *Professor, Akdeniz University School of Tourism and Hotel Management, Antalya, Turkey; e-mail: aktas@akdeniz.edu.tr*

Vitor Ambrósio, *Escola Superior de Hotelaria e Turismo do Estoril, Estoril, Potrtugal; e-mail vitor@ambrosio@eshte.pt*

Alexandra Arellano, *Assistant Professor, School of Human Kinetics (Leisure Studies), Montpetit Hall, University of Ottawa, 125 University Street, Ontario , Canada, K1N 6N5; telephone: +1 613 5625800 (ext. 2441); e-mail:* alexa37@hotmail.com *(temporary e-mail)*

Vincent John Batarelo, *Deputy CEO, Caritas Croatia, Kaptol 26, 10000 Zagreb, Croatia; telephone: +385 21 481 2022; fax: +385 21 481 2103: e-mail: v.bartelo@zg.t-com.hr*

Ruth Blackwell, *Senior Lecturer, Centre for Event Management, Tourism, Hospitality and Events School, Leeds Metropolitan University, Civic Quarter, Leeds, LS1 3HE, UK; telephone: +44 (0)113 283 3483*

Yakin Ekin, *Research Assistant, Akdeniz University School of Tourism and Hotel Management, Antalya, Turkey; e-mail: yakin@akdeniz.edu.tr*

Kevin A. Griffin, *School of Hospitality Management and Tourism, Dublin Institute of Technology, Cathal Brugha Street, Dublin, Ireland; telephone: +353 1 4027593; e-mail: kevin.griffin@dit.ie*

Liu Ji, *Department of Tourism Management, Shenzhen Tourism College of Jinan University, Shenzhen 518053, Guangdong, P.R. China; e-mail: szzm2005@hotmail.com*

Wang Jian-hong, *Department of Tourism Management, Shenzhen Tourism College of Jinan University, Shenzhen 518053, Guangdong, P.R. China; e-mail: szzm2005@hotmail.com*

Huang Li, *Department of Tourism Management, Shenzhen Tourism College of Jinan University, Shenzhen 518053, Guangdong, P.R. China; e-mail: szzm2005@ hotmail.com*

Nigel D. Morpeth, *Senior Lecturer, Tourism, Hospitality and Events School, Leeds Metropolitan University, Civic Quarter, Leeds, LS1 3HE, UK; telephone: +44 (0)113 283 2600 (ext. 5496); fax: +44 (0)113 283 3111; e-mail: n.morpeth@leedsmet.ac.uk*

Zhang Mu, *Department of Tourism Management, Shenzhen Tourism College of Jinan University, Shenzhen 518053, Guangdong, P.R. China; e-mail: szzm2005@ hotmail.com*

Jacqueline Mulligan, *Senior Lecturer, UK Centre for Events Management, Tourism, Hospitality and Events School, Leeds Metropolitan University, Civic Quarter, Leeds, LS1 3HE, UK; telephone: +44 (0)113 283 3487; fax: +44 (0)113 283 3111; e-mail: j.mulligan@leedsmet.ac.uk*

Jurica Pavicic, *Associate Professor, Marketing Department, Graduate School of Economics and Business, University of Zagreb, Kennedyjev trg 6, 10000 Zagreb, Croatia; telephone: +385 1 2383 33; fax: +385 1 2335 5633; e-mail: jpavicic@efzg.hr*

Margarita Pereira, *e-Geo (Centro de Estudos de Geografia e Planeamento Regional Faculdade de Ciêncas Sociais e Humanas), Universidade Nova de Lisboa, Lisbon, Portugal; e-mail: ma.pereira@fcsh.unl.pt*

Isabel Maria Ribeiro Tavares de Pinho, *Departamento de Artes e Motricidade Humana da ESE, Instituto Politécnico do Porto, Rua do Dr Roberto Frias, 4200-465 Porto, Portugal; e-mail: i.r.t.p@mail.pt*

Maria Inês Ribeiro Basílio de Pinho, *Departamento de Artes e Motricidade Humana da ESE – Instituto Politécnico do Porto, 4200-465 Porto, Portugal; e-mail: inespinho@ese.ipp.pt*

Razaq Raj, *Senior Lecturer, Director of Events Management, Tourism, Hospitality and Events School, Leeds Metropolitan University, Civic Quarter, Leeds, LS1 3HE, UK; telephone: +44 (0)113 283 2600 (ext. 5877); fax: +44 (0)113 283 3111; e-mail: r.raj@leedsmwet.ac.uk*

Tahir Rashid, *Senior Lecturer, Tourism, Hospitality and Events School, Leeds Metropolitan University, Civic Quarter, Leeds, LS1 3HE, UK telephone: +44 (0)113 283 3466; fax: +44 (0)113 283 3111; e-mail: t.rashid@ leedsmet.ac.uk*

Ian D. Rotherham, *Reader, Tourism Leisure and Environmental Change Research Unit, Sheffield Hallam University, Sheffield, UK; telephone: +44 (0)114 225 2874; mobile: 07751 089499; e-mail: i.d.rotherham@shu.ac.uk*

Martin Scheer, *Department of Tourism and Event Management, ISM (International School of Management), Otto-Hahn-Str. 19, 44227 Dortmund, Germany; e-mail: scheer72@gmx.de*

Kiran A. Shinde, *School of Geography and Environmental Science, Monash University, Building 11, Clayton Campus, Wellington Road, Clayton, Victoria-3800, Australia; telephone: +61 3 9905 2953/+61 3 9905 1019; fax: +61 3 9905 2948; e -mail: kiran.shinde@arts.monash.edu.au*

Lai Xiting, *Department of Tourism Management, Shenzhen Tourism College of Jinan University, Shenzhen 518053, Guangdong, P.R. China; e-mail: szzm2005@ hotmail.com*

Jie Yan-geng, *Department of Tourism Management, Shenzhen Tourism College of Jinan University, Shenzhen: 518053, Guangdong, P.R. China; e-mail: szzm2005 @hotmil.com*

1 Introduction: Establishing Linkages between Religious Travel and Tourism

RAZAQ RAJ* AND NIGEL D. MORPETH**

*Tourism, Hospitality and Events School, Leeds Metropolitan University, Leeds, UK; e-mail: *r.raj@leedsmet.ac.uk; **n.morpeth@leedsmet.ac.uk*

Within ever-changing global political landscapes, religion has retained a significant place as a social movement, with a complexity of structures and functions that pervades cultures and traditions. It is clear that whilst there is no single or simple definition of the complex concept of religion, it is a system of recognizable beliefs and practices that acknowledge the existence of a 'superhuman' power that enables people to both address and transcend the problems of life (Hinnells, 184, p. 270).

This book is a timely reassessment of the increasing linkages and interconnections between shared sacred and secular spaces on a global stage, and explores key learning points from a range of contemporary case studies of religious and pilgrimage activity related to ancient, sacred and emerging tourist destinations and new forms of pilgrimage, faith systems and quasi-religious activities.

This book is an eclectic collection of case study-based chapters in which authors express personal, theoretical and empirical research insights on pilgrimage, religion and tourism from a range of authors, most notably members of the ATLAS Religious Tourism and Pilgrimage Special Interest Group. Therefore, a key strength of this book is the presentation of current and *diverse* empirical research insights on aspects of religious tourism and pilgrimage. The book is designed to present the reader with both common and disparate elements of these phenomena, reflecting the powerful unifying and contradictory elements of this field of study.

This opening chapter initially explores the complex nature of the concepts of religion and tourism and the interaction between the two concepts. The exploration of the emerging experience economy has implications for how an expanding symbolic economy has the capacity to change the expressions of religious tourism and pilgrimage. The final part of this chapter highlights the key elements of contributing authors.

Religion

Religion is an age-old and dynamic concept embracing ancient, living (including traditional, living religions of primal societies) faiths and the emergence of new religious and quasi-religious movements (also recognized as secular alternatives to religion). Whilst there are common elements to the concept of religion that include transcendent deities, heavenly beings, demons and divinations, there are defining elements that characterize distinct religious movements.

Furthermore, in articulating the Western conceptualization of non-Western religions, Hinnells (1984) cautions against the potential distortion of non-Western religious concepts, in particular highlighting the fact that cultures such as the Aborigines of Australia and Amerindians have one of the oldest living religions that have been subsumed and influenced by Western religious narratives. Hinnells (1984) also demonstrates the challenge of giving adequate coverage to the full spectrum of ancient religions and living and quasi-religions, and that the emphasis might stray towards certain major religions to the exclusion of others.

Sherratt and Hawkins (1972) recognize that there is a balance to achieve between definitions of religion being too narrow and restrictive, and yet too general and broad. With these considerations in mind, they consider the defining elements of religion to include some belief in a supernatural being (beings) who is (are) 'usually worshipped or venerated because they are transcendental or powerful' (Sherratt and Hawkins, 1972, p. 245) and that 'primarily it is a state of mind which motivates action and belief [which have] a ritual and emotional element' (Sherratt and Hawkins, 1972, p. 245).

These authors acknowledge that these definitional elements are not a catch-all for every religion (see, for example, Theravada Buddhism), but their definition has common definitional elements encapsulated in Campbell's comprehensive definition of religion being: 'a state of mind, comprising belief in the reality of a supernatural being or beings, endued with transcendent power and worth, together with the complex emotive attitudes of worship intrinsically appropriate thereto' (Campbell, 1957, p. 248).

These complex emotive attitudes of worship in the Christian tradition (which can also be applied to other religions) are highlighted by Hinnells (1984, p. 47) as being expressed by five 'arguments for the existence of God' based on an ontological, cosmological, teleological, moral and experiential argument. Existentialist philosophical doctrines challenge what they perceive to be the dogmatic restrictiveness of organized religion, with quasi-religious movements such as dialectical materialism underpinning Marxism, offer competing narratives to dominant religious world-views (Hinnells, 1984, p. 108).

Consistent with this view, Rosenau highlights that 'Non-institutional religion, new spirituality, is a central focus [which] is offered as an alternative to modern, organized mainstream [religions]' (Rosenau, 1992, p. 149). Within forms of non-institutional religion are included New Age postmodernists who, in rejecting the rigidity of institutionalized religion, embrace the 'mystical and the magical' (Rosenau, 1992, p. 152). This diversity of interpretation as to the changing nature of religion is addressed within this text.

The study of religion encompasses a diverse range of academic disciplines that, traditionally, have attracted the attention of historians, orientalists, classicists, archaeologists, sociologists, anthropologists, linguistics, art historians, philosophers and theologians (Hinnells, 1984). Increasingly, the study of religion is combined with other emerging academic disciplines to express new insights into the significance of religion within the contemporary sociocultural milieu.

Sociological discourses include functionalists' perspectives applied to the study of the science of religion, with a sense that this functionality creates societal solidarity (Hinnells, 1984, p. 128). A postmodern discourse of religion would not position the concept within one academic discipline, and would 'question any possibility of rigid disciplinary boundaries' (Rosenau, 1992, p. 6). Within religionswissenschaft (the science of Religion) is a group of disciplines that include the phenomenology of Religion, which includes a classification of ideas, actions and symbols; this is a study or method of describing and gaining empathetic understanding of religious phenomena without offering explanation of truth or falsity of religious beliefs (Hinnells, 1984, p. 250). This is contrasted with theological discourses of belief systems, 'revealed truths' and different theologies, which also include the emergence of the 'death of God' theologies (influenced by Nietzche) that challenge the utility of the 'language of God' for modern, secular man.

The study of world religions requires an understanding of a diverse collection of practices, rituals and ideas that articulate 'professions' of faith and, to paraphrase, Sherratt and Hawkins (1972), the intellectualization of professions of faith is more than an understanding of 'abstract philosophical notions'. Their historical categorization of religion traces the origins of world religions to the emergence of rudimentary religion in which ancient and (primal societies) primitive man's profession of faith is linked to animism (which they view as belonging to the same epoch as that of the early evolution of man) and the notion that living things are animated by spirits distinct from living human beings (Sherratt and Hawkins, 1972, p. 10).

They argued that not only is 'Animism without scriptures an oral tradition' but that 'Religion is more concerned with unseen forces but, like magic, it deals with an area which cannot be manipulated by ordinary methods. Magic and religion have become intermeshed' (Sherratt and Hawkins, 1972, pp. 10–11). Animism's link to the emergence of more mainstream religions has a common characteristic in the notion of 'soul survival' beyond human death.

In cataloguing the emergence in the Near East and West of the religions of Judaism, Christianity and Islam, Sherratt and Hawkins (1972) described the association of these religions with the worship of a God with polytheist beliefs in many gods and monotheist belief in one God. The major religions of India and Southern Asia are Hinduism, Buddhism, Zoroastrianism and Sikhism, and the religions of the Far East are of Confucius, Taoism, Shinto and Mahayana Buddhism. Sherratt and Hawkins (1972) highlighted the emergence of religious sects – including Jehovah's Witnesses and Mormons – in the 19th century.

These authors' categorizations of religions include: (i) *theistic religions*, which cover religions of the Near East and the West 'where the object of ultimate concern is a transcendental being, e.g. Islam, Christianity and Judaism' (Sherratt and Hawkins, 1972, p. 246); and (ii) *non-theistic religions* of India and Southern Asia, 'where the object of ultimate concern is an all-pervading power or "higher principle"'. They also argued that movements such as Communism – which has ritual elements and characteristics of other religions – form part of a categorization of *secular or quasi-religions* (Sherratt and Hawkins, 1972, p. 248). Tourism can claim to be a major area of academic study (Hall, 2005), with important linkages to the study of religion.

The Phenomenon of Tourism and the Consequences of Tourism Growth

There are inherent complexities within the phenomenon of tourism which, because of its 'conceptual weakness and fuzziness' and the multi-faceted and multi-dimensional phenomenon of tourism (Cooper *et al.*, 1993, p. 4). It has unclear origins, variously associated with religious pilgrimages, the 'Grand Tour' and various other significant movements of people from their usual place of residence to some other destination (Lavery, 1987; Holloway, 1989; Towner, 1994).

Burns and Holden (1995) described tourism as both 'enigmatic and bizarre, enigmatic in as much as there remain aspects of it difficult to define, and bizarre in that it sets out to make theoretical sense of people having fun' (Burns and Holden, 1995, p. 1). Mill and Morrison's view that: 'Tourism is a difficult phenomenon to describe, all tourism involves travel, yet all travel is not tourism' (Mill and Morrison, 1985, p. xvii). Burkhart and Medlik concur with Mill and Morrison's definition of tourism, adding that 'much of this movement is international in character and much of it is a leisure activity' (Burkhart and Medlik, 1981, p. v).

Apposite to the analysis of Arellano and Mulligan (Chapters 7 and 8, this volume, respectively), Krippendorf (1987) viewed the obsession with travel as a feature of postmodern societies, which is consistent with Urry's view that 'People are much of the time tourists whether they like it or not' (Urry, 1990, p. 82).

Tourism as a global industry is a generator of large numbers of international arrivals, with 600 million recorded in 2000, and with prospects of international arrivals rising to 937 million by the year 2010 (WTO, 1996; Brown, 1998), However, despite its susceptibility to global acts of terrorism and war, it continues to be viewed as a growth industry. The ubiquitous nature of tourism as a global phenomenon is not without its problems, with Krippendorf identifying that the 1960s signalled the 'beginning of universal and unrestrained tourism development euphoria' (Krippendorf, 1987, p. 68).

Turner and Ash (1975) recognized that the early global growth of tourism's celebrated economic benefits also created unwelcome sociocultural and environmental problems. Mathieson and Wall (1982), in their analysis of the impacts of tourism, positioned the tourism industry as a powerful agent globally for economic growth in both developing and developed countries but with associated negative environmental and sociocultural externalities.

Burns and Holden recognized that: 'What started as pilgrimage, as education for elite, or amusement for the masses has been transferred into a global consumer product in much the same way that Pepsi-Cola, Benetton, McDonalds, etc. have all become a standardized, rationalized global phenomenon' (Burns and Holden, 1995, p. 9).

In line with its global credentials, Poon (1993, p. 32) recognized the 'Fordist' characteristics of mass tourism as a standardized packaging of tourist products, which are consumed without social, environmental and cultural concerns. Similarly, Shaw and Williams (1994) recognized that mass tourism is: 'now deeply embedded in the organization of life in the more developed world. Over time the objects of what Urry terms the tourism gaze, have changed: winter sports have been added to coastal holidays, and the field of mass tourism has become increasingly internationalized' (Shaw and Williams, 1994, p. 175).

Wheeller (1993) and Towner (1994) offered an opposing view to the vilification of mass tourism and warned against framing it in a negative and oversimplified manner, with the crude caricaturing of tourism as a major environmental predator. Towner in particular viewed this onslaught on mass tourism as an elitist and value-laden response: 'Spas "declined" when the upper classes forsook them for more exclusive destinations, seaside resorts "waned" when their social tone altered. No matter that the actual number of visitors increased; they were the wrong sort of visitors' (Towner, 1994, p. 724).

In addition to 'interactional models' are the 'cognitive–narrative models' of Plog (1974) and Cohen (1979), which explain motivations behind travel; Plog (1974) constructed a 'psychographic continuum' of tourists, containing psychocentrics, mid-centric and allocentric types of travellers.

Allocentrics were viewed as the most adventurous tourists, in search of remote locations, with mid-centrics offering 'limited adventure' and psychocentrics choosing destinations characterized by familiarity and security. Cohen (1979) modified Plog's typology, with the broad categories of 'modern pilgrimage' and tourists in search of 'pleasure'. Indeed, Richards identified that: 'Cultural attractions have become particularly important in this modern form of tourism' (Richards, 2001, p. 3), with ancient pilgrimage routes of the El Camino: the Way of St James to Santiago de Compostela, Spain, becoming part of the EU's expanding cultural itineraries. In citing Urry (1990), Richards (2001, p. 4) suggests that 'tourism is culture'.

The former category of 'interactional models' highlights a spiritual dimension to motivations for tourism, with the second category of tourists seeking diversionary recreational experiences in artificial 'pleasure environments'. Urry (1990) identified the search for artificial pleasure environments as part of the condition of postmodernism and the 'dissolving of the boundaries' (Urry, 1990, p. 82) of cultural forms in society, with tourists engaged in 'pseudo-events and disregarding the "real" world outside' (Urry, 1990, p. 7).

Tourism's reputation as a resource-intensive industry (McKercher, 1993) raises ethical questions about the responsibility of how the tourism industry and tourists interact with host communities and the natural environment. An ethical response to the prudent use of resources for tourism creates a special challenge in the aspiration of achieving intra-generational and intergenerational equity. Prosser (1992, p. 37) considers that holidays are the 'high point of our leisure lives, as we are removed from the norms and structures of everyday life', and that 'one of the central dilemmas of tourism is that, by definition, it is a selfish and self-indulgent experience' (Prosser, 1993).

McKercher speculates that as a resource-dependent and private sector-dominated industry, with investment decisions being based predominantly on profit maximization, that 'Tourism is an industrial activity that exerts a series of impacts that are similar to other industrial activities' (McKercher, 1993, p. 14). Furthermore, as a multifaceted industry, it is difficult to constrain and standardize within a coherent legislative framework or voluntary implementation of a code of ethics. In terms of the 'responsibilities' of tourists, McKercher (1993) views them as consumers, not 'anthropologists', and that essentially tourism is a form of entertainment. Whilst he raises questions of how agencies and organizations might ameliorate and 'manage' the externalities of tourism, he argues that modifications to tourist activity might be dependent on the emergence of new forms of tourism.

In this respect, Palmer (1992) argued that we have an obligation of bequeathing 'an undiminished bank of natural resources' (Palmer, 1992, p. 182) to future generations, as part of a sustainable society. He identified that the bequeathing of resources requires a more cautionary approach to development, with new forms of tourism adopting 'softer development paths' (Jafari, 1989; Poon, 1993).

Burns and Holden (1995) noted that 'These ideas have also increasingly found favour in postmodern societies, in search of the alternative as a means of giving new meaning and values to social order' (Burns and Holden, 1995, p. 208). Consistent with this statement, Urry (1990, p. 13) viewed the search for the 'alternative' as consistent with changes from 'post-Fordist' to more individual patterns of consumption, prompting more specialized purchasing and segmentation of consumer preferences.

In part, Urry viewed the search for new tourist products as disillusionment with mass tourism products and 'contemporary consumerism' (Urry, 1990, p. 13). He argued that an industry had emerged with specialist travel agents catering for a 'discriminatory, independent-minded clientele' (Urry, 1990, p. 96) engaging in 'connoisseur leisure' (Shaw and Williams, 1994, p. 198). Nevertheless, Shaw and Williams identified that 'the essential features of mass tourism – spatial and temporal polarization, dependency and external control and intense environmental pressures – will remain little changed' (Shaw and Williams, 1994, p. 200).

However, Hitchcock (1993) recognized a desire for a move away from uncontrolled and poorly managed tourism towards alternative and appropriate forms of tourism, signalling 'a shift in the centre of gravity of mass tourism' (Hitchcock, 1993, p. 25). He recognized that organizations such as Tourism Concern and The Economical Coalition on Third World Tourism (ECTWT) had lobbied for 'softer forms' of tourism that had replaced exploitative tourism. Hitchcock recognized the potential benefits of alternative tourism 'encouraging people both inside and outside the tourism industry to look more critically and questioningly at how tourism is affecting destinations' (Hitchcock, 1993, p. 26).

The Experience Industry

Boorstin (1964), in lamenting the 'lost art of travel', cited the example of Robert Louis Stevenson's *Travel by Donkey* as a metaphor to contrast the slow and meditative forms of travel with the more rapid travel characterized by air travel, seeing tourism as a 'superficial pursuit of contrived experiences – a collection of pseudo-events' (Richards, 2001, p. 14). The creation of *spectacle* through an array of manufactured tourist attractions is designed to mimic the awe-inspiring nature of religious and holy sites. These tourist attractions create manifestations of pseudo-events, satiating superficial experiences. Richards also cites the work of MacCannnell (1976), who viewed tourist attractions as both 'symbols of modern consciousness' and that 'Sightseeing is therefore a modern ritual', with attractions venerated though 'sight sacralization' (Richards, 2001, p. 15). The parallel is that the 'must-see' attractions replace the 'must-see' religious sites and, in citing the work of Ritzer, tourist attractions have become 'the modern cathedrals of consumption' (Ritzer, 1999, p. 17).

The new means of consumption can be seen as 'cathedrals of consumption' – that is, they have an enchanted, sometimes even sacred, religious character for many people. In order to attract ever-larger numbers of consumers, such cathedrals of consumption need to offer, or at least appear to offer, increasingly magical, fantastic and enchanted settings in which to consume (Ritzer, 1999, p. 8 cited in Richards, 2001, p. 17).

Furthermore, the extension of Richards' thesis is that not only cultural, but also religious, sites are not 'immune from this process' but that attractions take on 'symbolic value and meaning' (Richards, 2001, p. 17). Richards (2001) highlighted the work of Edensor (1998), who differentiated between 'enclavic' spaces such as hotels and attractions, which have dominant discourses controlled by the 'international tourist industry'.

This is contrasted with 'heterogeneous' spaces that are largely unplanned, where 'Tourists become literally "performers", creating experiences for themselves and their fellow visitors to consume' (Richards, 2001, p. 18). In Boorstin's treatise on the inauthentic experiences of modern tourism, there are parallels between the perceived qualities of the traveller from previous centuries and the authentic experience of religious worship. Travel in this different age had associated dangers, was arduous and involved a 'journey into the unknown', qualities associated with religious veneration as part of the act of pilgrimage (Boorstin, 1964, p. 14).

This decline of the traveller and the rise of the tourist (which Boorstin mapped to the mid-19th century) was also, according to Fjagesund and Symes, part of traditional elitist associations with travel, and a throwback to the 'exclusivity of the Grand Tour' (Fjagesund and Symes, 2002, p. 48), articulated through travel literature of the 19th century, most notably in the poems of William Wordsworth. This metamorphosis of the traveller into a tourist also embodies a process of touristification (Picard, 1996) and a sense of the self-identity as to what it means to be a tourist, perhaps redefining what a tourist 'does'.

Richards argued that 'The problems of growing cultural competition between cities have more recently led to a shift from consumption-led to production-led strategies' (Richards, 2001, p. 12) and, central to this thesis, is the fact that that there is increasing festivalization and commodification of destinations and that 'traditional culture is not sufficient – popular culture must be added to the production mix' (Richards, 2001, p. 13). Richards (2001) cited the work of Pine and Gilmore (1999) in suggesting that economies have 'gone through a transition from extracting commodities to making goods, delivering services and currently staging experiences as the primary arena of value creation' (Richards, 2001, p. 55).

The corollary of this thesis is that destinations are marketing themselves as places to visit to consume experiences and to engage in 'enchantment' (Richards, 2001, p. 58), rivalling not only other experience-based economies but also religious-based experiences. Therefore, religion as a tourist experience will increasingly become part of the symbolic economy.

Religion and Tourism

In April 2003, the European Association for Tourism and Leisure Education (ATLAS, 2003) Religious Tourism and Pilgrimage Special Interest Group held their 1st Expert Meeting at Fátima in Portugal, 'one of Europe's foremost apparitional shrines' (ATLAS, 2003, p. 9). A wide range of papers were presented at this meeting, to stimulate discussion and to: (i) consider the research implications of gaining greater understanding of the motivations and needs of visitors at religious sites; (ii) how administrators at religious sites cater for the needs of holidaymakers and pilgrims; and (iii) how '21st century' (New) pilgrims interact with devout pilgrims.

Whilst there was common agreement amongst a number of contributors that the term 'religious space' 'was taken to refer to both the confined space within a shrine, sanctuary, cathedral, etc., as well as the religious space as a pilgrim travels through on his/her pilgrimage' (ATLAS, 2003, p. 175), there emerged an eclectic range of potential areas for future research. This ranged from the need to explore and refine the sacred–profane continuum to the role of guides, interpreters and interpretation at religious sites. In a sense, what emerged was the eclectic nature of the study of religious tourism and pilgrimages, not least because of the complex and changing relationships between visitors and the visited on a global stage; and indeed, on the one hand, a strengthening of religious devotion and on the other the fragmentation of religion into new, quasi-religious and secular movements.

There are a range of historical examples of linkages between religion and travel. Sherratt and Hawkins characterized Islam as a 'vital, vivacious and expanding religion' (Sherratt and Hawkins, 1972, p. 93), in which Muhammed's migration (the *Hijra*) from Mecca to Medina in AD 622 was the genesis of the rapid spread of Islam throughout the world.

Embodied within the five pillars of Islam is the notion of pilgrimage and the obligation that, once in a lifetime, Muslims should undertake the pilgrimage to Mecca ('if able to do so'). Contrasted with this is formation of a Nonconformist church through the emergence of the Methodism in England that saw John

Wesley, its organizer, travelling over 250,000 miles on horseback to preach sermons (Sherrat and Hawkins, 1972). However, what is emerging is a body of academic literature that recognizes a systematization of religion, pilgrimage and tourism.

Nolan and Nolan (1992) described a European religious system as being comprised of religious attractions, pilgrimage shrines (both touristic and non-touristic) and festivals. They highlighted the interaction between 'pious' pilgrims and secular tourists acknowledging that: 'Regardless of their motivations, all visitors to these attractions require some level of services, ranging from providing for the most basic human needs to full commercial development that rivals the most secular resort' (Nolan and Nolan, 1992, p. 69). Nolan and Nolan suggested that: 'At a well-visited shrine, visitors on any given day may represent a gradient from very pious and seriously prayerful, to purely secular and basically uninformed about the religious meaning of the place' (Nolan and Nolan, 1992).

Although visitors representing these extremes usually exhibit different behaviours, there is no dichotomy between pilgrims and tourists: 'Many fall into the range of intermediate categories' (Nolan and Nolan, 1992, p. 69). They suggested that, despite the potential incompatibility of these different visitors, it is possible to manage potential conflicts. These insights are resonated in Chapter 4 of this volume through the work of Pavicic, Alfirevic and Batarelo in exploring practical issues of managing sacred and secular visitation of pilgrimage sites in Croatia.

These potential conflicts have more recently been catalogued by Wall and Mathieson (2006), who, through their historical analysis of linkages between the impacts of tourism on religious centres, cited meetings of the World Council of Churches (1970, cited in Sherratt and Hawkins, 1972) and the Caribbean Ecumenical Consultation for Development (1971, cited in Sherratt and Hawkins, 1972) as early examples of the Church being worried about how tourism, through the growing commercialization of tourism, might have detrimental sociocultural and environmental impacts in religious centres globally.

A third conference, the International Congress on Pastoral Care of Tourism on the Move in 1979, considered practical measures to organize tourism in religious centres: not least, the consideration of how to resource the preservation and conservation of religious buildings and artefacts, viewed as a more complex conundrum of how to retain special or sacred places for religious worship in the face of increasing globalization.

Therefore, whilst Wall and Mathieson acknowledged that: 'Religion has been a powerful force which has long caused people to travel to religious centres in many parts of the world', they recognized that 'There is concern that holy places are being developed for tourism and that this is detracting from the religious significance which has made them famous' (Wall and Mathieson, 2006, p. 251). The change in traditional forms of pilgrimage destinations, with diffusion in spiritual motivation, has seen cathedrals and churches increasingly becoming tourist attractions as well as places of worship.

In terms of the significance of the relationship between religion and tourism, their analysis presents a challenge of what aspects of religion should intersect with tourism as the central articulations of religious tourism and pilgrimage. Authors within this book apply not only strong multidisciplinary insights from tourism, events, economic, sociology, psychology and cultural theory backgrounds, but the diverse educational and academic cultural traditions from both Eastern and Western philosophies applied to discourses on religion, pilgrimage, tourism and events.

Subjects Discussed in this Volume

Undoubtedly, this book has compelling appeal for emerging and growing academic audiences within Asia and South Asia and the Indian subcontinent, as well as for fields of study within the West, which focus on the ever-increasingly important societal narratives of the 'sacred and secular', and the application of these narratives to the activities of tourism and events. Theoretical and empirical perspectives on travel, religion, pilgrimage and the celebration of festivals and events are supported by case studies that express either personal perspective on religious devotion or research insights into the relationships between religion and tourism.

In Chapter 2, Kevin A. Griffin initially considers the problematic of religious and pilgrimage travel as parts of the tourism industry and, within an Irish context, presents patterns and typologies of pilgrimage, ranging from the 'accidental' religious tourist to the pilgrim at the other end of the spectrum who travels for religious and spiritual reasons. He cites the work of the ATLAS Religious Tourism and Pilgrimage Special Interest Group to support insights into the motivation of religious pilgrims in Ireland. His chapter is underpinned by contrasts in the societal trends of increasing secularization, with the decrease in domestic religious travel and a wider discussion of the international consumption trends of globalization and internationalization.

In Chapter 3, Ruth Blackwell reassesses, within a theoretical framework of content theories of motivation, both the historical and contemporary motivations for religious tourism, pilgrimage, festivals and events, recognizing the act of travel as well as the arrival as part of the complex matrix of travel motivators. She introduces discourses on content theories, with process theories highlighting the work of Maslow and Herzberg's 'two-factor theory' to underpin the analysis of motivations for religious tourism and pilgrimage.

In Chapter 4, Jurica Pavicic, Nikisa Alfirevic and Vincent John Batarelo explore the complex challenges facing 'managers' of religious and pilgrimage sites, addressing a combination of sacred and secular motivations for visitation. Practical issues of site management are explored to determine how existing holy places are able to combine different functions successfully. Within this chapter they also explore the multidisciplinary nature of applying sociological and anthropological perspectives to the concept of pilgrimage. There are cross-currents of analysis on the nature of pilgrimage with Arellano (Chapter 7) in terms of pilgrimage having qualities of being 'in and out of time', with pilgrimage as a rite of passage, departing from everyday rituals to return to 'centres of society' 'transformed'.

In Chapter 5, Ian D. Rotherham highlights the range of global religious and ceremonial sites which have been the focus of journeys promoting spiritual well-being, particularly within the English village church location, drawing on additional examples of sacred sites within a UK context. The English village church location is examined as the focus for an emerging tourist economy that can help to sustain an infrastructure for both religious and pilgrimage worship and visitation.

In Chapter 6, Vitor Ambrósio initially focuses on the historical framework of pilgrimage incorporating different phases in the development of pilgrimage, and considers the systemization of religious practice and pilgrimage based on a range of societal factors. The further development of this chapter articulates emic insights into the spiritual fundamentals of pilgrimage, exploring in particular the emotions expressed through Christian pilgrimage viewed as a significant event in a 'believer's life', providing both a cognitive and aesthetic experience. These insights are contrasted with academic discourses on the characteristics of pilgrimage.

In Chapter 7, Alexandra Arellano applies detailed empirical insights on research conducted at Machu Picchu, Peru, exploring the notion of secular pilgrimage to 'power places' such as Machu Picchu and argues that the tourist is in search of a lost immobility, found in the perceived authenticity of the vagabond (the lost Inca, the indigenous people of the Andes). She draws on New Age philosophies of travel and pilgrimage to explore the emergence of New Tourists or 'Esoteric Tourists' able to engage in processes of spiritualization and enlightenment.

In Chapter 8, Zang Mu, Huang Li, Wang Jian-hong, Liu Ji, Jie Yan-geng and Lai Xiting contrast the traditional cultural differences between religious tourism and pilgrimage in western and eastern China and consider the emergence of religious tourism and pilgrimage within these different regions of this vast country. There are parallels with the research insights of both Arellano in Chapter 7 and Mulligan in Chapter 9, in the sense that Chinese pilgrims are in search not only of new forms of pilgrimage, but of revitalizing and spiritualizing experiences as a foil for the pressures of 'everyday life'.

In Chapter 9, Jacqueline Mulligan initially explores contemporary experiences and expressions of new pilgrims engaged in the search for 'selfhood' beyond traditional religious belief systems and, in common with Arellano, analyses the 'New Age' spirituality viewed as 'a fluid phenomenon'. In using the Caribbean ('the Garden of Eden before a fall'), she considers the emergence of an eclectic range of faith systems with quasi-religious characteristics and argues that the lines between culture and religion (as the focus for tourism) have become ever more blurred.

In Chapter 10, Razaq Raj provides insights as to what it means to be a practising Muslim, outlining the main tenets of this system of faith. It is also stated that the *hajj* is considered as the culmination of each Muslim's religious duties and aspiration. It is stated in the Holy Qur'an that every physically and financially able Muslim should make the hajj to the Holy City of Makkah once in his or her lifetime. Furthermore, it is argued that the hajj is not a tourist phenomenon: it is the Islamic faith for Muslims to perform the hajj as stated according to the Holy Qur'an and the Hadiths. This is not like any other pilgrimage in the world, where people visit pilgrim sites as attention of tourism.

In Chapter 11, Vitor Ambrósio and Margarida Pereira express emic insights into Christian and Catholic pilgrimage. They adopt Butler's 'destination life cycle' model (1980) to analyse the development and management of four Catholic international towns in Western Europe. This framework for analysis of Banneux, Knock, Lourdes and Fátima provides insights on the impacts of a range of religious tourists to these destinations.

In Chapter 12, Nigel D. Morpeth considers the significance of how an ancient pilgrims' route is becoming transformed as a focus for both continuing use by 'pious pilgrims' and, increasingly, for secular tourists who are walking, cycling and horse-riding the route whilst engaging with cultural sites and attractions. The policy implications for redeveloping and promoting an ancient route for both sacred and secular uses are explored, not least of these the resolution of potential conflicts. The El Camino Frances, the 709-km pilgrimage route from Ronscevalles in the Spanish Pyrenees to Santiago de Compostela in western Spain, is one of the oldest pilgrimage routes within the Western World and remains a powerful focus for spiritual engagement.

In Chapter 13, Martin Scheer uses the example of the 'Ciudad de Cultura' in Santiago de Compostela to explore the symbolic representation of the integration of religious, cultural and heritage architectural resources as a focus to celebrate local, regional and tourist identities.

In Chapter 14, Ahmed Aktas and Yakin Ekin consider the emergence of faith tourism within the wider context of tourism development within Turkey, arguing that Turkey has a competitive tourist product emerging through the resources of the Peninsula of Anatolio, which houses the sacred sites of Islam, Judaism and Christianity.

In Chapter 15, Kiran A. Shinde highlights how religious tourism in India accounts for 90% of domestic tourism and explores the movement of pilgrims into an organized and formal industry of religious tourism through the study of Vrindavan, a sacred site, visited by more than 3.5 million people in northern India. He argues that pilgrimage tourism is moving towards newer forms of entrepreneurship and management, which are precursors of mass tourism.

In Chapter 16, Tahir Rashid explores the case study of Takaful International, an Islamic insurance company based on the concept of mutual cooperation and solidarity to enable pilgrims travelling to Islamic holy places to do so under Islamic jurisprudence or Sharia guidelines.

In Chapter 17, De Pinho and De Pinho explore the emergence of Fátima, located in central Portugal, as one of Europe's major apparitional shrines. In mapping the development of Fátima as a centre for pilgrimage, they evaluate the challenges of creating the infrastructure for pilgrims.

These chapters connect important insights between religion, pilgrimage and tourism in both Eastern and Western cultural traditions. In particular, the insights on religion and tourism to emerge from authors in different parts of Asia, Southern Asia and the Indian subcontinent, revealing new perspectives on emerging tourist destinations and developments in acts of religious worship, are explained. In this sense, within this book, we argue for a reassessment of analysis underlying religious motivations of travel and a full exploration of the pressures for sacred spaces to become venues for commercialized and festivalized arenas, particularly within the re-emerging and increasingly secularized Western pilgrimage routes and destinations particularly highlighted by Arellano and Mulligan.

The aim of the book is to provide empirical and personal insights into the changing nature of religion in society and to further the debate for both policymakers and academics to consider these policymaking challenges within the future development of faith tourism and pilgrimage.

References

ATLAS (2003) *Religious Tourism and Pilgrimage: Fátima*. Tourism Board of Leiria/Fátima, Portugal.

Boorstin, D. (1964) *From Traveler to Tourist: the Lost Art of Travel, the Image: a Guide to Pseudo Events in America*. Harper and Row, New York, pp. 77–117.

Burns, P. and Holden, A. (1995) *Tourism: Towards the 21st Century*. Prentice-Hall, Hemel Hempstead, UK.

Brown, F. (1998) *Tourism Reassessed: Blight of Blessing?* Butterworth-Heinemann, Oxford, UK.

Burkhart, A. and Medlik, S. (1981) *Tourism: Past, Present and Future*. Butterworth-Heinemann, Oxford, UK.

Butler, R. (1980) The concept of a resort life cycle of evolution: implications for management of resources. *Canadian Geographer* 34 (1), 5–12.

Campbell, C.A. (1957) *On Selfhood and Godhood*. Allen & Unwin, St Leonards, NSW, Australia.

Cohen, E. (1979) Rethinking the sociology of tourism. *Annals of Tourism Research* 6 (1), 18–35.

Cooper, C., Fletcher, J., Gilbert, D. and Wanhill, S. (1993) *Tourism: Principles and Practice*. Pitman, London.

Edensor, T. (1998) *Tourist at the Taj: Performing and Meaning at a Symbolic Site*. Routledge, London.

Fjagesund, P. and Symes, R.A. (2002) *The Northern Utopia: British Perceptions of Norway in the Nineteenth Century*. Rodopi, New York.

Hall, C.M. (2005) *Tourism: Rethinking the Social Science of Mobility*. Pearson Education Limited, Harlow, UK.

Hinnells, J.H. (ed.) (1984) *The Penguin Dictionary of Religions*. Penguin Books Ltd, London.

Hitchcock, M. (ed.) (1993) *Tourism in South East Asia*. Routledge, London.

Holloway, J.C. (1989) *The Business of Tourism*. Pitman, London.

Jafari, J. (1989) Tourism models: the sociocultural aspects. *Tourism Management* 8, 151–159.

Krippendorf, J. (1987) *The Holiday Makers: Understanding the Impact of Leisure and Travel*. Butterworth-Heinemann, New York.

Lavery, P. (1987) *Travel and Tourism*. ELM Publications, Huntingdon, UK.

MacCannell, D. (1976) *The Tourist: a New Theory of the Leisure Class*. Macmillan, London.

Mathieson, P. and Wall, G. (1982) *Tourism: Economic, Social and Physical Impacts*. Longman, London.

McKercher, B. (1993) Some fundamental truths about tourism: understanding tourism's social and environmental impacts. *Journal of Sustainable Tourism* 1, 6–16.

Mill, R. and Morrison, A. (1985) *The Tourism System*. Prentice Hall, Englewood Cliffs, New Jersey.

Nolan, M. and Nolan, S. (1992) Religious sites as tourism attractions in Europe. *Annals of Tourism Research* 19, 1–17.

Palmer, J. (1992) Toward a sustainable future. In: Cooper, D. and Palmer, J. (eds) *The Environment in Question: Ethics and Global Issues.* Routledge, New York and London.

Picard, M. (1996) *Bali: Cultural Tourism and Touristic Culture.* Archipelago Press, Singapore.

Pine, B.J. and Gilmore, J.H. (1999) *The Experience Economy.* Harvard University Press, Boston, Massachusetts.

Plog, S.C. (1974) Why destination areas rise and fall in popularity. *Cornell Hotel and Restaurant Administration Quarterly* 14, 55–58.

Poon, A. (1993) *Tourism, Technology and Competitive Strategies.* CAB International, Wallingford, UK.

Prosser, R. (1992) The ethics of tourism. In: Cooper, D. and Palmer, J. (eds) *The Environment in Question: Ethics and Global Issues.* Routledge, New York and London.

Richards, G. (ed.) (2001) *Cultural Attractions and European Tourism.* CAB International, Wallingford, UK.

Ritzer, G. (1999) *Enchanting a Disenchanted World: Revolutionizing the Means of Consumption.* Pine Forge Press, Thousand Oaks, California.

Rosenau, P.M. (1992) *Post-Modernism and the Social Sciences: Insights, Inroads and Intrusions.* Princeton University Press, Princeton, New Jersey.

Shaw, G. and Williams, A. (1994) *A Critical Issues in Tourism: a Geographical Perspective.* Blackwell, Oxford, UK.

Sherratt, B.W. and Hawkins, D.J. (1972) *Gods And Men.* Blackie, Glasgow, UK.

Towner, J. (1994) Tourism history: past, present and future. In: Seaton, A.V. (ed.) *Tourism: the State of the Art.* Wiley, Chichester, UK.

Turner, L. and Ash, J. (1975) *The Golden Hordes, International Tourism and the Pleasure Periphery.* Constable, London.

Urry, J. (1990) *The Tourist Gaze: Leisure and Travel in Contemporary Societies.* Sage Publications, London and Newbury Park, California.

Wall and Mathieson (2006) *Tourism: Change, Impacts and Opportunities.* Pearson Education Ltd, Harlow, UK.

Wheeller, B. (1993) Egotourism, sustainable tourism and the environment – a symbiotic, symbolic or shambolic relationship? In: Seaton, A.V. (ed.) *Tourism: the State of the Art.* Wiley, Chichester, UK.

WTO (1996) *Yearbook of Tourism Statistics, Vol. 1.* World Tourism Organisation, Geneva, Switzerland.

2 The Globalization of Pilgrimage Tourism? Some Thoughts from Ireland

KEVIN A. GRIFFIN

School of Hospitality Management and Tourism, Dublin Institute of Technology, Dublin, Ireland; e-mail: kevin.griffin@dit.ie

> Whilst in many societies – especially in the developed world – belief in religion has been eroded in the face of growing agnosticism and atheism, religious sites have become an increasingly popular object of the tourist gaze, even if people do not subscribe to the beliefs that such places represent.
>
> (Williams, 1998, p. 166)

Introduction

There are many reasons why people travel, and these motivations have been researched extensively by geographers, sociologists and others, including the business community. The phenomenon of religious tourism – and, more particularly, pilgrimage tourism – while widely recognized has not received much attention in literature. Perhaps the reason for this neglect is the difficulty of classifying this aspect of the tourism industry in a growing secular world, where spiritual meaning is often seen as unfashionable and perhaps even seen as a little 'backward'. Referring to Ireland, this disquiet was captured by Pochin Mould as early as 1955, who commented: 'To write of the Irish pilgrimages is to tread on dangerous ground, it is to attempt to keep a true balance between agnosticism and excessive credulity. It is easy to sneer at somebody else's superstition, and equally easy to fall into a too-sentimental piety.'

In order to avoid these pitfalls, it would appear that the easiest solution for those concerned with examining tourism has been to deal briefly with, or totally avoid, the topic of religious tourism. This is not to say that it has been ignored by all authors (a lengthy and highly useful international bibliography of religious tourism was assembled by the ATLAS Religious Tourism Special Interest Group in 2005, unpublished), but the emphasis in most texts has been on either pilgrimage or tourism and, where both have been considered together, the emphasis would appear to be on descriptive case studies of religious tourism and on religion as being a motivator for early tourism.

In its true sense, pilgrimage is defined as journeying to a sacred place or shrine as a devotee (Park, 1994; Pontifical Council, 1998). However, it must be acknowledged that the identification and examination of this journeying in the overall context of conventional tourism is difficult. This chapter presents some patterns and typologies of pilgrimage tourism in an Irish context: domestic pilgrimage appears to be in decline, while Irish inbound and outbound pilgrimage appears to be experiencing major growth.

Research suggests that the once personal and local practice of visiting a well, shrine or holy place has been gradually superseded in importance by a more public desire to seek distant, national or international wells, shrines or holy places (Sopher, 1967; Murray and Graham, 1997). This public display of pilgrimage is even more interesting when set against the perceived move in Ireland away from religious practice, towards a more secular, affluent and materialistic society.

Thus, the overall pattern of pilgrimage travel in Ireland appears to be following international consumption trends of globalization and internationalization, resulting in newly emerging management issues for those both organizing pilgrimages and maintaining Ireland's holy places. However, there are a number of exceptions to this overall pattern, and they serve to further colour the interesting tapestry of Irish pilgrimage tourism.

Tourism and Globalization

Globalization is a much contested concept that has many meanings, with some critics even debating whether the concept even exists. Globalization is generally identified with a global transformation that has been recognized (though debated by some critics) since the mid-20th century (Claval, 2002). Despite evidence of protectionism, global monopolies, financial regulation, military fragmentation and imperialism throughout the 20th century, there appears to be an emergence of universal trends, including a greater international movement of commodities, money, information and people; and also the increasing development of technology, organizations, legal systems and infrastructures to allow this movement (Wikipedia, 2006). The International Forum on Globalization defines globalization as: 'the present worldwide drive toward a globalized economic system dominated by supranational corporate trade and banking institutions that are not accountable to democratic processes or national governments' (IFG, 2006).

Depending on one's viewpoint, globalization can alternately be seen as a force that has benefited a relatively small number and made life more difficult for most people around the world, or it can be seen as a force that has resulted in a more equalized, fair and just world (Reiser, 2003).

As it was traditionally considered an economic entity characterized by small-scale enterprises, tourism was not initially seen as a causal force of globalization. However, since the 1990s, the growing literature on globalization and tourism argues that tourism must be considered in the context of its contribution to and influence over the global economy (Brown, 1998). Some would claim that tourism is a major player in the trend towards globalization, and others would go further by stating that 'The concept of globalization encompasses tourism' (Reiser, 2003, p. 306).

Much of the recent academic discussion is centred on whether tourism is a positive or negative force in a globalized society, and whether tourism can be used as a force to actively combat global inequalities and poverty (Reid, 2003). This discussion of globalization has led to the emergence of organizations such as The Global Forum, a non-profit organization dedicated to the pursuit of balance between global and local forces in today's world in a process that they define as 'globalization' (CERFE, 2004). Tourism and globalization are thus connected in a variety of ways, as they both deal with the movement of people, ideas and capital across boundaries. In this chapter we focus on the implications of globalization in the context of Irish pilgrimage tourism.

Religious Tourism and Pilgrimage

Something as deeply personal as religious belief is bound to be difficult to define. One can consider the critical views of Freud that religion is 'illusion' or that of Thomas Edison that 'religion is all bunk'. Alternatively, one can accept a less judgemental viewpoint that religion is 'human beings' relation to that which they regard as holy, sacred, spiritual or divine' (*Encyclopaedia Britannica*, 2006).

The present discussion acknowledges, but is not concerned with, the 'accidental' religious tourist who happens on a sacred site: it is concerned primarily with people at the other end of the pilgrimage continuum, who intentionally travel for reasons related to religion or spirituality in their quest for meaning. This is religious tourism, irrespective of the range of motives, destinations and manifestations of their experience. These religious or spiritual travellers are often ignored as a distinct grouping by traditional tourism research, as the quest for what Edison would have considered 'bunk' is, at its very best, a nebulous concept: 'The religious sense is nothing more than man's original nature, by which he fully expresses himself by asking "ultimate" questions, searching for the final meaning of existence in all of its hidden facets and implications' (Giussani, 1997).

Despite such intangibility, pilgrimage has long been an important aspect of the major world religions. Much of the Old Testament is a journey by the Jewish 'chosen people', beginning with their exodus from Egypt, journeying through the desert and entering the Promised Land. Three times a year the Israelites made pilgrimage to the holy city of Jerusalem. Mohamed, inspired by Jewish (and subsequent Christian) pilgrimage, commanded Muslims: 'Accomplish the Pilgrimage and the Experience for God's sake' (Koran, 1996, p. 196). This has resulted in many million Muslims undertaking pilgrimage (which is one of the five pillars of Islam) to Mecca and Madinah every year.

The followers of Hinduism make pilgrimage to the Ganges, the holy river, which cleanses them from sin, Buddhists make pilgrimage to places Buddha consecrated by his life, Shintoists go into deep forests and meditate in silence and

Christians go to the holy places where God revealed Himself or places connected with Jesus Christ and His saints (Rebic, 1999).

At its most basic, pilgrimage can be viewed as any travel that involves a religious experience. In view of the fact that such journeys are obviously a combination of a religious experience and travel, it would be easy to characterize all journeys to religious sites as religious tourism (Davies and Davies, 1982). But definitions of religious tourism based simply on a combination of 'religion' and 'tourism' are of little help in understanding the phenomenon of pilgrimage. In their *Annotated Bibliography on Religious Tourism and Pilgrimage* (2005, unpublished), the ATLAS Religious Tourism and Pilgrimage Special Interest Group suggest that the number of tourists travelling purely for religious reasons is relatively small. They make the distinction that spiritual motivations for engaging in pilgrimage outweigh religious ones. It could be argued however, that this separation of spiritual and religious presupposes that the individual travelling (or even the researcher) has a clear understanding of these differences.

Rather than become distracted by such theological discourse in this chapter, the key focus is a rather narrow one, considering pilgrimage as: 'a religious phenomenon in which an individual – or group sets forth on a journey to a particular cult location to seek the intercession of God and the saints of that place in an array of concerns' (Murray and Graham, 1997, p. 514).

Thus, the chapter includes visitors to sacred sites who partake in some form of external ritual related to the site visited. Notwithstanding this, the author is aware of the importance of the internal journey in pilgrimage, which many writers have alluded to, as in the following, traditional view of pilgrimage, presented by Wiederkehr:

> Pilgrimages have been an important part of religious history throughout the ages. A pilgrimage is a ritual journey with a hallowed purpose. Every step along the way has meaning. The pilgrim knows that the journey will be difficult and that life-giving challenges will emerge. A pilgrimage is not a vacation: it is a transformational journey during which significant change takes place. New insights are given. Deeper understanding is attained. New and old places in the heart are visited. Blessings are received. Healing takes place. On return from the pilgrimage, life is seen with different eyes. Nothing will ever be quite the same again.
>
> (Wiederkehr, 2001, p. 11)

Journeys such as this, related to religious sites and festivals, pilgrimage or spirituality, have long been a feature of human travel.

In the context of inner journeys, the literature often questions narrow definitions whereby pilgrimage tourism can be considered only where travel is for truly spiritual motives. The suggestion that travel can only be pilgrimage when it involves pure, internalized spiritual motives would question whether the 14th century *Canterbury Tales* (see Fig. 2.1) recount a journey of pilgrimage or pleasure. One of the earliest English texts, the *Tales* recounts the story of a group of pilgrims on their way from Southwark to Canterbury to visit the shrine of Saint Thomas à Becket at Canterbury Cathedral. As suggested in the following image, and in the text itself, the tales of the pilgrims include reference to more base desires than simple spiritual well-being. Indeed, some of the *Tales* are of a

Fig. 2.1. The pilgrims in *The Canterbury Tales*: woodcut from Caxton's 1483 2nd edition (from British Library, 2006).

much more earthy nature. Thus, the Canterbury Tales in an interesting manner illustrates a complex matrix of motivations, with interplay between pilgrimage as spiritually motivated and journeying more for pleasure and entertainment.

The importance of 'pure' pilgrimage can be clearly seen in sites such as Lourdes, Mecca and Chiang Mai, but it is not only the key religious sites of major world religions that are important for pilgrimage. Sites ranging from major cathedrals and temples right down to local wells, rocks and trees are considered as destinations for pilgrimage.

In addition, the continuum of religious tourism ranges from pilgrims who are motivated to visit a location entirely for religious purposes to the secular tourist who visits a site irrespective of its religious provenance, perhaps for architectural or historic motives (Cohen, 2001). Though outside the remit of this chapter, authors have questioned whether Graceland in Memphis, USA and burial places of heroes such as Jim Morrison, W.B. Yeats and, more recently, George Best could be considered as sites of pilgrimage. Thus, pilgrimage sites throughout the world vary, but it may be argued that religious sites in many locations provide a foundation for modern tourism.

> [P]erhaps paradoxically, the decline in churchgoing in recent years has been paralleled in many cases by a growing interest in religion and religious travel. The reason for this seems simple: people are searching for meaning in their increasingly uncertain lives. Many people have not been able to find this through traditional forms of worship, so they are now taking to different forms of experience to find it. This includes the rediscovery of pilgrimage or journeys to sacred places.
>
> (ATLAS, 2005, unpublished)

The following sections examine how this search for 'different forms of worship' has been a feature of Irish pilgrimage in recent times, with people travelling overseas to engage in pilgrimage. The work explores whether this change in practice (or perhaps returning to earlier Irish peregrinations) can be considered as an indicative feature of globalization.

Pilgrimage in Ireland

Kathleen Hughes, in a discussion on 'The Changing Theory and Practice of Irish Pilgrimage', recounts the earliest religious peregrinations of the Irish throughout Britain and Europe from the 5th century AD onwards. The missionary zeal of these individuals is remembered to the present day in the dedication of churches to Columba, Moluag, Kilian and Columbanus. Holy Irish travellers such as 6th-century Fursey and Columbanus: 'Though seeking salvation and solitude ... founded a series of monasteries which rapidly became centres of learning, hostels for Irish pilgrims and headquarters of evangelistic effort' (Hughes, 1960, p. 144).

Interestingly, due to their numbers, the Irish at times became unwelcome in Europe. This may be related to the practice of imposing pilgrimage upon a sinner as a form of penance, or the Irish law that allowed a man to escape legal liabilities by setting out on pilgrimage. By the 10th century, however, the focus of Irish pilgrimage had changed and the main emphasis was no longer on the old-style wanderings, but on journeys to famous shrines at home or abroad.

According to Harbison (1991), early documentation of pilgrimage is 'sparse and sporadic', with information being gleaned from tangential references such as records of when and where pilgrims died. One of the earliest accounts of domestic pilgrimage, discussed by Harbison, was a traveller who died at Clonmacnois in the year AD 606. Some of the other early sites mentioned in the records include Glenda Lough (AD 951), Armagh (AD 976), Croagh Patrick (AD 1113) and Lough Derg, County Donegal (AD 1147). Thus, the origins of key sites for modern pilgrimage in Ireland, some dealt with in this chapter, can be traced back to the very early days of Irish Christianity.

By the 19th century, Catholic Irish pilgrimage was almost exclusively domestic, with the more extreme Catholic pilgrimage rituals in Ireland being a form of fascination for the aristocratic Protestants who documented them. The following piece by Dixon Hardy expresses his disquiet at the physical hardship endured by the pilgrims on Holy Island in East Clare:

> It is lamentable to consider the extent to which idolatry, attended by its inseparable concomitants, still prevails in this benighted country ... as regularly as the season of

Whitsuntide comes, here you find a concourse of people assembled to perform penance ... this is performed on the naked knees through a heap of rugged stones; the females tuck up their clothes, and expose their persons in the most indelicate manner. Men of the most dissolute morals go to witness this part of the exhibition, but none can witness the finale without feelings of the greatest horror being excited; when it comes to this, all must (without assistance) descend on the naked knees, a step nearly a foot in depth. This is a most painful operation. The writhing postures, the intense agonies, and the lacerated knees of the votaries are most distressing to the spectators. After the descent they must go on their bleeding knees through the rough stones in the church to the east end, when in a posture of most profound reverence, they kiss a particular stone.

(Dixon Hardy, 1836)

Pilgrimage in modern Ireland

Not quite as arduous as Holy Island, some of the best known pilgrimage sites in Ireland – Lough Derg (St Patrick's Purgatory) in County Donegal and Croagh Patrick in County Mayo – are both physically demanding, while Knock Marian Shrine, also in County Mayo, is gentler yet no less important. Many other ancient pilgrimage sites exist throughout Ireland, such as the monastic city of Glenda Lough in County Wicklow, Clonmacnois in County Offaly and the Skelligs in County Kerry (Harbison, 1970; Alton, 2001). However, since these last three sites are possibly more important in modern times as tourist sites than as pure sites of pilgrimage, the emphasis will remain on the more strictly sacred sites.

Lough Derg

Lough Derg has been a site of pilgrimage at least since the beginning of the second millennium. It is said that Saint Patrick, the Patron Saint of Ireland, fasted and prayed there for 40 days and slew a serpent that lived in the waters of the lake. The classic Lough Derg pilgrimage tales place between June and mid-August every year and lasts for 3 days. The pilgrims begin fasting at midnight on the first day and travel to the island by boat during that morning. Once there they remove all footwear, undertaking the pilgrimage barefoot.

The Religious observances require the pilgrims to undertake a series of 'stations', which are a sequence of prayers and gestures while walking and kneeling. This is all conducted in silence. During the 3 days, the pilgrims complete nine stations around 'beds' dedicated to various saints – Brigid, Brendan, Catherine, Columba, Patrick, Davog and Molaise. These beds are circular structures, which may have been cells or huts built and used by early monks. A further exercise is to undertake an all-night vigil of prayer, repeating the stations, but one does not make up for lost sleep the next day. An additional penance of this pilgrimage is frugal eating and drinking, with a single meal of black tea or coffee and dry toast permitted each day. When pilgrims depart, they commit to continue fasting until midnight that day.

Despite – or perhaps because of – this severity, the Lough Derg experience is valued by many as being a unique religious experience. The following testi-

monial by a pilgrim clearly demonstrates the difference between this experience
and that of tourism:

> When I arrived it was totally different to what I expected. There is a deep sense of
> holiness and peace there. It was wonderful to walk around day and night, in bare
> feet, in silence, praying in the company of so many other people of all ages and from
> all walks of life. The peace and joy remained with me for many days after I arrived
> home. I was kinder, more patient, and gentler than usual. It was as if there was less
> of me and more of God in me.
>
> (Maureen Boyle, personal communication, 2006)

Notwithstanding this deep spiritual reward, numbers visiting Lough Derg
for the 'traditional' 3-day pilgrimage have dropped throughout the late 1980s
and 1990s. This may be linked to the boom of the Irish economy at this time,
and a recognizable decrease in general religious observance. To cater for falling
numbers, the site has adapted its pilgrimage 'product':

> The tradition of the historical three-day pilgrimage has been preserved, but other
> services have been offered in recent years. The introduction of these new services,
> one-day retreats, youth retreats and special group retreats allows people the
> opportunity to experience this sacred place when age or disability might otherwise
> prevent them from participating in the traditional pilgrimage.
>
> (Lough Derg, 2006b)

As can be seen in the following graph (see Fig. 2.2), the provision of
alternative, perhaps 'softer' rituals appears to have halted the decline of this
pilgrimage observed by the Catholic World News:

> Ireland's Catholics seem to be losing interest in the country's toughest pilgrimage.
> Over the last ten years the number of pilgrims visiting St. Patrick's Purgatory on an
> island in Lough Derg, Donegal, has fallen almost by half ... Monsignor Richard
> Mohan, the prior of Lough Derg, said 'people might not be as conscious of
> pilgrimage and prayer as they were ten years ago'.
>
> (CWN, 1997)

The growth in 1-day pilgrimages appears to have somewhat arrested the
decline in numbers at Lough Derg. A further noteworthy development (not

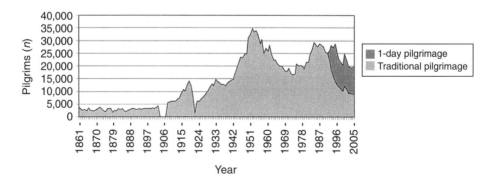

Fig. 2.2. Pilgrimage visitors to Lough Derg, County Donegal, 1861–2005 (data from Lough
Derg Office).

indicated in the chart) is a significant increase in the number of school retreats, with two schools participating in the year 2000 and 20 in 2005 (Maureen Boyle, personal communication, 2006).

Croagh Patrick

Croagh Patrick is a dramatic, conical-shaped mountain that rises out of relatively flat landscape near Westport, County Mayo, in the west of Ireland (see Fig. 2.3). This has been a site of Christian pilgrimage for at least a millennium, and was most likely an important site in pre-Christian times, possibly even as far back as the Neolithic period (Watt, 1995).

While approximately 100,000 people a year visit the site, the main pilgrimage takes place on the last Sunday of July each year. On that day, 20,000–30,000 pilgrims climb 764 metres to the top of this peak, overlooking Clew Bay, for mass. Those who complete this ascent are satisfied that they have undertaken a task for which they will receive spiritual reward: 'It is a mystical place of beauty and peace, where ... the people of Ireland flock and the descendants of emigrants return to kneel together in submission on the cold rock, asking for peace and giving thanks for their freedom' (Rose, undated).

To prepare for this pilgrimage, which is also linked with Saint Patrick, Ireland's national apostle, pilgrims often fast and many undertake the climb barefoot as an act of penance. Penitential exercises such as this have been handed down by many generations. One observer noted:

> [T]he main pilgrimage day sees thousands of visitors coming from all over the world to climb the three-mile long, tortuous path, with the last 500 yards, Casán Phadraig,

Fig. 2.3. Pilgrims on Croagh Patrick, County Mayo (from Smyth, 2006).

being at an angle of almost 45 degrees ... the ever-present danger for the climbers of being flattened by loose, moving stones being dislodged by climbers higher up! ... It is pure Hell! Take my personal, unbiased word for it! ... Until recent years ... the first climbers began the ascent after midnight but some time ago the Archbishop of Tuam [banned] night-time climbing.

(Mayo Gazette, undated)

Knock

From Fátima to Bethlehem and from Lourdes to Kiltimagh
I've never seen a miracle like the airport up in Knock.

(Moore, 1983)

As the presence of an international airport suggests, unlike the previous two sites steeped in long traditions and possibly even pre-dating Christianity, Knock is a modern, well-serviced pilgrimage site, based on a specific Marian apparition. In 1879 a group of local people saw a vision of the Lamb of God, St Joseph, St John the Baptist and Our Lady at the gable wall of Knock Church. This occurrence has been accepted by the Catholic Church and, as a result, Knock has grown in status to become recognized as an important international Marian Shrine.

A new Basilica was constructed in 1975 (see Fig. 2.4), and a visit by Pope John Paul II in 1979, on the centenary of the apparition, resulted in renewed devotion and Vatican endorsement of the Shrine. Mother Teresa of Calcutta

Fig. 2.4. The basilica at Knock, County Mayo (from Smyth, 2006).

visited in 1993 and now approximately 1.5 million pilgrims visit annually, making it one of the most visited locations in Ireland.

Religious practice is also an important feature of the pilgrimage at Knock, with dedicated prayers and mass an essential part of the tradition. However, unlike Lough Derg or Croagh Patrick, which provide little or no ancillary services, for practical reasons, with such a large number visiting (many of them infirm), the provision of additional facilities is essential. At Knock, pilgrims may avail of the following:

- Rest and care centre for invalid and sick pilgrims with a doctor on call/wheelchairs/refreshments/minibus with wheelchair lift.
- St Joseph's Hostel, which provides accommodation for people with disabilities and employs helpers on a nightly basis.
- Professional counselling service year-round – drop-in basis or appointment.
- Youth Ministry that caters for young people.
- Guided tours during pilgrimage season – twice daily.
- Audio-visual centre with a varied programme of films in the prayer guidance centre.
- Knock Folk Museum, which encourages understanding and appreciation of the Shrine.

In addition to the religious support services, the village of Knock can provide accommodation in three-star hotels, a number of bed and breakfasts and self-catering establishments, or a camping site. It also has a number of restaurants, a golf club, shops that are famous around the country for inexpensive (and often plastic) souvenirs and, nearby, built ostensibly to serve the Shrine, and immortalized in the song by Christy Moore quoted above, is Ireland West (International) Airport, Knock.

Knock Shrine is open all year and consists of two pilgrimage periods: the main season, which runs from the last Sunday in April until the second Sunday in October and the remainder of the year. Each Saturday and Sunday during the 'season' is allocated to a particular group, including most Catholic dioceses of the country, religious orders, special Catholic organizations or devotions to particular saints and holy people (Duffy, 1996; Knock Shrine, 2006). This is a very well-organized and managed site, which would appear to provide a modern product for the modern pilgrim and their materialistic demands. This is supported somewhat by the following comment by a visitor:

> People have travelled the world to visit Knock to pray for a miracle. Knock is a must-visit for Catholics vacationing in Ireland ... Holy water is a very popular item and across the street from the Shrine is a bazaar-like atmosphere that thrives by selling plastic holy water bottles and other inexpensive souvenirs.
>
> (Magner, 2002)

Decline of local pilgrimage?

With the rising popularity of sites such as Knock and Croagh Patrick and the changed nature of Lough Derg, there is a perception that 'local' sites are being neglected or forgotten in Ireland. To explore this concept, it is worth examining holy wells. These sites have been presented in a plethora of popular and academic literature, but much of the work is descriptive and static, illustrating individual interesting sites, drawing parallels with pre-Christian, Celtic shamanism, focusing on artistic imagery or hidden Christian meaning, rather than on the use of sites. The following 19th-century quotes from County Clare suggest that local abandonment of wells, whatever the reason, is not a new phenomenon:

> [Flannan's memory was formerly celebrated in Killaloe, now his holy well is visited] on any day the pilgrims think proper.

> [In Kilfenora, people] have no remembrance of a Patron Saint here but the name, and that only as being borne by his well, which however, is no longer looked upon as a holy well but is used for domestic purposes as well as if it never had received sanctification from the blessed hands and words of the Holy Saint Fachtna, whose name it bears and whose festival was formerly kept there on the 14th of August.
> (O'Donovan and Curry, 1997)

It would appear from this that the holy wells of Ireland have been in a state of decline for over a century. However, such a generalization is unfair. Literally thousands of wells are recorded by the Office of Public Works in their *Sites and Monuments Record* of Ireland (Office of Public Works, 2001). County Clare alone contains 381 holy wells and, while some may be forgotten over time, many wells around the country are still visited by locals and 'pilgrims' from further afield. One commentator (Walsh, 2006a), who is somewhat sceptical of the spiritual value of the site, has recorded activities at St Brigit's holy well in Liscannor, County Clare (Cunnayne, 1974; Fig. 2.5) for a number of years, and illustrates through his website the constantly changing votive offerings left by pilgrims.

Fig. 2.5. St Brigit's holy well, Liscannor, County Clare (from Kevin M. Griffin, 2006). The circular flowerbed in the left-hand picture is a structure similar to the 'beds' described in Lough Derg. Pilgrims making 'rounds' circumnavigate the bed on their knees, reciting prayers as they do so. The entrance to the well is through the archway to the left. The right-hand picture shows the inside of the well with the 'offerings' left by pilgrims.

The survival and continued devotion at holy wells such as this may in fact be a direct connection with rituals at sacred sites that have survived since prehistoric times. The ritual of leaving personal items (pictures, items of clothing, prayer cards, crutches, babies' dolls and even a bank card) is as intriguing as it is colourful.

The continued practice of pilgrimage to wells can be seen throughout the country by examining local newspapers. The following announcement is just one of many 'local notes' in the *Limerick Leader* newspaper, in this instance referring to Ballylanders:

> Celebrations have now been finalised for this year's annual Pattern Festival. This year's programme is packed with entertainment for young and old. The highlights of the festival will commence with the celebration of Holy Mass in the cemetery where Our Lady's Well is located. The main events will be a Vintage Rally filmed race, Fashion Show, fancy dress, street entertainment and a special card game as usual on Wednesday night ... Ballylanders Pattern can trace its origins back to more than 300 years and ranks amongst the oldest events in the County.
>
> (*Limerick Leader*, 2003)

The juxtaposition of Holy Mass with a vintage rally, fashion show and card game (suggesting gambling) could be seen by some as sacrilegious, but for many small Irish communities this reflects the acceptance of an annual pilgrimage of this nature as a well-established norm.

The travelling community and holy wells

In a world where globalization, assimilation and conformity appear to be paramount, the Irish travelling community (indigenous Irish gypsies) represents a unique ethnic group that has resisted absorption into mainstream society. Sometimes confrontational, always proud of their traditions, travellers trace their ancestry to early Ireland, identifying with the wandering heroes of the pre-Christian period (MacLaughlin, 1995). It is interesting therefore, that this community, which places great emphasis on the oral tradition, is still closely linked to a faith that venerates local pilgrimage sites. The following extract from a study of traveller oral tradition in County Wexford presents an account by children of the annual pilgrimages they make throughout the country:

> We go to holy wells in the summer and in the winter. We go to pray for other people and for ourselves. Holy wells are very special. Some wells are very important to other people too. The names of some of the wells we visit are St. Ann's Well in Killanne in Wexford and Our Lady's Well up the Half-way Road outside Bunclody, St. Kevin's Well in Wicklow, St. Patrick's Well in Rathvilly, County Carlow, St. Bridget's Well in Myshall, County Carlow and St. David's Well in Oylegate in County Wexford.
>
> (Bunclody, 2006)

Further evidence for the importance of a faith mixed with superstition and visits to religious sites is evidenced in the words of another traveller, Kathleen McDonagh:

Travellers are very religious. I love a lot of blessed pictures and statues and plenty of holy water in the place. If I miss Mass it takes a lot out of me. Travellers believe a lot in priests and cures. We are very superstitious – marriages and black cats. We believe in ghosts – it gives us an idea that there's life after death. We wouldn't miss the patterns of the graves.

(Pavee Point, 2006)

Irish pilgrimage overseas

In recent years, with their recently acquired wealth, Irish people have embraced the concept of international pilgrimage with new-found enthusiasm. Traditionally, the sites that they visit are well-established Catholic sites such as Lourdes, Rome and The Holy Land, but in addition they flock to sites such as Medjugorje, Fátima and San Giovanni.

Examples of modern Irish pilgrimages include the following:

- 1500 young people travelled to World Youth Day 2005 in Cologne, Germany (organized on a diocesan basis).
- Due to the easy access to Italy, many parishes and organizations travel to Rome, San Giovanni and Assisi for pilgrimage. In 2002, 2000 Irish people travelled to Rome for the canonization of Padre Pio (over 400,000 people present).
- Irish Pilgrimage Trust began in 1972 in Ireland – bringing 500 children to Lourdes, France, annually.
- 2000 people travel on Dublin diocesan pilgrimage to Lourdes annually.
- 50,000 Irish pilgrims travel to Lourdes annually.
- 11,000 Irish pilgrims travel to Medjugorje, Bosnia-Herzegovina, annually.
- 'Large numbers' visited Rome for the funeral of Pope John Paul II. Numbers are difficult to calculate, but 10,000 people visited the Phoenix Park, Dublin, to watch the funeral on large television screens.

A 2002 report in the *Sunday Business Post* presented the following:

Joe Walsh Tours services about three-quarters of the Irish pilgrimage market. The most popular destination is Lourdes in France, with 50,000 pilgrims (35,000 in parish groups and 15,000 on diocesan pilgrimages). Next most popular is Rome with 12,000 pilgrims, then Fátima in Portugal and Medugorje in Bosnia, both with 10,000 Irish visitors annually ... The reasons for the increase [in pilgrimage] are higher incomes, better-quality accommodation, day flights ... more choice of destinations and ... personalized service for group leaders.

(Wood, 2002)

Lourdes

The world-famous Catholic Shrine of Lourdes is located in the Pyrenees Mountains in the south-west of France. The story of Lourdes and the appearance of Our Lady to a young shepherdess, Bernadette Soubirous, has been recounted the world over, and made into a film by Hollywood Director Franz Werfel (*The Song of Bernadette*). Today, the town of Lourdes is a thriving place with three basilicas, attracting pilgrims from around the world. As part of the pilgrimage, participants take part in a torchlight procession, follow the Stations of the Cross and also participate in a Ceremony for the Sick.

The number of Irish pilgrims travelling to Lourdes increases every year. In 2004, 50,000 Irish pilgrims travelled, with virtually every diocese in the country organizing pilgrimages every year. In addition, groups and organizations as diverse as boy scouts, the army, religious orders, individual parishes, prayer groups and youth groups have travelled on pilgrimage to this important site (Joe Walsh Tours, 2006b).

Medjugorje

From June 1981, the small village of Medjugorje in Bosnia-Herzegovina has become a focal point for Marian pilgrimage, with the appearance of Our Lady, Queen of Peace. Since then, large numbers of Irish pilgrims have visited the site. Joe Walsh Tours alone claim that 11,000 Irish pilgrims travelled to Medjugorje in 2003. While Limerick-based Sharon and Martin Clohessy, official Marian Pilgrimage organizers, estimate that as many as 5000 pilgrims from Limerick and Clare have visited the shrine since its foundation to join more than 25 million people from around the world who have visited this small village (Joe Walsh Tours, 2006a; *Limerick Post*, 2006).

Is Irish pilgrimage becoming globalized or glocalized?

To talk of pilgrimage in language other than religiously focused, pious reverence may be seen by some as sacrilegious. For example, while religion and tourism may seem to be inextricably linked for some, at a major Irish conference in 2000 dealing with pilgrimage, only three of the 82 papers mentioned the word 'tourism' in their abstracts, the majority dealing instead with pilgrimage in the context of safer themes such as history and theology.

Likewise, the topic of globalization does not appear to be associated very much with pilgrimage, despite the growth in popularity of international pilgrimage. This chapter has examined the perceived downturn in local and national observance in Ireland and, while a certain amount of decline is evident, many sites show evidence of continued religious practice.

In an attempt to synthesize some of the thoughts in this chapter, the following table (Table 2.1) suggests connections between globalization and pilgrimage tourism, proposing that while some of the evidence suggests that Irish pilgrimage is becoming more globalized, conversely there is a continuing value in the traditional, national and local pilgrimage. Thus, the adoption of the term 'glocalized' would appear to be more appropriate to Irish pilgrimage.

Thus, when one looks at the pilgrimage to Croagh Patrick and sees 'lines of gleaming SUVs in car parks at the base [of the mountain]', one could think that the pilgrimage had changed from one of local practice by an impoverished people to a 'fashion parade' demonstrating people's wealth. However, while the shining cars may be testament to the increasing affluence of the modern

Table 2.1. Globalized or glocalized – trends in Irish pilgrimage.

Characteristics of globalization[a]	Characteristics of Irish pilgrimage
International trade growing faster than the world economy	Tourism, and indeed pilgrimage tourism, is an area of major growth in Ireland
Increased international flow of capital and foreign direct investment	International flow of capital does not appear to influence Irish domestic pilgrimage, but international pilgrimage is managed by corporate travel agents, often using international finance for accommodation and service provision
Greater individual access to international cultural exchange (Hollywood and Bollywood movies), multiculturalism and cultural diversity; but also reduction in diversity through assimilation, hybridization, Westernization, Americanization or Sinosization	Greater access to information and awareness of international sites of pilgrimage has resulted in many more international pilgrimages, but native Irish practices, while altered, appear to remain strong, thus maintaining and perhaps increasing diversity
Erosion of national sovereignty and borders (WTO and OPEC)	National sovereignty appears to remain uninfluenced by pilgrimage; however, the international popularity of Ireland for 'Early Christian'-centred pilgrimages may help to bolster Irish identity
Greater international travel and tourism	Access to cheap travel, particularly flights, is facilitating greater participation in international pilgrimage. Some national and local sites may be in decline, but many remain popular
Greater immigration	Growth of immigrant groups in Ireland is increasing the viability of travel provision to parts of Eastern Europe and the Middle East. As yet there is no discernible impact on pilgrimage patterns
Global financial systems	The introduction of the euro facilitates easier travel to locations within the euro zone
Increased importance of multinational corporations and practices such as outsourcing	Ryanair flying from Ireland to airports near shrines is weakening the hold of tour organizers
Increased role of international organizations (WTO, WIPO, IMF)	Recognition of Christian sites such as Knock by the Vatican validates their worth as pilgrimage sites
Increased international standards (copyright laws, patents)	Improved safety and standards at destinations is encouraging more pilgrims to engage in repeat travel
Spread of local foods such as pizza and Indian food to other countries (often adapted to local taste)	Awareness and experience of international cuisine is decreasing the perception of 'food' as a deterrent to international travel
Global telecommunications and trans-border data flow (Internet, communication satellites, telephones)	Information technology and telecommunications are facilitating international travel at a phenomenal rate, but technology is also is used by many sites to market their pilgrimage product
Formation or development of a set of universal values	While the Irish appear to be more aware of universal values, they would also appear to be maintaining their own traditional values

[a] Adapted from the globalization work of Reiser (2003) and Wikipedia (2006).

pilgrim, the numbers taking part are constant (albeit with fewer undertaking the pilgrimage in bare feet). In the region of 20,000 pilgrims make the climb each year. In the words of the Archbishop of Tuam, Dr Michael Neary: '[Despite] the seeming weakness of faith in an Ireland of growing prosperity [there is] still a vibrant church calling men and women to seek God with the strength and companionship of others' (Shiel, 2005).

Inbound pilgrimage – or tourism?

In undertaking the research on Irish pilgrimage, a number of inbound tours to Ireland were examined, and while these included the use of pilgrimage in a number of ways such as a 'Walking and Art Pilgrimage' and a week-long pilgrimage of 'Native Irish Spirituality and Mythology', comments were also received from organizers of more traditional Christian pilgrimages into Ireland. These following excerpts provide an insight into the strongly religious motives and ideals of those organizing pilgrimages to Ireland:

> I tell people not to come with us unless they want Mass every day, three rosaries every day, evening holy hours, processions, and bible studies. I really don't want others to come. This way, we are all of a like mind. As a result ... our faith experience is enriched on every level ... even the guide and the chaplain expresses this.

> The chaplain and the guide must themselves be pilgrims and not tourists. Unfortunately, many pilgrimages are run by unholy individuals, and then the pilgrimage is little different than a tour.

> Pilgrimage is very different from touring ... [it] is journeying for a spiritual purpose ... almost to a person, those who have gone on pilgrimage with me have returned home claiming to have touched a deeper spiritual place in themselves. It has much to do with being in the places that have been sacred for so many centuries and finding the inner ancient and holy place where the divine dwells.

> I have had the privilege of working with leaders who facilitate this experience ...

However, not all tour organizers were quite so zealous, with one taking a milder approach:

> My observation is that pilgrims will do some shopping along the way and have just as much fun as tourists. Remember, the pilgrimage of the Middle Ages was quite commercial and fuelled European commerce and trade in that day. Some say it led the way for the Renaissance and the Reformation.

> The pilgrims who go on my fall tour to Ireland usually buy all their Christmas presents for that year while there.

Summary

In Ireland, much pilgrimage is for a mixture of religious and tourism-focused motives, but there is an abundance of evidence for pilgrimages that are undertaken purely for spiritual and religious reasons. There is a growing trend of people engaging in international pilgrimage, both into and out of the country; however, there is also a continued appreciation and observance of many forms of domestic pilgrimage. Thus, while this chapter began with a suggestion that there is a growing trend towards globalization of society, religion and pilgrimage, this would appear to be an over-simplification.

At one level there is a desire to visit internationally important sites, to take part in global events such as the funeral of a Pope, the canonization of a holy person or the ritualistic practices one has seen on television, read or heard about. At the other end of the scale, people would also appear to be interested in attending and finding out more about and attending their local sites of pilgrimage. While some sites have been neglected and are long forgotten, throughout the country there are many holy wells, churches, reliquaries, mass rocks and graveyards that are visited for the purpose of pilgrimage. Perhaps this practice is a reaction to the increased pace of life, the growing pressures to conform and the general homogenization of society.

In conclusion, the use of the term globalization in the title of this chapter does apply to the increasing practice of international pilgrimage from Ireland, and somewhat to the arrival of overseas pilgrims into Ireland, but it does not provide a complete picture. Adoption of the term 'glocalization' is proposed to bridge the gap between the increasing importance of 'global' pilgrimage, while at the same time preserving the concept of 'local' pilgrimage. It is suggested here that the current trend in Ireland is taking advantage of both: moving people towards a larger, homogenized world while at the same time focusing on the parochial and local.

Therefore, the present-day patterns of pilgrimage in Ireland reflect empowerment, increased choice and information that facilitate a more varied pattern of travel (*Economic Times*, 2002). In this context, the future of pilgrimage in Ireland – and throughout the world – is one that is happy to combine both the excitement of the international experience with the stability of ethnic practice; in other words, the future of pilgrimage lies with glocalization.

References

Alton, D. (c. 2001) *Pilgrim Ways: a Personal Guide to Catholic Pilgrimage Sites in Britain and Ireland.* St Paul's, London.

Brown, F. (1998) *Tourism Reassessed: Blight or Blessing?* Butterworth-Heinemann, Oxford, UK.

Claval, P. (2002) Places of memory. Paper presented at *'Perspectives on Landscape, Memory, Heritage and Identity' Meeting of International Geographical Union Cultural Study Group*, University College, Dublin.

Cohen, E. (ed.) (2001) The Chinese Vegetarian Festival in Phuket: religion, ethnicity and tourism on a southern Thai island. *Studies in Contemporary Thailand*, No. 9, White Lotus Press, Bangkok.

Cunnayne, J. (1974) Pilgrim circulation in Ireland. *Baile* (the magazine of the Geography Society, University College, Dublin), 17–20.

Davies, H. and Davies, M.H. (1982) *Holy Days and Holidays, the Medieval Pilgrimage to Compostela.* Bucknell University Press, Lewisburg, Pennsylvania.

Dixon Hardy, P. (1836) *The Holy Wells of Ireland.* Hardy and Walker, Dublin.

Duffy, M. (1996) *Knock Shrine Visitor Survey 1996*. Knock Folk Museum, Knock, Ireland.

Economic Times (2002) Glocalisation: globalization plus localization. 16 and 23 June.

Giussani, L. (1997) *The Religious Sense*. McGill-Queen's University Press, Montreal, Canada.

Harbison, P. (1970) *Guide to the National Monuments of Ireland*. Gill & Macmillan, Dublin.

Harbison, P. (1991) *Pilgrimage in Ireland: the Monuments and the People*. Barrie & Jenkins, London.

Hughes, K. (ed.) (1960) The changing theory and practice of Irish pilgrimage. *Journal of Ecclesiastical History* 11.

Limerick Leader (2003) Your local notes – Ballylanders, 9 August.

Limerick Post (2006) Marian pilgrimage to Medjugorje announced, 3 April.

MacLaughlin, J. (1995) *Travellers and Ireland: whose Country, whose History?* University Press, Cork, Ireland.

Moore, C. (1983) The Knock Song. In: *The Time Has Come*, album by Christy Moore, available from WEA, London.

Murray, M. and Graham, B. (1997) Exploring the dialectics of route-based tourism: the Camino de Santiago. *Tourism Management* 18 (8), 513–524.

O'Donovan, J. and Curry, E. (1997) *The Antiquities of County Clare: Ordnance Survey Letters 1839*. Clasp Press, Ennis, Ireland.

Park, C.C. (1994) *Sacred Worlds: an Introduction to Geography and Religion*. Routledge, London and New York.

Pochin Mould, D.D.C. (1955) *Irish Pilgrimage*. M.H. Gill, Dublin.

Pontifical Council (1998) *Pilgrimage in the Great Jubilee of the Year 2000*. Pontifical Council for the Pastoral Care of Migrants and Itinerant People, Rome.

Reid, D.G. (2003) *Tourism, Globalisation and Development: Responsible Tourism Planning*. Pluto Press, London.

Reiser, D. (2003) Globalisation: an old phenomenon that needs to be rediscovered for tourism. In: *Tourism and Hospitality Research*, Vol. 4, No. 4. Henry Stewart Publications, London, pp. 306–320.

Shiel, T. (2005) Reek Sunday on Croagh Patrick draws 20,000. *Irish Times*, 1 August.

Sopher, D. (1967) *Geography of Religions*. Prentice Hall, New Jersey.

Watt, N. (1995) Pre-Christian remains found on Ireland's Holy Mountain. *The Times*, 2 September.

Wiederkehr, M. (2001) *Behold Your Life: a Pilgrimage Through Your Memories*. Ave Maria Press, Paris.

Williams, S. (1998) *Tourism Geography*. Routledge, London.

Wood, K. (2002) God Inc. weathers the economic storm. *Sunday Business Post*, 25 August.

Websites

British Library (2006) *Treasures in full: Caxton's Chaucer*. Facsimile of the Canterbury Tales. http://www.bl.uk/treasures/caxton/homepage.html (accessed 15 March 2006).

Bunclody (2006) *Ireland's Last Nomadic People Project*. Website of Bunclody National School. http://www.bunclodyns.com/nomads03/html/wells.htm (accessed 15 March 2006).

Catholic Communications Office. http://www.catholiccommunications.ie (accessed 15 March 2006).

CERFE (ed.) (2004) *The Glocalization Manifesto*. http://www.glocalforum.org/ (accessed 15 March 2006).

CWN (*Catholic World News*) (1997) Numbers down at annual Irish pilgrimage. http://www.cwnews.com/ (accessed 8 April).

Encyclopaedia Britannica (2006) http://www.britannica.com/ (accessed 15 March 2006).

IFG (International Forum on Globalisation) (2006) http://www.ifg.org/analysis.htm (accessed 15 March 2006).

Joe Walsh Tours (2006a) http://www.joewalshtours.ie/Pilgrimages/Medjugorje/Medjugorje.html (accessed 15 March 2006).

Joe Walsh Tours (2006b) http://www.joewalshtours.com/About_Us/Press_Centre/Press_Centre.html (accessed 15 March 2006).

Knock Shrine (2006) *Knock.* http://www.knock-shrine.ie/ (accessed 15 March 2006).

Koran (2006) Translated version of the Koran available at http://arthurwendover.com/arthurs/koran/koran_irving10.html (accessed 15 March 2006).

Lough Derg (2006a) *Personal Testimonials of Lough Derg.* http://www.loughderg.org/AboutUs/PersonalTestimonials.asp (accessed 15 March 2006).

Lough Derg (2006b) *Lough Derg Services.* http://www.loughderg.org/LoughDergServices/ (accessed 15 March 2006).

Magner, M. (2002) *Knock.* http://www.magnergraphix.com/Ireland/Knock.html (accessed 11 December 2002; website has been changed, with no reference to Knock).

Mayo Gazette (undated) *Mayo Gazette* – online magazine outlining history and traditions of County Mayo. http://www.mayogazette.com/mayo/issue18A.html (accessed 11 December 2002, now no longer 'live').

Office of Public Works (2001) *Sites and Monuments Record for County Clare.* http://www.heritagedata.ie/en/NationalMonuments/Download/ (the Sites and Monuments Record has been temporarily removed for updating and correction, as of 19 January 2001).

Pavee Point (2006) *Traveller Voices.* http://www.paveepoint.ie/voices2.html (accessed 15 March 2006).

Rebic, A. (1999) The document of the Holy See on: Pilgrimage 2000. In: *All About Medjugorje.* http://www.medjugorje.org/medpage.htm (accessed 15 March 2006).

Rose, J. (undated) *Croagh Patrick, Ireland's Holy Mountain.* http://www.anu.ie/reek/ (accessed 15 March 2006).

Smyth, J. (2006) *North Atlantic Skyline.* http://www.monasette.com

Wikipedia (2006) http://en.wikipedia.org/wiki/Globalisation (accessed 15 March 2006).

3   Motivations for Religious Tourism, Pilgrimage, Festivals and Events

RUTH BLACKWELL

Centre for Event Management, Tourism, Hospitality and Events School, Leeds Metropolitan University, Leeds; e-mail: r.blackwell@leedsmet.ac.uk

Introduction

The aim of this chapter is to provide an understanding of the motivations for religious tourism, pilgrimage, festivals and events. Theories of motivation will be identified and discussed in order to identify the prime motivating factors underpinning people's decisions to make pilgrimages and to take part in religious tourism. Theories of motivation are divided into content theories or process theories. Content theories focus on what actually motivates people, seeking, therefore, to identify and explain the relevant factors. Process theories of motivation place their emphasis on the actual process of motivation, with the aim of identifying the relationship between various dynamic variables, such as values and expectations, that influence individual motivation.

Both sets of theory can inform our understanding of motivation in the religious context of travel. Definitions of pilgrimage and religious tourism will be compared and contrasted so that the essential features of each form of tourism can be identified and analysed within the context of motivation: this will provide us with a fuller understanding of the various motivations for these kinds of travel. Understanding and classifying the motivations of pilgrims and religious tourists can inform tourism management in developing ways to meet the needs of pilgrims and religious tourists on journeys to religious destinations and during their stay at those destinations.

It is clearly imperative that, given the rise in this kind of tourism, we understand what motivates travellers to sacred sites and to what extent, if at all, their expectations can be met.

It is believed that, since the dawn of time, human beings have defined some elements of the natural and built environment as spiritual sites, regarding them as sacred and, in many cases, endowing them with supernatural qualities. Even though the spiritual meaning of some of them has been lost over time, there is still immense interest in many of these ancient sites and their artefacts, examples of which can be found all over the world: the statues of Easter Island, Stonehenge in England, Uluru in Australia, the Ring of Brodgar in Orkney, the Teotihuacanos in Central America, Angkor Wat in Cambodia and sacred mountains in China.

As knowledge about our world increases, more and more sacred sites are being discovered, so that the list is literally endless. It seems, therefore, that travel to sacred places was, and is, an inherent aspect of all cultures; as early as 30,000 years ago, Australian aboriginal people made yearly journeys on foot for the purpose of ceremonies, ritual and festivals. These journeys can tell us something about the relationship between humans and nature, that there is an awareness of natural artefacts as embodying a life force. The world's greatest religious sites inspire feelings of awe in those who visit them (Wilson, 1996).

People have always been interested in making sense of their lives and the world in which they live and, it is claimed, have looked to the sacred for meaning. The search for meaning involved travel to sacred sites and taking part in rituals at those sites. Today we see that, all over the world, more and more people are travelling to sacred sites (not always sacred to their own religion, even when they have one), taking part in religious festivals and events, and more and more people are making pilgrimages to their religion's sacred sites. That this is happening at the same time as there are falling congregations in Christian worship in much of the Western world is significant. At the same time, it has been observed that there is not the same trend of declining formal participation in other religions. Buddhist, Hindu, Jewish, Muslim and Christian pilgrimage sites, however, continue to attract increasing numbers of visitors.

Even in areas where it is recognized that there is a higher risk of danger, people are not always deterred from visiting sacred sites: recent studies of adventure tourism in Nepal found that pilgrimage to Hindu and Buddhist religious sites was less affected than trekking by the threats to personal safety posed by global and internal security matters (Bhattarai *et al.*, 2005). What is it, then, that motivates people from all walks of life, all religions (and none) and all cultures to undertake travel to sacred sites?

Pilgrimage and Religious Tourism: Defining the Terminology

There is considerable debate about what is meant by religious tourism and whether it differs from pilgrimage: are they the same thing, 'new wine in old bottles' as it were, or do they have substantive differences? As a starting point, we can turn to the definition of tourism as set out by the World Tourism Organisation (WTO): 'The activities of persons travelling to, and staying in, places outside their usual environment for not more than one consecutive year for leisure, business or other purposes' (as cited in Goeldner and Brent Richie, 2003, p. 7).

Pilgrims and religious or sacred tourists clearly fit into this definition, since both involve the decision to travel from home with the intention of returning to it within a given time period (i.e. less than a year) for 'other purposes', that is, incorporating religious motivations. The WTO definition is wide enough, therefore, to incorporate both pilgrimage and religious tourism; however, more focused definitions are needed if we are to understand and differentiate between the motivations and expectations of pilgrims and religious tourists.

Lefebvre, in Vukonic (1996), defines religious tourism as consisting of a range of spiritual sites and associated services, which are visited for both secular and religious reasons. Within this definition two different kinds of sites can be identified: shrines and pilgrimage sites. Shrines encompass sites where a relic or image is 'venerated', whereas pilgrimage sites are places where it is recognized that a miracle has occurred, still occurs and may do so again: an example of the latter is Lourdes in France.

Some sites have both elements ascribed to them and, since this definition refers mainly to the Christian context, it has limited application. Pilgrimage sites are not so narrowly prescribed within the majority of world religions and can be part of the natural environment, like the river Ganges or the Himalayas, or part of the built environment, like temples and mosques. Festivals with religious associations, like Tamil Nadu's unique religious festival, are also classified as religious tourism attractions. Shackley (2003, p. 161) sets out a broad classification of religion-based attractions:

- Natural phenomena (sacred lakes, mountains, islands, groves).
- Buildings and sites originally constructed for religious purposes.
- Buildings with a religious theme.
- Special events with religious significance held at non-religious sites.
- Sacralized secular sites associated with tragedy or politically significant events (e.g. Nelson Mandela's prison on Robben Island).

There is a growing trend towards developing purpose-built religious tourism attractions on non-sacred sites, like the 'Holy Land Experience' in Florida, creating, in effect, a religious theme park. Visits to this kind of religious tourist attraction are desirable to the home population, since they can take place without the inconvenience (long journeys, smells, dirt, illness, crowds, 'foreign' food, etc.) and without exposure to environmental or political danger. The latter can be perceived as applying more to Western tourists in the wake of 'September 11'.

Managers of purpose-built religious attractions need to be aware of the conflict between visitors' desires for authentic experiences and their need for security. This desire for authenticity might include an understanding of, and opportunity for, meaningful contact between indigenous religions and religious travellers: sacred sites, otherwise, are in danger of becoming entertaining religious theme parks.

Religious tourism, therefore, encompasses all kinds of travel that is motivated by religion and where the destination is a religious site. These sites may not necessarily be associated with current religions, since there are many religions in the history of the world that have become extinct – some have left behind impressive artefacts (temples, churches, shrines, statues) and cultural heritages.

Religious tourism need not incorporate belief in a specific religion, as recent 'Da Vinci Code' tourists demonstrate. King (2000) makes the valid observation that there are secular 'religions' like football, where fans boast that the football club is their religion and where, far from being a reference to a sacred site, the 'hallowed ground' is a common description of the football pitch. Many major clubs build on these sentiments in organized tours of their grounds and facilities, emulating the characteristics of organized tours to religious sites.

Whatever the similarities and differences between these forms of religious tourism, there is a common underlying theme: travel, being a vital component of tourism, can be seen as an integral part of religious tourism since people, whatever their motivation, travel by foot, bicycle, car, bus, train or plane to these sites. Whether the journey itself can be considered as religious tourism is a matter of debate. Some authors exclude the journey from their definition of religious tourism. Religious tourism is said to have five characteristics (da Graca Mouga Pocas Santos, 2003, p. 40):

- Voluntary, temporary and unpaid travel.
- Motivated by religion.
- Supplemented by other motivations.
- The destination is a religious site (local, regional, national or international status).
- Travel to the destination is not a religious practice.

It is intended to take these characteristics, which exclude pilgrimage, as a working understanding of religious tourism that will be used in the exploration of motivation. These characteristics clearly bring religious festivals and events into its remit. It has been argued elsewhere that pilgrimages and religious tourism can both be seen as sacred journeys (Graburn, 1989). Although some authors argue that tourism and pilgrimage should be placed at the opposite ends on a continuum of travel – between the sacred and the secular – others see them as being more intertwined: religious festivals can be attached to the end of a pilgrimage or operate as a stand-alone event. It is generally believed, however, that the distinguishing feature of pilgrimage is that it incorporates religious involvement *into the journey*.

Singh's (2004) study of pilgrimage in India (Hindu and tribal-Hindu) identified pilgrimage as having been institutionalized over 1000 years ago. Historically and currently, pilgrimage has an integrating function, connecting people from diverse cultures and ethnic groups in India. A distinctive feature of traditional Hindu pilgrimage is its circular, clockwise direction – very different from the linear tradition of most pilgrimages. Pilgrimage is always expected to involve austerity to a greater or lesser degree (strenuous walking and labour) – records show that early pilgrims (although not always the wealthy) did indeed experience a great deal of hardship. Many pilgrimages in India involve carrying artefacts over some distance – even children share in the experience, carrying miniature versions.

Pilgrims to Lhasa's Buddhist temples prostrate themselves flat, standing up at the point reached by their hands, and then repeat these movements in the pilgrimage circuit. Austerity was to be incorporated in all aspects of pilgrimage – choice of food, places to stay *en route*, social intercourse, etc. Concern for maintaining the natural and social environment was also built into traditional pilgrimage. Pilgrimage should mediate between the natural and the cultural world and, at the same time, between the natural and the supernatural world. This provides us with a definitive means of distinguishing pilgrimage from religious tourism.

In many cases it is possible to distinguish between pilgrims and religious tourists (as characterized by their destination) by the way they behave. Participant observers of tourists travelling by bus through the mountains to the Garhwal Himalayas noted that pilgrims ritually chanted the Lord's name at what were perceived as critical junctures and dangerous points during the journey, whilst the tourists did not do so (Singh, 2004). In this case, religious ritual was invoked during the pilgrimage. The journey itself, the pilgrimage, can be considered to be a ritual as well as incorporating ritualistic elements.

Traditional views of pilgrimage have identified that the experience should also involve hardship and suffering. Putting these elements together – ritual and austerity – help us to see that simply *travelling* to a sacred site is not sufficient to identify the traveller as a pilgrim. The distinction can become blurred where people taking part in organized pilgrimages are allowed extra time to visit other religious tourist sites.

Distinction between Pilgrimage and Religious Tourism: Implications

Spiritual destination management involves responsibility for satisfying the needs of pilgrims and religious tourists. Motivations for pilgrimage will differ from those of religious tourism, and it is these differences that can have a significant impact on the ability of destination managers to satisfy their 'customers'. We can see that, whilst it is the experience at their *destination* that has significance for the religious tourist, perceptions will be different for the pilgrim, since the destination constitutes only one part of the experience of pilgrimage. Experiences along the pilgrim route are an integral element, affecting the whole travel experience.

Visitors to sacred sites can be classified as:

- Pilgrims visiting sacred sites that have meaning for them.
- Religious tourists.
- Secular tourists.
- Pilgrims visiting sacred sites that have no religious meaning for them (tacked on to the end of pilgrimage).
- Religious festival and religious event participants.

Motives for visiting the sacred site have been found to affect behaviour, in that pilgrims are more likely than any other visitor to subscribe to overt and covert norms at sites that hold religious significance for them. Conflict over clothing conventions, in particular, are a frequent cause of conflict: it is not uncommon to see people wearing shorts and vests at religious sites where prominently placed signs ask visitors to cover their heads, shoulders and legs. Taking photographs of religious rites is forbidden in certain areas of the world, yet several incidents of violence have been reported where local custom has been flouted.

It is clearly imperative that, given the rise in pilgrimage and religious tourism, the management of religious destinations and pilgrimage routes is informed by an understanding of what motivates these categories of traveller and to what extent, if at all, their expectations can be satisfied. Even though the prime motivation is religious, motivations and expectations change over time: it is claimed, for example, that improved transport facilities and the greater wealth of prospective pilgrims have led to increasing commodification of sacred sites, thus raising expectations of quality.

Theories of Motivation

Motivation can be defined as something that commits people to a course of action, i.e. the driving force that exists in all individuals. Without appropriate motivation, pilgrims and religious tourists would not be able to achieve their goals, whether physical or spiritual. Theories of motivation are commonly drawn from studies of workplace motivation, whereby the focus is on identifying those factors which managers can apply to enhance worker productivity.

Much research has been carried out into what motivates people, and theories of motivation can be used to help us understand what motivates people to undertake pilgrimages and participate in religious tourism, and how an understanding of the processes of motivation can be used to facilitate and support these forms of tourism. It is important to be aware that there are many competing theories of motivation which aim to explain the nature of motivation. Motivation is a complex concept, and there is no simple or universal answer to the question of what motivates people.

The following section will focus on motivation theories that are most relevant to the study of pilgrimage and religious tourism: content theories and process theories. Content theories focus on *what* actually motivates people, seeking, therefore, to identify and explain factors that motivate the individual. Process theories of motivation, on the other hand, place their emphasis on the actual *process* of motivation, so that they aim to identify the relationship between various dynamic variables which influence individual motivation.

Content theories of motivation

Content theories of motivation focus on what things motivate people to act in a certain way. These theories aim to identify people's needs, classifying them in order of relative strength, and to identify the goals people follow to satisfy their needs. People have needs, sometimes described as feelings of deprivation, which propel the individual to do something to satisfy the need. One of the most popular content theorists is Maslow (1954), who focused on need as the basis of motivation. Maslow's theory is in two parts: (i) the classification of human needs; and (ii) the relationships between the classes of needs.

Maslow (1954) contended, in his theory of individual development and motivation (the hierarchy of needs theory), that people's needs can be divided into five different levels, from lower- to higher-order needs, with the lower-order needs having to be satisfied before people are motivated to satisfy the next need in the hierarchy. Once a need is satisfied, it no longer remains a motivator – people then seek to satisfy higher-level needs. The hierarchy contains, at its lowest, the deficiency needs – physiological, safety and social or belonging needs and, at the higher levels, growth needs – esteem and self-actualization needs. Table 3.1 provides examples of the outcomes of satisfying each level of need, ranging from the lowest (at the bottom of the hierarchy) to the highest order.

Maslow contends that a person starts of the bottom of the hierarchy and initially seeks to satisfy basic physiological needs, such as hunger, thirst and shelter. Once the physiological needs have been met, they no longer act as motivators and the individual is motivated to satisfy the higher-order needs. Maslow stated that, although most people's basic needs do run in this order, the hierarchy of needs should not be seen as a fixed order: in other words, the order may change according to circumstances.

It has been argued that the higher-order needs change and extend with the development of societies and the concomitant development and form of social relations – this is because, given their social rather than physiological basis, they are more likely to be influenced by social norms. Although there is little empirical evidence to support Maslow's theory, nevertheless it can provide insights into the motivations of pilgrims and religious tourists.

People who feel a need for social interaction, to make new friends or feel part of a group of like-minded individuals may seek to satisfy their social needs by taking part in an organized pilgrimage or organized travel to a religious destination, whilst pilgrims who do travel alone or with a small party are frequently part of a large group travelling to the sacred site. Once their lower-order needs have been met, people might be motivated by the need to gain the esteem of their religious community through taking part in a prestigious pilgrimage, for example, to the hajj, or by undertaking a physically demanding pilgrimage, such as the Pilgrimage Circuit of Lhasa or the pilgrimage to Santiago de Compostela.

At the highest level of motivation, the experience of pilgrimage itself would be expected to provide satisfaction of self-actualization needs. A cursory study of Chaucer's *Canterbury Tales*, however, shows us that motives for pilgrimage may always have been mixed – the wife of Bath, for example, had a secular motive (to find another husband) – as well as the more traditional spiritual reasons for pilgrimage.

Table 3.1. Maslow's hierarchy of needs (adapted from Maslow, 1954).

Needs	Outcomes
Growth needs	
Self-actualization	Achieve full potential, creativity, development
Esteem	Self-respect, self-esteem, prestige, status
Social	Affection, sense of belonging, friendship, love
Deficiency needs	
Safety	Safety, security, stability, protection
Physiological	Food, water, sleep, healthy environment, sex

A major influence on theories of motivation is Herzberg (1974), who developed his two-factor theory, from research into occupational motivation, represented in Table 3.2. He divided factors influencing people's motivation into two sets: hygiene factors and motivating factors (mostly known as motivators). The hygiene factors do not actually motivate people but will lead to feelings of dissatisfaction if they are absent or inadequate, whilst the motivators are those things that motivate the individual, but will not cause dissatisfaction if absent. Comparison with Maslow's hierarchy of needs suggests that hygiene factors can be approximated to the lower-level needs and the motivators to the higher-level needs.

Whilst there are methodological criticisms of Herzberg's two-factor theory, the consequence of his research has been to encourage a focus on restructuring work to enable people to satisfy higher-level needs through their work. What has this to do with religious motivation? Clearly, his ideas have resonance for our understanding of the motives for pilgrimage and religious tourism and, hence, for the management of the process, whether travel is seen as an integral element – as in pilgrimage – or not, as in religious tourism.

The two-factor theory of motivation suggests that religious tourists may be motivated by the opportunity to gain recognition of their achievement, perhaps by a photograph of their participation in a religious ceremony that they can show to friends at home, or by opportunities for personal and spiritual growth realized during a pilgrimage or a religious event.

Table 3.2. Herzberg's two-factor theory of motivation as applied to pilgrimage and religious tourism (adapted from Herzberg, 1974).

Hygiene factors	Application to pilgrimage and religious tourism	Motivators	Application to pilgrimage and religious tourism
Salary	Income to afford travel, accommodation, time off work	Sense of achievement	Personal satisfaction, overcoming physical hardship of travel
Job security	Security of destination, travel arrangements	Recognition	Photograph, certificate, participation in ceremony
Working conditions	Quality of travel, destination, accommodation, freedom from conflict	Responsibility	Responsibility for own religious achievement, responsibility for others *en route* and at destination
Level/quality of supervision	Couriers, accommodation management	Nature of the work	Pilgrimage, experience at religious destination, participation in ceremony
Company policy and administration	Policy affecting religious travel and pilgrimage, administrative efficiency	Personal growth and advancement	Religious experiences *en route* and at destination
Interpersonal relations	Local inhabitants, fellow travellers, staff and volunteers at destination, travel company, accommodation		Satisfaction of spiritual needs, survival skills acquired and used on pilgrimage

Some hygiene factors may cause dissatisfaction and demotivation: the physical conditions encountered during travel, for example, may discourage some. Others, however, may perceive hardship as an integral part of the experience that, in itself, offers an opportunity for personal growth and the development of survival skills. Crowd surges at the hajj in recent years have led to hundreds of deaths and injuries amongst participants: there are fears that such incidents will have a demotivating effect. Study of content theory clearly shows that such an outcome would not be unexpected and, therefore, destination managers should focus on ensuring that the lower-level needs (Herzberg's hygiene factors) are met, whilst not stifling opportunities to achieve satisfaction of higher-level motivators.

Content theories are useful in that their focus on need fulfilment helps in understanding what actually motivates individuals, but they are open to criticism because they do not enable us to identify which need is most dominant in an individual at any one time. Since each person is different, due to the uniqueness of their experiences, it is difficult to generalize from these theories.

It is also claimed that these theories underestimate the effects of social and cultural factors on motivation – cultures, for example, that value the individual over the group may inculcate in their members a belief that self-actualization is desirable, whereas in other cultures, which emphasize the importance of the group above the individual, self-actualization may considered to be an undesirable, selfish goal.

Maslow's work, however, remains useful because it is a pragmatic way of classifying the different needs that people try to fulfil through pilgrimage and religious tourism. Herzberg's research enables us to distinguish between motivators and dissatisfiers: the primary focus needs to be on providing opportunities for the satisfaction of motivators such as a sense of achievement whilst, at the same time, paying attention to hygiene factors such as security, which, of themselves, do not motivate but will cause dissatisfaction if they are not attended to.

Process theories of motivation

As stated earlier, process theories of motivation emphasize the actual *process* of motivation and, in doing so, focus on identifying the relationship between various dynamic variables that influence the individual's motivation. The process theory most relevant to our understanding of motivations for pilgrimage and religious tourism is Vroom's (1964) expectancy theory.

Expectancy theory

Expectancy theories of motivation were first identified in the 1930s in the USA and further developed in the 1960s. Expectancy theory asserts that individuals are motivated by the *expectancy* that there will be a particular outcome of their actions: that this outcome will then result in a reward (*instrumentality*) and that the rewards (extrinsic or intrinsic) are such that it justifies the effort put into carrying out the act (*valence*). Valence was defined by Vroom (1964) as the anticipated satisfaction from an outcome – the emphasis here is on the *anticipated* rather than the *actual* satisfaction. Expectancy is the perceived probability that the outcome will happen if the individual works hard to achieve it.

Expectancy theory, therefore, explores the relationship between effort, performance and satisfaction. Expectancy theory can be said to be culturally dependent in that individuals, whether consciously or unconsciously, rate their preferences in a rational way and then decide how much effort to put into achieving goals. People are more likely to act in this way in more individualistic cultures rather than in more collectivist cultures.

Expectancy theory assumes that people are motivated by rewards that they value – for example, if individual A's family offered to pay for a visit to Lourdes, the offer would be taken up only if individual A valued the experience. The role of perceptions is crucial – the individual's perceptions of the link between their effort and the reward. If an individual believed that undergoing the hardships of pilgrimage would be rewarded by spiritual enhancement, then their perception of that reward would be motivating to them. To illustrate the application of expectancy theory to pilgrimage we can see that:

- A person has an *expectancy* that by undertaking a pilgrimage their spirituality will be enhanced.
- Taking part in the pilgrimage is *instrumental* to that person achieving their spiritual goal.
- Intrinsic rewards (enhanced spirituality, self-actualization) plus extrinsic rewards (recognition, increased status within their religious community) create *valence.*

In this example, the individual has to believe that undertaking a pilgrimage will enhance their spirituality. If it is believed that their efforts will be instrumental in achieving their goal, then they will be motivated to do their absolute best to achieve it. They must value the reward for achieving this goal above all other competing ways of spending their time and money.

Process theories do not make assumptions about what motivates people but focus on how people's needs and wants affect their behaviour and, therefore, they are considered to be more universally applicable than content theories. Theories of motivation can be criticized because they focus on the individual rather than examining the environment in which the person is located: some needs, like self-actualization, are said to be culturally determined. Nevertheless, theory provides frameworks for our understanding of expectations and behaviour in this context.

Motivation for pilgrimage, religious tourism, festivals and events

Religious travel of all kinds has a long history: experts point to pilgrimage being institutionalized in parts of India more than a 1000 years ago, whilst some sources trace travel to sacred sites back 30,000 years. Islam has been identified as the religion where the most pilgrimages are made, although, in fact, most religions require their adherents to visit its sacred places to help relieve spiritual or material troubles. Before the development of mass systems of transportation in the 19th century, most religious travellers had to walk to their destination (only the wealthy could afford to travel on horseback or by carriage). Even so, the wealthy were expected to walk at least some of the way during pilgrimage.

Religion has long influenced, and been influenced by, population movements and continues to do so, as we can see today with significant increases in the numbers of pilgrims and religious tourists. Although today there is a growing trend for religious believers to travel in groups organized by or through their respective religious organizations, this is not a modern phenomenon; most travelled in groups, satisfying the desire for companionship and social life alongside the primarily religious motivation and, at the same time, demonstrating the strength of that religion to outsiders. An essential feature of pilgrimage was the large numbers who gathered together at sacred sites: hundred of thousands, for example, continue the tradition of being together for the celebration of Kumbh Mela in India.

Religious motive is a complex concept with more than one meaning, and has different levels of intensity depending on individual belief and social context. It is generally agreed that religion has been, and is, a prime motive for undertaking travel and, in this context, travel to sacred sites and religious events and festivals. Even where religion is the main motive, other motives can come into play: for example, whilst it is clear that medieval Crusades to the Holy Land were underpinned by religious motives, they were also seen as opportunities for adventure, advancement and wealth creation.

Even modern-day religious pilgrimage can be seen as an opportunity for adventure – many pilgrimage sites are situated in remote areas, requiring several days' travel on foot. Motivation for pilgrimage, historically, has also been linked with religious conflict: for example, a large pilgrimage aiming to preserve Jerusalem for Christianity followed the Pope's proclamation that the Holy City had been desecrated by Turkish occupation. This is not unusual in the history of religions: religious tourism and many pilgrimages have resulted from conflict between religions. Religious practice influences both the motives for pilgrimage and the quality of the experience. The Catholic Church's granting of indulgences in the Middle Ages affected people's motivation for pilgrimage: although the main motivating factor was forgiveness of sin, an unintended effect was a weakening of spiritual motivation (Sumption, 1975).

Motivation for religious tourism and religious pilgrimage, therefore, is complex, multifaceted and multilayered. It can be anticipated that, given the intensity of motivation needed for pilgrimage, expectations will be higher than for the religious tourist. This was demonstrated in Poria *et al.*'s (2003) study of visitors to the Wailing Wall in Jerusalem: Jewish pilgrims' motivations were based on their desire for an emotional experience, since the site was part of their own heritage, whereas Christians' motivation was primarily due to the site being an historic tourist attraction.

Motivation, furthermore, can change where the individual switches activities, for example, from being a pilgrim to a tourist and vice versa, often without the individual being aware of the change. Several studies show that religion explains people's behaviour as tourists – acting as a motivating force and also as a constraint. The whole spectrum of motivations, from eagerly anticipated spiritual experience to idle curiosity, therefore, should be expected at religious sites.

It should not be forgotten that pilgrims and religious tourists need to have their basic needs met *en route* and at the destination – in that way they behave like other tourists. Care should also be taken to avoid conflict with local beliefs – it has been reported that some higher-class hotels in Nepal import beef for visitors in a Hindu country where the killing of a cow is believed to be a crime (Bhattarai *et al.*, 2005).

Summary

[Globally, religiously motivated travel is increasing (Mintel International Group Ltd, 2005) manifested in religious festivals and events, visits to religious sites and the undertaking of pilgrimages.] Religiously motivated travel is affected by factors such as access to free time, finances and travel arrangements. Religious tourism and pilgrimage have similar features yet are different. Travel to the destination is an inherent element of pilgrimage: austerity and hardship are traditionally expected *en route* as well as at the destination. Unlike religious tourism, pilgrimage has a mediation function: between the natural and cultural worlds, on the one hand, and between the natural and supernatural worlds, on the other.

Content theories of motivation focus on what actually motivates people: they provide a way of identifying, classifying and explaining the factors that are most likely to motivate. They distinguish between lower- and higher-level motivators and explain their impact on behaviour. Application of content theories to this context serves to remind us that religiously motivated travellers, like all tourists, have basic needs: attention must be paid to providing the right conditions for satisfying those needs so that more spiritual motivations can be fulfilled.

Process theories of motivation emphasize the *process of motivation*, aiming to identify the relationship between various dynamic variables such as values and expectations, which influence individual motivation. Studies of religious travel consistently emphasize the importance of identifying and understanding religious values in underpinning motivations for religious travel. Motivation for religious travel is multifaceted and multilayered. Religiously motivated travellers themselves exhibit differences in motivation and expectation.

There is a need for further research in these differences to understand and classify the motivations of pilgrims and religious tourists to inform tourism managers, as well as their staff and volunteers, and help them to develop systems that will meet the diverse needs of pilgrims and religious tourists on journeys to religious destinations and during their stay at those destinations. It is clearly imperative that, given the rise in religious tourism and pilgrimage, we understand what motivates these travellers and to what extent, if at all, their expectations can be met.

References

Bhattarai, K., Conway, D. and Shrestha, N. (2005) *Annals of Tourism Research* 32 (3), 660–688.

Da Graca Mouga Pocas Santos, M. (2003) Religious tourism: contributions towards a clarification of concepts. In: Fernandes, C., McGettigan, F. and Edwards, J. (eds) *Religious Tourism and Pilgrimage ATLAS – Special Interest Group 1st Expert Meeting*, April 2003, Fátima, Portugal.

Goeldner, C.R. and Brent Richie, R.R. (2003) *Tourism Principles, Practices, Philosophies* 9th edn. John Wiley and Sons, Inc., Hoboken, New Jersey.

Graburn, N.N.H. (1989) Tourism: the sacred journey. In: Smith, V.L. (ed.) *Hosts and Guests: the Anthropology of Tourism*, 2nd edn. University of Pennsylvania, Philadelphia, Pennsylvania.

Herzberg, F. (1974) *Work and The Nature of Man*, Granada Publishing Ltd, St Albans, UK.

King, A. (2000) Violent pasts: collective memory and football hooliganism. *Sociological Review* 49 (4), 568–585.

Maslow, A. (1954) *Motivation and Personality*. Harper and Row, New York.

Mintel International Group Ltd (2005) *Religious Tourism – International*, March. Mintel International Group Ltd, London.

Poria, Y., Butler, R. and Airey, D. (2003) Tourism, religion and religiosity: a holy mess. *Current Issues in Tourism* 6 (4), 340–363.

Shackley, M. (2003) Management challenges for religion-based attractions. In: Fyall, A., Garrod, B. and Leask, A. (eds) *Managing Visitor Attractions – New Directions*. Butterworth-Heinemann, Oxford, UK.

Singh, S. (2004) Religion, heritage and travel: case references from the Indian Himalayas. *Current Issues in Tourism* 7 (1), 44–65.

Sumption, J. (1975) *Pilgrimage: an Image of Medieval Religion*. Faber, London.

Vroom, V.H. (1964) *Work and Motivation*. Wiley, Chichester, UK.

Vukonic, B. (1996) *Tourism and Religion*. Pergamon, Elsevier Science Ltd, Tourism Social Science Series, Oxford, UK.

Wilson, C. (1996) *The Atlas of Holy Places and Sacred Sites*. Dorling Kindersley Ltd, London.

4

The Management and Marketing of Religious Sites, Pilgrimage and Religious Events: Challenges for Roman Catholic Pilgrimages in Croatia

JURICA PAVICIC,[1] NIKISA ALFIREVIC[2] AND
VINCENT JOHN BATARELO[3]

[1]Graduate School of Economics and Business, University of Zagreb, Zagreb, Croatia; e-mail: jpavicic@efzg.hr; [2]Faculty of Economics, University of Split, Split, Croatia; e-mail: nalf@efst.hr, nalf@nalf.net; [3]Caritas Croatia, Zagreb, Croatia; e-mail: v.batarelo@zg.t-com.hr

Introduction

This chapter explores the complex managerial and marketing challenges facing all relevant stakeholders relating to religious and pilgrimage sites, while also addressing a combination of sacred and secular motivations for visitation. Practical issues of site management are explored to determine how existing holy places are able to combine different functions successfully.

Social Extraction of the Contemporary Phenomenon of Pilgrimage: Secularization and Religion in Modernity

Without getting into an in-depth analysis of the difference between secularization theory (or paradigm) and the role of religion in modernity, it is important to present a framework positioning the role of pilgrimages and religious events within modern societies. In the recent past, science has been a kind of 'grand narrative' (Lyotard, 1979), that is, science has offered itself and was looked upon as the means to solve each and every material, physical, psychological and social problem. Through science, the world would become better for everyone, in each domain.

It has been claimed that, in the face of scientific rationality, religion's influence on all aspects of life – from personal habits to social institutions – is in dramatic decline. The underlying assumption was that people have become, or are going to become, 'less religious'. Social theorists doubted that modernity could combine religious traditions with the overpowering impersonal features of our time: scientific research, humanistic education, high-tech multinational capitalism, bureaucratic organizational life, and so on.

Reacting on the basis of a functional definition of religion, religion appeared to these theorists denuded of almost all the functions it had previously appeared to perform. In this view, religion harked back to a prior level of human evolution and was now uselessly appended to the modern cultural repertoire. People today are in awe of human achievements, not divine forces: societies of the future would be constructed around these, not antiquity's notion of the 'sacred' (Swatos and Christiano, 1999).

Contrary to what was hoped for during modernity, people in contemporary industrial and post-industrial societies are being confronted with the incapacity of science to solve every problem. Very often, science has no direct significance for them, since its developments have no immediate applicability and are often unable to offer the urgent answers required by practical and particular problems that people face 'here and now', ranging from health issues to general meanings of life.

This fact stimulates people to look for a solution elsewhere – outside of science and impersonal 'red-tape' organizations. In this respect, popular religion appears as an important and valuable resource. People go on pilgrimages, for instance, hoping to solve or to avoid health difficulties for themselves and their nearest relatives and friends, to reconstruct familial harmony, to find a job or to pass exams (Voye, 1999).

This current reign of doubt and insecurity induces people to seek elsewhere a response for which, previously, they would have searched for initially in science or/and in the benevolence of the state. This is the case not only for individuals confronted by the hazards of their personal everyday life: there exist many testimonies showing that people with important responsibilities, notably in business or finance, are searching for responses in their professional affairs along non-rational lines, such as practices of popular religion (Voye, 1999). The shaking of confidence in rational thinking, which has been promoted in recent times, thus induces the reappearance of many kinds of non-rational practices, which affords and opportunity for popular religion to regain popularity and legitimacy, and which modernity had been intended to eradicate.

For instance, Central and Eastern European (CEE) countries up until the middle of the 20th century could very well be considered in sociological terms as traditional–rural and premodern societies. The process of extensive indus-trialization, increased urbanization and mass public education started after World War II – in the communist period. However, modernization in the communist period had characteristics of so-called forced or deviant modernization. Due to specific political circumstances, it was not led by its own inherent logic of development, nor did it result in modernism as its natural consequence (Županov, 2001).

In such circumstances, the Catholic Church first appeared as a marginalized, but socially strongly rooted, institution, primarily connected to traditional society. The erosion of that world represented the erosion of the strongest social basis of the Church. This process, though, was far from certain, mostly due to the specific characteristics of communist modernization.

Other than this, the connection between the Catholic Church and traditional society was strongly supported by the role of the Church in the maintenance of the disparate national identities within states that consisted of several nationalities/formal entities. The suppression of national feelings and identity by the communist governments had its clear counterbalance in the defence of national identity by the Church: there was a clear expression of the connection between faith and nation (Baloban, 2005).

In this context, the Catholic Church in Croatia during the period of communist rule (until 1990) happened to be one of the very few institutions outside the communist system that was not directly controlled by it and, as such, represented in a symbolic manner a means of opposition and counterculture. This was achieved many times through symbolic means, especially at pilgrimage sites. Between 1976 and 1984 nine major events – a Novena of religious/national festivities celebrating 13 centuries of Christianity in Croatia – were held.

From the Marian shrine in Solin (1976) and Nin (1979), celebrating the votive cross of a Croatian prince, to the culmination in 1984 of a National Eucharist Congress in Marija Bistrica, which symbolically represented 300 years since the discovery of Mary's statue, which was hidden due to the Ottoman threat. Over 400,000 pilgrims gathered in the shrine for the Congress. Shrines as such became a strongly symbolic public arena, shifting the ground of conflict from the political plane. An analogous situation took place in a similar manner in Poland (Herbert, 2003, p. 200).

The process of secularization, however, is an increasing factor within most modern societies. The above-mentioned could obviously be seen in the discrepancies between publicly declared acceptance of specific church teachings and traditions and their practical implementation in everyday life, especially in the sphere of morals and values. These elements of a church that has traditionally held a powerful position in society, and still does, combined with increasing secular influences, also have ramifications for the management and marketing of religious tourist sites, pilgrimages and religious events.

With the constant or even increasing demand for religious 'products', church and faith-based organizations and institutions have had to increase their offers, level of service and all-round professionalism to cater for various modern 'clients', both sacred and secular.

Religious Sites, Pilgrimages and Events: Sacred and Secular Motivations for Pilgrimage

Sacred motivations for pilgrimage

The most prominent religious 'tourist' or pilgrimage sites in CEE are Catholic shrines dedicated to Jesus, Mary the Mother of Jesus and the saints. In the religious usage of the word, shrines are repositories for a revered body or venerated relic. In its broader meaning a shrine refers to a sacred site that houses holy artefacts, promotes ritual practice and attracts religious travellers (pilgrims), who often mark the time and extend the space of the journey by returning home with mementos.

These sacred sites function as mediating spaces or transitional zones by allowing a vertical movement toward the sacred, elevating devotees and 'bringing low' the transcendent, as pilgrims petition and thank God and the saints. Shrines also allow horizontal movement outward into the social terrain and built environment. In this sense, they culturally situate devotees by creating interpersonal bonds, negotiating social status and constructing collective identity. Shrines differ from other places of worship such as local churches, mosques, temples or synagogues, which attract visitors on a more regular basis and from a narrower geographical range (Eliade, 1987; Smith, 1995).

The religiously motivated travellers who come to shrines are defined as pilgrims. They often undertake infrequent round-trip journeys to sites they consider sacred. At their destination, and along the way, pilgrims engage in religious practices that might include ritualized speech, dress and gestures. Pilgrimage is one of the well-known phenomena in various religious cultures and exists in all of the main religions of the world. It is defined as 'a journey resulting from religious causes, externally to a holy site, and internally for spiritual purposes and internal understanding' (Barber, 1991, p. 1).

Pilgrimage sites sometimes stand far from the follower's home, and sometimes the length and arduousness of the journey is itself spiritually significant. In recent literature, a high level of uniformity was found to exist between pilgrims' beliefs among different religions. As such, it is possible to view pilgrimage as a phenomenon cutting across religions and cultures, with uniform patterns and concepts. Even more so, contemporary research emphasizes the importance of what the pilgrims themselves say about their pilgrimage, since they are the main element in the pilgrimage phenomenon, and this subject has received meagre coverage in sociological studies.

There have been several approaches as to the study of pilgrimage (based upon Tweed, 2000). A historical approach has highlighted change over time and the distinctiveness of each pilgrimage, plus its embeddedness in the cultural context and the sponsoring religion. The sociological view, inspired by writings of Emil Durkheim, presupposes that pilgrimages reflect broader social processes, such as bolstering of social status and construction of collective identity.

A phenomenological approach, guided by the writings of Mircea Eliade (1987), has identified pilgrimage's common features by theorizing across religions and cultures. Claiming to be more sympathetic to the participants' interpretations, these scholars have seen pilgrimage as an encounter with the sacred. In opposition to functionalist sociological theories (Durkheim), they have also highlighted religion's inherent character, criticising those who reduce the phenomenon to social, cultural or economic impulses.

According to the most influential anthropological theory, developed by Victor Turner and Edith Turner, pilgrimage is a rite of passage: the pilgrim begins in the social structure, departs from it during the ritual and then returns (transformed) to society. During the pilgrimage, devotees stand in a 'liminal' state, where the usual social hierarchies are suspended and an egalitarian spirit of 'communitas' temporarily holds.

A plausible context for the theory of pilgrimage is Eliade's (1969) concept of the 'centre of the world'. From this perspective, a pilgrimage is a religiously motivated journey to the centre of the world itself, or to one of its homologous representations. For the individual pilgrim, that centre may also be remote, in the sense that he or she lives at a distance from it, but this remoteness is, in Eliade's interpretation, only locational–geographical and has no theoretical significance.

In contrast, within Turner and Turner's (1969) concept of the location of the pilgrimage centres, this remoteness gains theoretical significance. Turner and Turner (1969) introduced several fundamental ideas into the study of pilgrimage, directing the study of these phenomena into entirely new paths. Their basic idea was that pilgrimage might be analysed in homologous terms, proposed in their concept of the 'ritual processes'. They argued that pilgrimages typically involve a stage of liminality, resembling that in which novices find themselves in the transitory stage between two established social statuses.

Turner and Turner present pilgrimage as a symbolic, ritual activity with a variety of identifiable features. Firstly, pilgrimage requires a journey, and needs to be distinguished from rituals that do not. Rituals focused on pilgrimage sites are inclusive and emphasize 'shared values' (Turner and Turner, 1973, p. 207). Then, pilgrimages are a 'special locus of non-confrontational interaction' (Pechilis, 1992, p. 63), where unfamiliarity breeds a sense of communitas and inclusiveness that may not be found in familiar religious settings or institutions. As regards the 'ritual process', Turner and Turner introduce three stages of 'separation, margin or limen and reaggregation' (Turner and Turner, 1973, p. 213).

The pilgrim leaves home, separating him/herself from the familiar and, during the journey, has the experience of being 'betwixt and between all familiar lines of classification' (Turner and Turner, 1978, p. 2). He/she then returns home, spiritually transformed. The second stage of the rite of passage, the event itself, is, for the pilgrim, a 'liminal' experience: 'it represents a "threshold", a place and a moment "in and out of time" and, as such, an actor – as evidence of many pilgrims of many religions attest – hopes to have their direct experience of the sacred, invisible or supernatural order' (Turner and Turner, 1973, p. 218).

It appears therefore, that the role of pilgrimage in society at large appears to be that of showing the individual the importance of his or her role in the community. Turner and Turner believe that pilgrimages take people out of the structures of their everyday lives and bring people together in communitas. Communitas is 'a spontaneously generated relationship between levelled and equal, total and individual human beings, stripped of structural attributes' and is to be distinguished from a 'community', which Turner defines as a 'geographical area of common living' (Turner and Turner, 1973, p. 216). For Turner and Turner, the experience of pilgrimage is one of unity and communitas that expands the pilgrim's world view in a way that benefits both the individual and society as a whole.

Turner and Turner proposed the fundamental idea that pilgrimages centres are typically located 'out there'. This peripherality is both geographical–locational and cultural; the sites are marginal to population centres, and indeed to the socio-political centres of society. These peripheral centres are often located beyond a stretch of wilderness or in some other uninhabited territory, in the 'chaos surrounding the ordered "cosmicized" social world'. Nevertheless, because it is a focus, the pilgrimage centre is a paradoxical conceptualization that emerges as a 'centre out there' (Turner and Turner, 1973, pp. 211–214, 1978, p. 241).

This idealistic notion about pilgrimage has been increasingly subjected to criticism from anthropologists and others. Although Dubisch (1995, p. 46) cautiously finds the category of pilgrimage valuable because of what she sees as 'similarities in the practice of journeys to sacred places even among quite different religious traditions', she does raise the question of whether or not there are significant variations between journeys made for 'religious' or 'non-religious' reasons and events, or whether or not the journey itself matters (Dubisch, 1995).

A change in the focus of research in analysing the pilgrimage process took place recently in the studies of Eade and Sallow (cited in Collins-Kreiner and Kliot, 2000, p. 56). They formulated a new approach with a wider view from different levels and aspects: political, cultural and behavioural, taking into account the tourist perspective as well. Thus, pilgrimage ceased to be investigated from only the religious perspective.

Non-religious, secular and touristic motivations for pilgrimage

Superficial relationships between tourists and pilgrims have been acknowledged by numerous medieval scholars and by tourism historians (Smith, 1992). In its current usage, the term 'pilgrimage' connotes a religious journey, but its Latin derivation from *peregrinus* allows broader interpretations, including foreigner, wanderer, exile and traveller, as well as newcomer and stranger. The term 'tourist' also has Latin origins, from *tornus* – an individual who makes a circuitous journey, usually for pleasure, and returns to the starting point.

The contemporary use of the terms, identifying the 'pilgrim' as a religious traveller and the 'tourist' as a vacationer, is a culturally constructed polarity that veils the motives of the travellers (Smith, 1992). The nature of the 'tourist experience' has received increasing attention in tourism research, with the tourist perceived as a pilgrim in the current modern secular world (Collins-Kreiner and Kliot, 2000, p. 56). Tourism has been defined as an activity dependent on three operative elements: discretionary income, leisure time and social sanctions permissive of travel.

Pilgrimage also requires these elements. Turner and Turner claimed that a tourist is half a pilgrim, if a pilgrim is half a tourist, while other authors have described tourism as a 'sacred journey' in which the individual escapes from the secular everyday world to the land of play (ibid). Tourism and pilgrimage can be identified as opposite end points on a continuum of travel (Smith, 1992; Fig. 4.1).

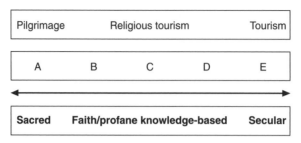

Fig. 4.1. Tourism and pilgrimage as a continuum of travel (from Smith, 1992). A, pious pilgrim; B, pilgrim > tourist; C, pilgrim = tourist; D, tourist > pilgrim; E, secular tourist.

The polarities on the pilgrimage–tourism axis are labelled as sacred versus secular. Between the extremities lie almost an infinite [number of] possible sacred–secular combinations, with the central area (C) now generally termed as 'religious tourism' or 'knowledge-based tourism' (as the term is sometimes used as a synonym). These positions reflect the multiple and changing motivations of the traveller, whose interests and activities may switch from tourism to pilgrimage and vice versa, even without the individual being aware of the change.

Most researchers identify 'religious tourism' with the individual's quest for shrines and locales where, in lieu of piety, the visitors seek to experience the sense of identity with sites of historical and cultural meaning (Collins-Kreiner and Kliot, 2000, p. 57).

Contemporary research is now increasingly addressing the complicated relationship between pilgrimage and tourism, including the economic, social, political, psychological, emotional and other aspects. One of the representative articles on this aspect came from Eade (1992), whose paper describes the interaction between pilgrims and tourists at the Marian shrine in Lourdes, France.

One cannot describe 'the tourist' as a 'general type' (Cohen, 1979, p. 180). Therefore, there are several tourist experiences that will help in the understanding of the phenomena of pilgrimage. Four main modes are defined, presenting the spectrum between the experience of the tourist as a traveller in pursuit of 'mere' pleasure and that of the modern pilgrim in quest of meaning at someone else's 'centre'. Cohen (1979) classifies them as the 'recreational mode', the 'diversionary mode', the 'experiential mode' and the 'existential mode' (Cohen, 1979, p. 183).

Cohen claims that tourists travelling in the 'existential mode' are analogous to pilgrims. Both are fully committed to an elective spiritual centre, external to the mainstream of their native society and culture because they feel that the only meaningful 'real' life is at the centre. The pilgrim and the 'pilgrim-tourist' peregrinate toward their sociocultural centre, while the traveller and the 'traveller-tourist' move in the opposite direction. It seems that the difference between old-fashioned pilgrimage and tourism is narrowing. Numerous points of similarity are emerging, and the word 'pilgrimage' itself is widely used in broad and secular contexts, such as for visits to war graves or to the graves and residences of celebrities (Collins-Kreiner and Kliot, 2000, p. 57).

'Tangible' artefacts of pilgrimage

Regardless of the journey, most pilgrims experience a temporary or permanent change in the outlook of their lives and their relationship to the sacred, to God. All in all, pilgrimage sites offer tangible reminders for pilgrims to take back home, to remind them of the pilgrimage and the changes that have spiritually taken place. For the modern-day pilgrim, this can mean a wide range of artefacts ranging from rosaries and statues of saints to bottles of holy water, candles, postcards, t-shirts, books, etc. When returning home, devotees recall and extend the sacred journey by wearing or carrying mementos, giving them to loved ones or placing them in the home, thereby 'sacralizing' their homes and linking them with the pilgrimage site.

Case Study: Management and Marketing Practices at the Shrine of the Mother of God in Marija Bistrica, Croatia

> Through examining pilgrimage as an aspect of popular culture in the past, we are able to see tourism of the 20th century in sharpened focus.
>
> (Theilmann, 1987, p. 100)

Historical context

Marija Bistrica, a village of 7000 inhabitants[1] in the region of Hrvatsko Zagorje (near Zagreb, the capital of Croatia), is one of the premier pilgrimage destinations for both devoted Catholic believers from the entire CEE as well as for all those seeking a spiritual refuge from the everyday routine. The first mentioning of the site dates back to the early 13th century (Kurečić, 2004), with the site being recorded as a feudal possession, with changing feudal lords until the revolution in 1848, which saw its transformation into a civil community.

However, the social life of the community has always been concentrated on church-going (as was the norm at the time), but also on the worship of Virgin Mary,[2] with the simple statue of a Black Madonna[3] becoming the object of

---

[1] Source: http://www.marija-bistrica.hr/stranice/opceinformacije/folder/index.htm (available in Croatian only, accessed 30 January 2006).

[2] The very term *Virgin Mary* is a difficult issue: while the Roman Catholic church usually uses the title *Blessed Virgin Mary* (*The Blessed Virgin*), the Protestant tradition inclines to the simple name *Mary, the Mother of Jesus*, but the Islamic tradition is also linked to worship of Mary, as one of the 114 Qur'an chapters is devoted to *Maryamm, Umm Issa* (*Mary, the Mother of Jesus*, who is considered to be one of the Prophets of Islam). Therefore, throughout this chapter, the 'neutral' term *Virgin Mary* is used, as it refers to the immaculate conception as a common belief in all major religions (compiled from Wikipedia, http://en.wikipedia.org, accessed 30 January 2006).

[3] The term *Black Madonna* (in this context) refers to the medieval representation of the Virgin Mary (mostly from the 12th–15th centuries), with many paintings believed to have miraculous effects. The statue of Marija Bistrica is comparable to Our Lady of the Hermits in Switzerland, Our Lady of Jasna Gora in Poland, Our Lady of Montserrat in Spain and other 'Black Madonnas' (Duricy, 2006).

pilgrimage of hundreds of thousands of pilgrims. The wooden statue can be traced to one of the local 15th-century craftsmen, with tradition implying that it was located in a chapel at the hill called Vinski Vrh, nearby Marija Bistrica (Kurečić, 2004).

Social context and challenges

The challenges for managing such a pilgrimage site are twofold: on one hand, the pilgrims' need for spiritual and social experience should be met, but on the other, the practical considerations should not be forgotten. However, managing the spiritual/religious component is not easy, either, especially for the 'old' shrines, such as Marija Bistrica.

Pilgrimage patterns have been changing, along with the social structure of believers, which is very noticeable in the demand patterns. Up to the second half of the 20th century, pilgrimages to Marija Bistrica have often been the only form of leisure available to the lower classes of Croatian society, which could also explain the attractiveness of yet another Marian shrine, located in Trsat (which is today a part of the city of Rijeka, located in the north-western part of the Adriatic).

The pilgrimage to Trsat was a rare opportunity for many to see the Adriatic Sea for the first time in their lives, which reflects the theoretical notion of pilgrimage as the origin of tourism in pre-modern societies (Theilmann, 1987). At those times, the pilgrimage patterns strictly reflected the 'rhythm' of the rural society, with peaks during the summer months (as required by the determinants of agricultural production), seeing the entire families on pilgrimages that used to last for several days or even a week.

Therefore, the pilgrimage motives – at the time – might have been mixed (including both a spiritual component and a certain aspect of using the only available form of a family holiday), but this fact did not pose an exceptional challenge to the shrine management team, taking into account that the 'customers' were perfectly happy to use substandard accommodation, made available by the local community members.

The second half of the 20th century brought about the processes of modernization (for an overview of this and its reference to the processes of transition and transformation, see Langer *et al.*, 2005), and the introduction of Communism, which made the public declaration of either nationality or religious beliefs/practice at least socially unacceptable (or even punishable, depending on the level of tolerance of the government structures). Therefore, the pilgrimage patterns have been changing to reflect a new social reality, as well as to show the level of opposition to the ruling social order.

Marija Bistrica, along with the other pilgrimage sites in the region during this period, has been often interpreted by its guests not only as a 'sacred place', but also as a space of personal freedom, in which feelings and beliefs related to nationality and religion could be expressed.

In spite of formal obstacles, the pilgrimages continued during socialism, with Marija Bistrica being officially recognized as the national Croatian place of pilgrimage by the Catholic church (i.e. by the former Bishop's Conference of Yugoslavia) in 1971, further boosting its status among the pilgrims (Kurečić, 2004).

The year of 1990 brought about comprehensive social changes, including the introduction of a democratic political system and a market-based economy into most of the CEE countries. For good or worse, CEE countries have rejoined 'the West' (Hagen, 2003) and entered the process of political, economic and social ... transition toward the postmodern, 'Western' blueprints. The social change affected (more or less) traditional families which, according to the recent theoretical viewpoint (Giddens, 1992; Beck and Beck-Gernsheim, 1995; Haralambos and Holborn, 2004), become diverse and fragmented, due to the increasing individualization and variety of life opportunities presented to the family members.

However, this also implies little or no stability at all, lack of traditional behavioural archetypes and increased pressure of the capitalist economic system on individuals, who are supposed to sacrifice the quality of their family life to business accomplishment(s). In such a context, the act of pilgrimage could be interpreted in a new, postmodern manner – as a spiritual refuge from a secular society that increasingly valued material accomplishment.

The 'business' context of managing a pilgrimage site

Although belonging to the spiritual realm and offering refuge from the routines of (post-)industrial society, pilgrimage sites/shrines pose practical challenges to the individuals and/or managerial teams occupied with the daily management of all the activities required in serving pilgrims' needs. Given that many of those managers actually belong to the clergy, the self-perception of their activities does not include the concept of a 'businesslike' approach to managing both the pilgrims' experiences and the 'secular' aspects of their visit, including schedule/time management, transportation, lodging, etc.

In order to describe the 'typical' challenges of 'business' tasks in such a specific context, a fairly simple, customer-oriented framework will be used. It is based on the 'standard' idea of implementing the overall (marketing) approach (strategy) to accomplishing destination objectives by: (i) identifying the target groups whose needs are to be served; (ii) making decisions related to product/service offering; (iii) making decisions related to the place in which those products/services are being offered; (iv) initiating promotion and other forms of communication with the potential and existing clients; and (v) adopting a pricing/fundraising approach (Kotler and Armstrong, 2005; Kotler and Keller, 2005).

Target groups/audience

During the 322 years of pilgrimage tradition, Marija Bistrica has gained a considerable reputation as *the* place of pilgrimage, especially for the churchgoers from the wider area of Zagreb, Croatia, although its national status attracts visitors from the entire country.[4] However, there are four target groups that could be identified as potential 'customers'/guests: (i) groups of 'parish pilgrims' from the entire country, usually visiting the site on an annual basis; (ii) elementary school students (usually visiting Marija Bistrica as a part of their regular school trips); (iii) pensioners' associations (usually as civil society organizations); and (iv) individual visitors, normally families with young children.

The demand is highly seasonal, with the peak number of visits from the last weekend in July up to the end of the August, with different estimates regarding the number of pilgrims visiting the site annually, of which the most 'conservative' is of 500,000 people (although the figure could be anywhere between 500,000 and 1.2 million, as there are no reliable data regarding the number of visitors). Pilgrimage events have, traditionally, shown seasonal variations related to climate and the agricultural cycle, with the pilgrimage vows being important means for coping with environmental hazard and uncertainty.

Destination marketing and management decisions

Service and product management

The management of pilgrimage sites has to consider the varying demands of their guests, but also they should not give up the traditional reliance on piety, as 'what is vital for the religious tourist is the spirit of a sanctified ritual ...', which 'matters more than whether a saint was buried at a certain place ...' (Kamill, 2000). The experience matters: contemporary places of pilgrimage enable visitors to immerse in the feelings considered 'ancient' and 'sacred' (however these attributes might be construed by the individual pilgrim).

Violation of these principles in the everyday destination management would undermine its competitive advantage over the similar experience offerings and, hence, it could be argued that preserving and/or enhancing the 'holy experience' represents the core of the competitive strategy for a place of pilgrimage, i.e. its *core competence*, as usually labelled by theory (Prahalad and Hamel, 1990).

The contemporary economy – even beyond the tourist industry – tries to emulate the practices that have been well known to the managers of pilgrimage sites for centuries. Specifically, with the economy of 'the West' being primarily service-oriented, producing ('staging') and selling memorable experiences becomes a viable tool for the promotion of services (either as an individual offering or combined with tangible products) (Pine and Gilmore, 1998). In the process, customers (labelled as 'guests') perceive the 'clues' (architecture, music, speeches, scents, etc.) which, in turn, produce an emotional state. The context and personal interpretations of such emotions create the *experience* – either positive or negative (Boswijk *et al.*, 2006).

[4] The main source of information on site management in the following sections is from an in-depth interview with the parish priest and managing director of the Shrine of the Mother of God in Marija Bistrica, the Reverend Ziatko Koren, held on 30 January 2006.

Like local/regional pilgrims, people from foreign countries, usually accompanied by their parish priests, are provided with the opportunity to celebrate the Holy Mass in their own language, while the tour through the shrine is provided by a professional guide. Therefore, the activities related to the site management could be, roughly, divided into: (i) those related to the everyday schedule of 'standardized offering' to the pilgrims, including the special religious/spiritual events, celebrated according to the traditional schedule; and (ii) *ad hoc* activities, usually created to satisfy the needs of larger, organized groups of pilgrims. In addition, the management successfully innovates the traditional spiritual offering of the shrine by offering new, more meditative forms of prayer, which are considered to be more appropriate to the needs of contemporary pilgrims.

The new segments of potential audience(s) are also being targeted by the cooperation of, and 'strategic alliances' with, the cultural institutions and organizations, with Marija Bistrica hosting folk performances and concerts of classical music within the programme of *Varaždin baroque evenings*, being held traditionally in September. All related services/products are oriented towards improving the 'whole experience' of all relevant stakeholders.

Local alliances/partnerships are also essential for the success of the pilgrimage site, as evidenced by the simple means of forecasting the demand: taking into account that the number of guests on any given Sunday depends on a number of factors (such as the weather conditions, holiday schedules, etc.). A working partnership with the local police station is also an advantage: through observation of the number of cars arriving in the area early in the morning, police officers (who need to regulate the incoming traffic anyway) are able to estimate how many visitors can be expected and thereby inform the shrine management.

In order to preserve the devotion to the spiritual content of their work and avoid the 'businesslike' orientation, there are no related 'secular businesses' (including cafes, restaurants, souvenir stands, etc.) within the pilgrimage complex, although this implies sacrifice of a certain amount of revenue.

Place/accessibility management challenges through the centuries

The statue of the Black Madonna has been located in the parish church, having being concealed in 1545 and 1650 due to the fear of an Ottoman invasion (Croatia has had a border with the Ottoman Empire) and rediscovered in 1588 and 1684, with miracles being linked to both rediscovery events (source: http://www.marija-bistrica.hr/stranice/novosti/povijest003.htm; available in Croatian only, accessed 30 January 2006). The resultant pilgrimages had a beneficial influence to the community, especially after the Croatian Parliament (Sabor) decided to grant Marija Bistrica the status of the national place of pilgrimage in the 18th Century, as well as to finance the public roads leading to the parish church (Kurečić, 2004).

The Bistrica pilgrimage site has reached its present appearance, including the construction of the new bell tower and arcades at the end of the 19th century, with the renowned Austrian architect, Hermann Bolle (who also designed some of the central areas of Zagreb), being hired for the job. Another 'pilgrim attraction' – the Calvary, was erected on the hill facing the extended parish church, and could be visited from 1943 up to the late 1970s (source: The Way of the Cross on the Bistrica Calvary, http://www.svetiste-mbb, accessed 30 January 2006).

During last few decades, most group visits to Marija Bistrica have been organized by local parishes and local/international travel agencies that are considered reliable intermediaries between the shrine and potential pilgrims. Management and control of all related infrastructure – roads, means of transportation, accommodation facilities, restaurants, etc. – are not directly connected with the shrine, but all activities are derived from the common interests of all stakeholders at local and national levels.

Promotion and communication management

The Marija Bistrica shrine communicates with the potential pilgrims mostly through church media, as it is felt that paid advertising would undermine the mission and the spiritual identity of the organization. In addition, the shrine (intertwined with the local parish) publishes its own newsletter, *Milosti puna* (trans., full of grace – recalling the words of a common prayer to the Virgin Mary), which is distributed to all parish communities in Croatia that have previously visited Marija Bistrica. It also runs a radio station, Radio Marija Bistrica and World Wide Web pages (accessible at http://www.svetiste-mbb.hr). In addition, a new multimedia presentation of the shrine is being set up, in order to better explain its history and importance to the younger pilgrims.

The management of the pilgrimage site in Marija Bistrica understands the challenges of creating experiences, by trying to demonstrate the openness and emphasize the 'spiritual content' of a typical visit to the shrine. The practices used are simple, but effective, and can be described by the keywords of *personal accessibility* (of the entire staff) and *personalized communication*, relying on a traditional, low-tech approach that gives in to postmodernity only by introducing cell phones into the everyday operation of the site; the shrine staff are always available by telephone, enabling both tourist agencies (and other intermediaries on the tourist market) and individual visitors to announce the arrival of pilgrims, who are given the option either to 'fit into' the standardized 'product offer' (Holy Mass and different forms of prayers – located throughout the pilgrimage complex, the Holy Communion, etc.) or to 'customize' their own choice of activities, depending on the motivation and time available.

In addition, all pilgrims arriving at the shrine are personally welcomed by the manager of the pilgrimage site at the beginning of the day, whether they are partaking as individuals of the 'standardized' activities or as groups for whom the *ad hoc* programme has been offered.

Taking into account a certain level of 'competition', due to the existence of regional places of pilgrimage (also devoted to Virgin Mary) – which include Sinj (located in the region of Dalmatia), Trsat (Rijeka and Primorje), Aljmaš (Slavonija) as well as Medjugorje (in neighbouring Bosnia and Herzegovina), promotion of the shrine is also essential. However, the concept of competition is not entirely applicable to Marija Bistrica, due to the fact that it holds the status of the national place of pilgrimage, being – as such – visited by believers from the entire country.

There is also an opportunity of 'packaged' pilgrimages to multiple sites, which is often the plan of foreign pilgrims wishing to see more of the country they are visiting; the popular option (especially for the guests from CEE countries) is a 'combo visit' to Marija Bistrica and Medjugorje. However, it is not clear whether the relevant institutions recognize such a form of package offer, as this has not, as yet, been promoted at all, but has been left to the decision of tourist agencies and individual pilgrims, depending on the information that might have been gleaned from various media.

Considering all the abovementioned aspects of such specific pilgrimages, a very important content of almost every related marketing communication is the concept of 'family reunion'. Such an opportunity for a family to travel together in search of an experience that is both sacred and collective unquestionably strengthens the family ties and, probably, has therapeutic effects for its members.

The pilgrimage experience is, therefore, being *deconstructed* and opened up to various communication processes and multiple interpretations, highly dependent upon individual needs and expectations. In the same manner, the contemporary patterns of pilgrimages at the Marija Bistrica shrine are more complex and very difficult to forecast, as the majority of guests/pilgrims are nuclear families from the urban communities (especially the city of Zagreb), arriving at weekends by their own cars and spending either a few hours or an entire day at the pilgrimage site. They might have a variety of motives and may wish to combine the visit to the shrine with some other form of touristic offer (such as a family excursion, family lunch, etc.).

Pricing and fundraising management

The shrine is financed primarily by pilgrims' donations, although it is actively seeking partnerships with governmental institutions, local authorities and corporate donators/sponsors. Being a significant part of the local economy, the shrine of the Mother of God in Marija Bistrica is deeply 'embedded' within the community, employing (either part- or full-time) over 120 people (in the period of peak demand) and providing business opportunities to many local entrepreneurs.

Instead of a Conclusion

In the (post)modern society, places of pilgrimage/shrines perform significant social functions, although they have to 'compete' with alternative offerings targeting the same needs and motives of (potential) pilgrims. Although it may be argued that the 'competition' in the field of religious tourism is irrelevant, as long as clients' spiritual needs are satisfied, both the organization running such a site and the local community – often depending economically on the inflow of pilgrims – would certainly disagree (Pavicic *et al.*, 2001). Therefore, there is a need for identification and transfer of best practices among such sites, as well as the imperative of developing more professional approaches to management and marketing of such sites in terms of tourist destinations. However, the spiritual/religious experience emanating from the pilgrimage remains the core of the shrine's success in meeting the spiritual needs of its clients and cannot be substituted by any other critical success factor.

References

Baloban, J. (ed.) (2005) *In Search of Identity. A Comparative Study of Values: Croatia and Europe*. Golden Marketing, Tehnička knjiga, Zagreb.

Barber, R. (1991) *Pilgrimages*. The Boydell Press, London.

Beck, U. and Beck-Gernsheim, E. (1995) *The Normal Chaos of Love*. Polity Press, Cambridge, UK.

Boswijk, A., Thijssen, T. and Peelen, E. (2006) *A New Perspective on the Experience Economy*. http://www.experience-economy.com/wpcontent/UserFiles/File/Article%20 Lapland5.pdf (accessed 1 February 2006).

Cohen, E.A. (1979) Phenomenology of tourist experiences. *Sociology* 13 (2), 179–201.

Collins-Kreiner, N. and Kliot, N. (2000) Pilgrimage tourism in the Holy Land: the behavioural characteristics of Christian pilgrims. *GeoJournal* 50, 55–67.

Dubisch, J. (1995) *In a Different Place: Pilgrimage, Gender and Politics at a Greek Island Shrine*. Princeton University Press, Princeton, New Jersey.

Eade, J. (1992) Pilgrimage and tourism at Lourdes, France. *Annals of Tourism Research* 19 (1), 18–32.

Eliade, M. (ed.) (1969) *The Quest: History and Meaning in Religion*. University of Chicago Press, Chicago, Illinois.

Eliade, M. (ed.) (1987) Shrines. In: *Encyclopedia of Religion*. MacMillan, New York.

Giddens, A. (1992) *The Transformation of Intimacy: Sexuality, Love and Eroticism in Modern Societies*. Polity Press, Cambridge, UK.

Hagen, J. (2003) Redrawing the imagined map of Europe: the rise and fall of the 'center'. *Political Geography* 22, 489–517.

Haralambos, M. and Holborn, M. (2004) *Sociology*, 6th edn. Collins Publishers, London.

Herbert, D. (2003) *Religion and Civil Society – Rethinking Public Religion in the Contemporary World*. Ashgate, Aldershot, UK.

Kamill, J. (2000) Religious tourism as big business In: *Al-Ahram Weekly* 469, 17–23 February, Cairo, http://weekly.ahram.org.eg/2000/469/tr2.htm (accessed 31 January 2006).

Kotler, P. and Armstrong, G. (2005) *Principles of Marketing*, 11th edn. Prentice Hall, Upper Saddle River, New Jersey.

Kotler, P. and Keller, K.L. (2005) *Marketing Management*, 12th edn. Prentice Hall, Upper Saddle River, New Jersey.

Kurečić, Z. (2004) *The Mother of God of Bistrica: the Croatian National Shrine*. Turistička zaklada Zagreb & Svetište Majke Božje Bistričke – Marija Bistrica.

Langer, J., Alfirevic, N. and Pavicic, J. (2005) *Organizational Change in Transition Societies*. Ashgate, Aldershot, UK.

Lyotard, J.F. (1979) *The Postmodern Condition* (previously published in French as *La Condition Postmoderne: Rapport sur le Savoir*, Minuit, Paris, 1979). Manchester University Press, Manchester, UK.

Pavicic, J., Renko, N. and Alfirevic, N. (2001) Role Of marketing orientation and competitive analysis in improving competitiveness of the non-profit sector – theoretical background and empirical evidence from the Croatian public libraries. In: *Proceedings of the 4th International Conference 'Enterprise in Transition'*, 24–26 May 2001, Faculty of Economics Split and World Bank, pp. 115–116 (extended abstract in the book of abstracts, pp. 422–437; full paper on CD-ROM).

Pechilis, K. (1992) To pilgrimage it. *Journal of Ritual Studies* 6 (2), 59–91.

Pine, B.J. and Gilmore, J.H. (1998) Welcome to the experience economy. *Harvard Business Review* July/August, 97–105.

Prahalad, C.K. and Hamel, G. (1990) The core competence of the corporation. *Harvard Business Review* May/June, 79–90.

Smith, J.Z. (ed.) (1995) Shrine. In: *The Harper Collins Dictionary of Religion*. HarperCollins, San Francisco, California.

Smith, V.L. (1992) Introduction: the quest in guest. *Annals of Tourism Research* 19 (1), 1–17.

Swatos, W.H. and Christiano, K.J. (1999) Secularization theory: the course of a concept. *Sociology of Religion* 60 (3), 209–228.

Theilmann, J.M. (1987) Medieval pilgrims and the origins of tourism. *Journal of Popular Culture* 20 (4), 93–102.

Turner, V. and Turner, E. (1969) *The Ritual Process*. Routledge, London.

Turner, V. and Turner, E. (1973) The center out there: pilgrim's goal. *History of Religions* 12 (3), 191–230.

Turner, V. and Turner, E. (1978) *Image and Pilgrimage in Christian Culture: Anthropological Perspectives*. Columbia University Press, New York.

Tweed, T.A. (2000) John Wesley slept here: American shrines and American Methodists. *Numen* 47, 41–68.

Voye, L. (1999) Secularization in a context of advanced modernity. *Sociology of Religion* 60 (3), 275–288.

Županov, J. (2001) Industrijalizirajuća i deindustrijalizirajuća elita u Hrvatskoj u drugoj polovici 20. stojeća'. In: Čengić, D. and Rogić, I. (eds) *Upravljacke Elite i Modernizacija*. Institut društvenih znanosti Ivo Pilar, Zagreb, Croatia.

5 Sustaining Tourism Infrastructures for Religious Tourists and Pilgrims within the UK

Ian D. Rotherham

Tourism and Environmental Change Research Unit, Sheffield Hallam University, Sheffield, UK; e-mail: i.d.rotherham@shu.ac.uk

Introduction

This chapter initially explores concepts of pilgrimage, religion and tourism within a UK context, considering how visitation to UK religious sites provides opportunities for economic regeneration and community sustainability.

Pilgrimage, Religion and Tourism

Pilgrimage is one of the oldest forms of tourism and is an integral component of the tourist industry; the three terms, above, can be defined in different ways and from differing viewpoints. Pilgrimage is a journey made by a pilgrim, who travels from place to place, usually journeying a long distance and to a sacred place as an act of devotion (Onions, 1983). Harvey (2000) describes religion as structured, orderly, socially sanctioned ways of reaching out for what people want most. Cohen (1992) raises important ideas, in particular noting relationships between pilgrim and tourist as travellers.

Tourism generally relates to the activities of persons travelling to and staying in places outside their usual environment for not more than one consecutive year, for leisure, business and other purposes according to Cambridge Policy Consultants and Geoff Broom Consultants (Anon., 1998). The main purpose of the trip is not an activity that will be remunerated from the place to which the trip is made. These authors combine the UK Day Visits Survey definition of a day trip (i.e. an irregular trip of 3 or more hours' duration undertaken by people travelling to and staying in places outside their usual environment) with overnight stays away from home, to define a tourism trip.

The Social and Planning Research team of the former Countryside Commission (Countryside Agency, 1998a, b) described a day visit as a round trip from home or work, for leisure purposes, with return within the same day. Roe *et al.* (1997) define tourism as any form of travel that involves a stay of at least one night, but less than one year, away from home. They note that it is generally domestic or international travel for leisure or recreation, including day trips.

From a spiritual perspective, such an experience may offer a location, place or experience to a believer that relates to someone or something that they venerate, such as a saint. Sociologically it may provide cultural access to sacred art and sculpture, which may attract atheists or those of other religions as well as the devout of a particular faith. Cultural roots may be embedded in places or images regardless of whether or not the contemporary tourist is a believer.

For the pilgrim, this experience may be to a place such as a holy shrine or a journey between two significant places; for Catholics for example, from Mont-Saint-Michel to Lourdes, or from Lourdes to Rome. It is also helpful to examine briefly the terms *visitor attraction* and *tourist attraction*, and Busby (2003) is useful in this respect. Whilst these terms are often used interchangeably, the latter may exclude leisure day visits, and this is unhelpful in addressing the issues raised here. What amounts to a *visitor attraction* is also important, and the Scottish Tourist Board definition is informative:

> A permanently established excursion destination, a primary purpose of which is to allow public access for entertainment, interest or education, rather than being principally a retail outlet or a venue for sporting, theatrical or film performances. It must be open to the public without prior booking, for published periods each year, and should be capable of attracting tourists as well as local residents.
>
> (Scottish Tourist Board, 1991)

From this definition, it is clear that many religious places such as churches and mosques are tourism and leisure visitor attractions. So are iconic sites of former faiths, such as Druidic stone circles or the pyramids of Ancient Egypt. Consideration of religious tourism and the visiting of sacred sites suggest potential for problems. At an intersection of two contrasting approaches to life, they present realities that are difficult to reconcile. The image of the mass tourist suggests consumption, triviality and leisure; that of the pilgrim is of sobriety, often with asceticism, and an engagement with deep religious process and, above all, serious. These seem to conflict.

Religious tourism and the visiting of sacred sites offer experiences to meet both demands. They can cater for those demanding spiritual retreats or provide a priest to accompany a group of pilgrims. On the other hand, they may facilitate understanding of the significance of a particular religious building, perhaps in relation to a living church of relevance to the participant. Alternatively, they can package the religious experience within a tour or study trip, incorporating the broader topics of history and heritage, food, etc. Tourism can simply provide the experience of a guide for an itinerary of artistic and cultural works from religious and sacred places, the locations serving as museums.

Religious tourism – including pilgrimage – is embedded within a complex of heritage tourism and mass tourism activities. The interrelationships are complex, and interactions with local people and communities are central to the understanding of religious tourism in creating community-based sustainable development. What constitutes heritage for one group is conversely a religious place or artefact for another, and there is potential for serious conflicts of interests and priorities.

Yet, religious tourism and the visiting of religious sites, such as churches in rural England, is important, with synergies to many aspects of heritage leisure and historical tourism in both urban and rural areas and the bringing of economic benefits. Tourism is recognized as important to many economies: an industry with potential to impact significantly on local communities and the environment (Beard *et al.*, 2000; Rotherham *et al.*, 2005), and religious pilgrimage offers established economic benefits in other parts of the world.

The Breadth and Importance of Religious Tourism

A typical image of religious pilgrimage is tourism associated with Lourdes in France. This small town (population 16,581 in 1990) in Hautes-Pyrénées, south-west France, lies at the foot of the Pyrenees. Famous for its Roman Catholic shrine where 'Our Lady of Lourdes' is believed to have appeared repeatedly in 1858 to St Bernadette, millions of people today make the pilgrimage each year, drawn by their faith in miraculous cures attributed to the waters of the shrine.

Similarly huge numbers of Muslims (over 2 million in January 2006) visit Mecca every year (*The Guardian*, 2006). Woodward (2003) notes the importance of the hajj for example, to the economy of Saudi Arabia. This is worth around US$1.5 billion, with 40% being spent on the rental of rooms to pilgrims, and so a major input to local economies. Yet, as discussed later, there are serious conflicts of interest over this impact, and considerable damage to the resource has resulted. Both the breadth of the topic and of associated research are important. Bhardwaj (1998) notes that research has neglected non-hajj pilgrimage in studies of Islam and of tourism, and it is the same scenario for other faiths. Much focuses on better-known sites and bigger events, while lesser-known activities are neglected.

Tourism associated with religions, sites and pilgrimage is recognized as ever more important. This is for both religious reasons *per se* and economic impacts. The small village of Epworth in north Lincolnshire, UK, was the birthplace (1703) of John Wesley, the founder of Methodism. Hundreds of thousands of tourists come from around the world, especially from the Far East and the USA, to visit the site or to take part in celebrations. These visitors are the cornerstone of an emerging tourist economy in an area of severe economic and social decline (Smith, 2004).

In the Western world, we live in an increasingly secular, often non-religious society. Whether this lacks spirituality is a different question. Harvey (2000) and Blain *et al.* (2004) consider these issues in terms of diverse religions and religious experiences. In the UK, for example, the diminished role of the organized Christian church is paralleled by a growth in multiculturalism and moves towards other sources of spiritual enlightenment and fulfilment.

In some cases, these include a return to paganism such as the Druid movement. This re-emerged in the Victorian era, influenced by both the

Romantics and the work of antiquarians such as William Stukeley, whose research associated ancient Druids with places like Avebury and Stonehenge. In some cases – such as Stonehenge (Jenkins, 2006) and Stanton Moor in the Peak National Park (England) – there are major conflicts over spiritual 'ownership' of these heritage sites.

Jenkins (2006) raises interesting points about the heritage issues and about the cultural 'ownership' of sites such as Stonehenge by neo-ancients and Druids. The numbers of visitors, both religious and secular, can be huge (817,981 in 2004 for Stonehenge). For instance, visitors to Stonehenge may be secular, non-practising Druids; many Western tourists visit Mount Fuji, Japan (the latter has over 25 million day visitors per year).

The search for spirituality may include extreme sports such as mountaineering, and many visits to beautiful locations, both cultural and natural, have a degree of spirituality whether conscious, overt or hidden. Tresidder (1999) and Aichison *et al.* (2000) discuss these, and Woodward (2003) addresses broader roles of visits to sacred sites in the wider context of tourism products.

Inspection of UK visitor data provides insight into the importance of visits to sacred sites (see Table 5.1). The UK has 61 cathedrals which, excluding worshippers, attract around 19 million visitors per year. Taking data from the year 2000, 19 of the UK's 50 most visited buildings were cathedrals York Minster receives around 1.6–2.2 million visitors per year, the city having over 1 million leisure visitors and 2.5 million retail tourists. This is part of a tourism economy in the city worth over £250 million per year, supporting 9000 jobs.

Lincoln Cathedral has nearly 250,000 tourism visits per year. In 2000, it began charging £4 for entry; income is vital in maintaining the fabric of the buildings and the quality of facilities and experience for visitors. Tourists and their spending are major contributions to a regional tourism economy based on 3 million staying visitors and 18 million leisure day visitors to the county (Lincolnshire) per year, and worth around £800 million.

There is a challenge to spread benefits more sustainably throughout the community and to sustain the more remote, but often historic, rural churches. Around 12 million people annually visit nearly 17,000 churches and chapels across the UK, though the real importance to tourism is undoubtedly much greater. Miller (2001) is actively promoting the wider church network in the context of places to visit and recreational walks around Lincolnshire. A typical

Table 5.1. Position of sacred sites in top ten most frequently visited historic properties in the UK, 2000 (from ICOMOS-UK, 2000).

Site	Position in top ten sites	1999 visits (*n*)	2000 visits (*n*)
York Minster	2	1,900,000	1,750,000
Canterbury Cathedral	3	1,320,000	1,260,000
Westminster Abbey	4	1,260,000	1,230,000
Chester Cathedral	6	1,000,000	1,000,000
St Paul's Cathedral	7	1,070,000	940,000
Stonehenge	9	840,000	800,000

English village church location may reveal settlement and significance extending back beyond Christian cultural use, having drawn visitors from distance for millennia. Increasingly now, these places attract secular visitors, tourists being the new economic if not spiritual lifeblood of village and community.

Furthermore, the Church of England, for example, has other agendas. With falling congregations, particularly in rural areas that may suffer depopulation, visitors to churches present opportunities to draw new people to the faith, or to claw back those that have slipped away. This additional benefit involved in providing a visitor experience was noted in the assessment of church visiting by the English Tourist Board (1984). The pilgrim and the tourist offer financial and congregational opportunities and benefits in exchange for a leisure experience and a spiritual encounter. Research by Keeling (2000) helps gives some insight into the motivations of visitors. Taking a survey of visitors to English churches, motivations included:

- Spiritual motivation.
- Impulse visiting.
- Family connections.
- Connections with famous people or literary connections.
- Interest in architecture.

The difficulty is in marrying the potential conflicts. The pressure of visitors can damage an important heritage site, and the spirituality, whilst sometimes enhanced by sheer numbers in the case of mass pilgrimage, can be lost in the crowd. A site or location (such as Stonehenge) can be both a cultural and secular heritage site to one audience, with rules and concerns, and a religious place of spiritual significance for another.

Extreme conflicts of this sort have occurred with Islamic sites of tourism and of pilgrimage in Iran, Afghanistan and – especially – in Saudi Arabia. Mashhad is Iran's holiest city and its name literally means 'place of burial of a martyr'. Over 12 million pilgrims annually visit the shrine of the eighth Shiite imam and direct descendent of the prophet Mohammed, Imam Reza, who died in AD 817, and these numbers have increased with the conflicts in Iraq (Cochrane, 2004).

This creates opportunities, but problems too. The recently established London Middle East Institute (LMEI) aims to help the preservation of Middle Eastern and North African cultural heritage, including religious buildings and artefacts. The Taliban's destruction of non-Muslim sites in Afghanistan, including the well-published destruction of ancient Buddhist statues, is an extreme example (Rathje, 2001). Fundamentalist groups are also destroying many Islamic sites in Saudi Arabia (Howden, 2005). These actions not only destroy heritage, but they remove forever the potential social and economic benefits of both pilgrimage and secular tourism.

The two types of function of the site or experience, religious and secular, are not always compatible. Reflecting the trends in trying to maximize benefits, while recognizing the potential problems, is the emergence of literature to both promote visits and to guide owners and providers in visitor management. Both the potential and the challenges are considerable. The Arthur Rank Centre has published a guidebook for Church of English parishes to help in the promotion of tourism and to help support the management of visitors to rural churches (Francis and Martineau, 2001). This method of engaging the religious community with the visitor is relatively low-cost and eminently transferable.

Opportunities and Drivers

For many people and communities, tourism provides huge opportunities for economic development, but there are major obstacles and potential problems. In an increasingly multicultural, secular and globalized world, there is enormous potential for tourism associated with religious sites and heritage. Visits related to religion and sacred heritage can be in the form of either mass tourism in the industry mainstream or low-key, related to sustainable tourism and local sustainability.

The focus may be a long-standing or permanent attraction, or a one-off or sequential event or events. The public display of the Turin Shroud is an example of a major tourism happening (Shackley, 2001). Interestingly, this has involved careful management of artefact and visitor to allow free access to the religious devotee, while at the same time offering a major paying, touristic event. The proposed Sea of Galilee Theme Park (Urquhart, 2006) is an extreme example of a mass tourism initiative. Low-key examples include attempts in the UK to promote visitors to regional networks of rural churches such as in Essex (Essex Tourism, undated), in Derbyshire (Tomkins, 2000) and the Hidden Britain Project, discussed later in the case study section.

Drivers for mainstream religious tourism and pilgrimage are deep within a faith and outside this discussion. However, for religious heritage tourism and low-key rural tourism, the motivation is often financial and/or social. In rural parts of the UK, for example, the rural economy has suffered badly, and initiatives to promote rural church tourism are often attempts to support the community through economic benefits of tourism spend. Additionally, it may help to re-establish the church at the core of rural communities.

Problems and Issues

Religious and heritage tourism based on religious sites or artefacts faces difficulties and raises controversial issues. These include competition between faiths for a location and heritage, and conflicts between pilgrimage and secular, commercial tourism. The building, shrine, or artefact may have great spiritual value, but a commercial value too. As such, and often in an openly accessible situation, it is vulnerable to theft and to vandalism. Furthermore, as with other specialist or low-key tourism assets (Rotherham, 2006), financial benefits associated with, say, church visiting do not pay for the resource and its management. The church may be the attraction, but the money is spent in the local cafe, pub or gift shop and, with little reinvestment in presentation or conservation of the site, building or artefact, the situation is not sustainable.

There are aspects of sacred site visiting and management already noted that render some problems particularly important. There can be serious conflicts between a desire to keep facilities freely open to religious visitors, a need to raise money to maintain the fabric and the vulnerability of often-remote sites to vandalism, theft and desecration. According to the English Tourist Board survey (English Tourist Board, 1984), more than half the churches assessed had suffered from theft and almost as many from vandalism, with up to 80% of sites affected. There were problems of wear and tear, damage to buildings, noise, disturbance and litter. A more recent study (ICOMOS-UK, 2000) considered the problems of cathedrals and churches, but with a smaller sample (around 100 sites) than the 1984 survey (see Table 5.2).

Visiting of Churches in Britain as a Case Study

That rural communities and their economies depend more on tourism spend is increasingly recognized (Countryside Agency, 1998a; Countryside Agency and English Tourist Board, 2001) and is a key consideration of this case sudy. In the UK, the situation has become particularly acute in recent decades. Declines in farming and forestry over the 1990s were paralleled by increases in leisure day visits and tourism to countryside areas. This came to a pitch with chaos over foot-and-mouth disease and the economic impacts of advice given to the public not to visit the countryside. Incomes plummeted and businesses closed (Countryside Agency and English Tourism Council, 2001). In the aftermath of the crisis and in response to other problems of rural areas (BSE etc.), many organizations considered ways of responding to and supporting these hard-pressed communities.

For churches of various denominations, but perhaps for the Church of England in particular, the rural economy and the rural community of England pose serious problems, considered in research by such as Binney and Burman (1977) and English Tourist Board (1979). However, there are related issues too, affecting mainstream secular and tourism interests. In a socio-economic environment in which it is felt imperative to promote leisure visits to the

Table 5.2. Visitor-related problems for cathedrals and churches (from ICOMOS-UK, 2000).

Problem	Problem level (%)	
	ICOMOS-UK study (2000)	ETB[a] study (1977)
Insufficient parking for cars/coaches	54	46
Wear and tear on fabric	27	33
Occasional congestion or overcrowding	20	33
Theft	10	–
Vandalism	10	–
Noise	9	–
Disturbance to services	9	–

[a]English Tourist Board.

countryside for both tourists and day visitors, for much of England the parish church is hugely important. It has a significance of place in the rural setting beyond almost anything else other than the landscape itself. Church towers or spires on the highest ground reach out across the rural landscape, and churchyards are sanctuaries of historic depth in the core of the rural settlement.

The cultural relationship of church and community is embedded deep in the fabric of village and town. Old buildings, lanes – trees, even – giving character and distinction, are often a part of this attachment. St Helens Church at Darley Dale in Derbyshire has elements from AD 950, a wealth of objects and artefacts from over 1000 years of worship and a 2000-year-old yew tree in its churchyard. The site is visited by Christian pilgrims, by historians interested in artefacts and by people fascinated by the ancient, pre-Christian tree. Custodians of sites such as this have responsibilities and liabilities for maintenance and upkeep of a unique heritage resource. In most cases – and this applies to different situations and faiths around the world – they have little expertise, and often no finance even for necessary recording or conservation.

In the rural areas in England there is a serious problem of falling congregations and perceived lack of relevance of church to society, making related issues of heritage management – often in secluded and remote locations – problematic. The potential costs of maintaining and perhaps staffing a site, building or facility, and of conserving or protecting the heritage resource, are considerable. Many, including the remaining congregation and religious visitors, expect the village church to be open and available, its artefacts, artworks and treasures on view, but free of charge. These pressures and responsibilities combine with obvious vulnerability to vandalism and theft in an increasingly secular society.

The church has a complex role as provider of spiritual experience and guidance, but also as curator and custodian of a unique heritage for a wider community than its congregation. This is a problem is faced by many churches around the world. Where these buildings, locations and artefacts become the focus of an increasing tourism industry too, the problems come sharply into focus. It is surprising that so little has been done to consider the visiting of rural church in the wider context of tourism.

Relationships between religion and pilgrimage to sites, artefacts and tourism raise important issues of resource and community sustainability. Some have been raised by Shackley (1998, 2001), considering the management of heritage sites and specific issues of sacred sites. However, the broader issues of sustainable development and local economies have not been considered in detail. Researchers such as Busby (2003, 2004) have looked at church visitors in detail, in a particular region (Cornwall in England) and considered definitions, issues and difficulties in relation to tourism. He raises issues of definition of churches as heritage attractions, and this crosses national and cultural boundaries. With over 4 million visitors to Cornwall each year, he discusses visitor attractions (mostly heritage sites), and places the visiting of parish church in context (Busby, 2002). This details visitor age profiles and social status, raising important issues about long-term sustainability and challenges to growth in this sector.

Perhaps the church, too, has been reluctant to accept the mantle of tourism provider. According to Busby (2003), churches in Cornwall are very much a part of the regional heritage and tourism experience. Data extrapolated from church visitor books indicate numbers from 2000 visitors per year to over 40,000 in some cases visiting individual, smaller churches in Cornwall. The 1984 survey (English Tourist Board, 1984) suggested that at least £2 million was spent by at least 10 million visitors to English parish churches annually. Many of the 974 churches surveyed indicated that this income was important – and in some cases vital – for their survival. The more recent survey by ICOMOS-UK (2000) examined cash flows at churches and cathedrals in more detail (see Table 5.3).

Increasingly, publications and guides link rural churches together and to their mother cathedral in the urban core. In rural Essex, for example, *A Guide to Essex Churches* (Essex Tourism, undated) brings together key information on a selection of the county's churches, with notes on location and access, history, facilities and a contact point; there is website support too. Information is distributed through the usual tourism outlets, but particularly via major visitor sites in the urban centre, such as Chelmsford Cathedral. Books that are more ambitious are also available, for example *Derbyshire Churches and Chapels open to Visitors* (Tomkins, 2000). This again presents a substantial selection of churches and chapels, in this case from a number of denominations, with comprehensive information on access, facilities and history.

It is clear that these initiatives recognize the importance of smaller – and especially rural – churches in today's tourism; Hidden Britain is one such initiative.

There are a number of typical approaches in providing information and support to church and cathedral visitors across the UK. Woodward (2003) notes the following, and the levels of use for each approach, from ICOMOS-UK (2000):

Table 5.3. The varying income streams from a sample of charging cathedrals and churches (from ICOMOS-UK, 2000).

Site	Annual visitors (*n*)	Gross revenue (%)					
		Admissions	Donations	Food and drink	Sales and gifts, etc.	Events/ activities	Other
Canterbury Cathedral	1,350,000	53	1	1	40	–	5
Westminster Abbey	1,270,000	61	3	6	27	2	1
St Paul's, London	1,075,000	65	1	2	30	2	–
St Mary the Virgin, Oxford	300,000	60	5	10	25	–	–
Lincoln Cathedral	200,000	50	15	10	15	–	10
Oxford Cathedral	175,000	90	5	–	5	–	–
St Mary's, Rye	170,000	45	19	–	28	2	6
Glastonbury Abbey	120,000	77	6	–	11	1	5
St Patrick's, Armagh	10,000	10	10	10	30	40	–
Mean for all sites	n/a	57	7	7	23	9	5

n/a, not available.

- Guided tours   47%
- Recommended routes   36%
- Guide books   31%
- Foreign language guidebooks or leaflets   30%
- Displays or exhibitions   26%
- Volunteers or stewards to welcome visitors   24%
- Education programmes   16%
- Children's programmes   15%

What do we know of rural church visiting? The answer is: frustratingly little. There have been some studies, but these are generally not up to date, and leave many questions unanswered. Much research is on urban sites of historic importance, particularly on cathedrals. The English Tourist Board (1984) published a detailed assessment of English churches and visitors. This survey assessed important aspects of church visiting, including: (i) access; (ii) location and relation to tourist board areas; (iii) numbers of visitors recorded in church visitors' books; (iv) features of interest to visitors; (v) relationships to other tourist attractions; (vi) interpretation, guided tours, events and concerts; and (vii) community group uses. It also examined publicity and marketing, visitor management issues, wear and tear/damage and gross visitor revenues. This was a comprehensive overview, with substantial recommendations.

However, much of the work required updating, so the ICOMOS-UK (2000) study is important but, for rural churches in particular, critical questions remain. The 1984 report relies almost entirely on the visitor books for visitor numbers. Yet observations in and around churches suggest that most visitors do not 'sign in', and rural church visiting is much higher than these estimates. Work by Busby and colleagues in Cornwall demonstrated the importance of detailed local and regional studies.

English Tourist Board research in the 1980s suggested the importance of visitors for the survival of small churches in rural areas. Busby (2003) notes the importance of the church to the cultural regional heritage and to tourism and economy. Again, data from visitor books underestimate numbers. Furthermore, visitors to churchyards only, or the importance to visitors of the church in the landscape, are not considered.

The Hidden Britain Approach

There is evidence of 'low-key projects' around the UK that promote visitation to rural churches. The problem is often how to embed these within a local community and to develop maximum economic benefit. The Hidden Britain Project aims to encourage tourism and to help people discover lesser-known countryside areas. The intention is to provide a different and more meaningful visitor experience.

The project, developed by the Arthur Rank Centre based in Warwickshire, works with a range of denominations. It works with and through local communities, focusing on local business promotion, local employment and local community life. This approach, developed through the church – especially the Church of England in rural areas – seeks engagement with communities to help them face problems of declining rural economies and industries.

In the UK, the past 20 years has witnessed massive declines in the traditional rural economies of farming and forestry and, in some regions, the increased economic importance of tourism. This major impact of tourism has been seen only in areas with established attractions and infrastructures, with other areas missing out and benefits bypassing many in the rural community.

Hidden Britain has developed low-key tourism projects embedded in local, rural communities across England, engendering many aspirations of sustainable rural development. Whilst not attempting to grow mainstream or mass tourism in these areas, the project has quietly and effectively evolved a niche market. If this brings economic benefit so that local shops, post offices, petrol stations and village pubs remain open, then for these communities the urban drift may have been halted.

The project is 'not for profit', with a national membership and supported by a 'How To' handbook, with advice and support, regional and national marketing and literature, a national website, a support network and quality assurance monitoring. Monitoring of economic impacts is limited to positive feedback from participants. Whilst not focused specifically on churches or religion, it is led and coordinated by religious organizations, seeking to engender projects that maximize benefits for religious buildings and sites and their communities and congregations. This approach potentially re-engages churches with communities, and re-awakens local pride in history, culture and heritage.

It is too early to judge long-term effects, but the aspirations make it an exciting contributor to rural development through sustainable rural tourism. Publications such as *Beating the Bounds* by Terry Miller (2001) on Lincolnshire show church visiting as a part of rural tourism and leisure day visits.

This approach is transferable to other providers and other regions. It is low-key and relatively low-cost; as each project grows within the community, it demonstrates the benefits of sustainable rural tourism. The local initiative, supported by a national framework and based on particular local interests, character and distinctions, is easy to follow and modest to resource. This initiative, led by rural church communities in England, demonstrates how low-key rural tourism, centred on religious sites and their congregations, fosters sustainable rural development. It highlights faith and facilities stimulating sustainable tourism, with social and economic benefits.

Summary

Tourism offers religious sites more than visitors and financial opportunities: it brings a wide and potentially receptive audience. The English Tourist Board report (1984) quoted the vicar of Little Walsingham, Norfolk, who stated that: 'I feel strongly that parish churches have tremendous potential for proclaiming the Christian faith to visitors, who are often impressionable and have time to look and think. I am most anxious to develop this potential here.'

Visitors to religious sites may become 'converts', and this is important to many faiths. There is also opportunity to extend understanding and awareness of faith and heritage to a wider audience, and there are also pragmatic issues, with religious tourism and secular visiting of sacred sites generating social and economic development opportunities. Whilst modest in the case of the English parish churches, these are vital; however, managing these visitors whilst minimizing damage is a challenge. Case studies in England suggest that local community ownership of process and opportunity is important in the sustainable provision of this visitor and tourism experience.

The basic needs for sustainability are similar to tourism generally, ranging from trying to make large-scale mass tourism less socially and environmentally damaging to developing low-key, sacred visits to support rural communities. Many ideas and lessons are transferable between faiths and across national boundaries. Where religion has struggled to find contemporary relevance, initiatives can help re-establish faith within the community. If this is not effective, then many buildings, artefacts and heritage sites will not be sustained.

With 'sacred' visitation to historic towns, approaches are often through holistic town planning such as in York and Durham in the UK, with Woodward (2003) suggesting micro-level responses tailored to local circumstances reflecting cultural traditions and market opportunities. Within rural communities, provision of opportunities to embed 'sacred' visitation and religious tourism more fully within sustainable models has emerged through initiatives such as Hidden Britain to establish sustainable development in practice.

References

Aitchison, C., Macleod, N.E. and Shaw, S. (2000) *Leisure and Tourism Landscapes*. Routledge, London.

Anon. (1998) *A Feasibility Study for Compiling a Tourism Satellite Account for the UK*. Cambridge Policy Consultants and Geoff Broom Consultants, for Department of Culture, Media and Sport and British Tourist Authority, London.

Beard, C., Egan, D. and Rotherham, I.D. (2000) The changing role of outdoor leisure: a critical review of countryside tourism. In: Robinson, M., Swarbrooke, J., Evans, N., Long, P. and Shapley, R. (eds) *Reflections on International Tourism. Environmental Management and Pathways to Sustainable Tourism*. Centre for Travel and Tourism, University of Northumbria, Sunderland, UK, pp. 1–19.

Bhardwaj, S.M. (1998) Non-hajj pilgrimage in Islam: a neglected dimension of religious circulation. *Journal of Cultural Geography* 17 (2), 69–87.

Binney, M. and Burman, P. (1977) *Chapels and Churches: Who Cares?* British Tourist Authority, London.

Blain, J., Ezzy, D. and Harvey, G. (eds) (2004) *Researching Paganisms*. Altamira Press, Walnut Creek, California.

Brice, J., Busby, G. and Brunt, P. (2003) English rural church tourism: a visitor typology. *Acta Turistica* 15 (2), 144–162.

Busby, G. (2002) The Cornish church heritage as destination component. *Tourism* 50 (4), 371–381.

Busby, G. (2003) 'A true Cornish treasure': Gunwalloe and the Cornish church as visitor attraction. In: Payton, P. (ed.) *Cornish Studies Eleven.* University of Exeter Press, Exeter, UK, pp. 168–191.

Busby, G. (2004) The contested Cornish church heritage. In: Payton, P. (ed.) *Cornish Studies Twelve.* University of Exeter Press, Exeter, UK, pp. 166–183.

Cochrane, P. (2004) With Iraq in turmoil, pilgrims head to Iran. http://www.Worldpress.org (accessed 19 September 2004).

Cohen, E. (1992) Pilgrimage and tourism: convergence and divergence. In: Morinis, A. (ed.) *Sacred Journeys: the Antrhopology of Pilgrimage.* Greenwood Press, Westpoint, Connecticut.

Countryside Agency (1998a) *The Economic Impact of Recreation and Tourism in the English Countryside 1998.* Countryside Agency Publications, Cheltenham, UK.

Countryside Agency (1998b) *UK Leisure Day Visits: Summary of the 1996 Survey Findings.* Social and Community Planning Research, Countryside Agency, Cheltenham, UK.

Countryside Agency (2002) *Land Management Initiatives.* Countryside Agency, Cheltenham, UK.

Countryside Agency and English Tourism Council (2001) *Working for the Countryside – a Strategy for Rural Tourism in England 2001–2005.* Countryside Agency and English Tourism Council, London.

English Tourist Board (1979) *English Cathedrals and Tourism.* English Tourist Board, London.

English Tourist Board (1984) *English Churches and Visitors.* English Tourist Board, London.

Francis, L. and Martineau, J. (2001) *Rural Visitors* (a parish workbook for welcoming visitors in the country church). Acora Publishing, Stoneleigh, UK.

Harvey, G. (ed.) (2000) *Indigenous Religions. A Companion.* Cassell, London.

Howden, D. (2005) The destruction of Mecca: Saudi hardliners are wiping out their own heritage. *The Independent,* 6 August.

ICOMOS-UK (2000) *To Be A Pilgrim. Meeting the needs of Visitors to Cathedrals and Churches in the United Kingdom.* ICOMOS-UK, London.

Jenkins, S. (2006) The curse of Stonehenge will remain until it is handed back to the Druids. The *Guardian,* 27 January, p. 34.

Keeling, A. (2000) Church tourism – providing a Ministry of Welcome to visitors. In: *English Tourism Council (2000) Insights,* Section A13, London.

Lambrick, G. (2001) Comment: is your historic environment in Little England? *Archaeology* 57, February.

Miller, T. (2001) *Beating the Bounds – Walks and Rides in Lincolnshire in the Millennium Year.* Nth Degree Publishing, Lincoln, UK.

Onions, C.T. (1983) *The Shorter Oxford Dictionary on Historical Principles,* 3rd edn. Book Club Associates with Oxford University Press, Oxford, UK.

Orbasli, A. (2000) *Tourists in Historic Towns. Urban Conservation and Heritage Management.* Spon, London.

Palmer, M. and Palmer, N. (1997) *Sacred Britain. A Guide to the Sacred Sites and Pilgrim Routes of England, Scotland and Wales.* Judy Piatkus (Publishers) Ltd, London.

Rathje, W.L. (2001) Why the Taliban are destroying Buddhas. *USA Today,* 22 March.

Roe, D., Leader-Williams, N. and Dalal-Clayton, B. (1997) *Take Only Photographs, Leave Only Footprints: the Environmental Impacts of Wildlife Tourism.* Wildlife and Development Series No. 10, International Institute for Environment and Development, London.

Rotherham, I.D. (2006) Opportunities and pitfalls in ecotourism development. In: Dixit, S.K. (ed.) *Promises and Perils in Hospitality and Tourism Management.* M.S. Aman Publications, New Delhi, India. 148–167.

Rotherham, I.D., Rose, J.C. and Egan, D. (2000) A critical evaluation of the wildlife leisure industry: an emerging component of leisure and tourism. In: Robinson, M., Swarbrooke, J.,

Evans, N., Long, P. and Shapley, R. (eds) *Reflections on International Tourism. Environmental Management and Pathways to Sustainable Tourism.* Centre for Travel and Tourism, University of Northumbria, Sunderland, UK, pp. 229–245.

Rotherham, I.D., Doncaster, S. and Egan, D. (2005) Nature-based leisure and tourism in England's Humberhead Levels. *Current Issues in Tourism* 8 (2–3), 214–230.

Scottish Tourist Board (1991) *Visitor Attractions: a Development Guide.* Scottish Tourist Board, Edinburgh, UK.

Smith, R. (2004) *Enjoying the Humberhead Levels.* Halsgrove, Tiverton, UK.

The Guardian (2005) Cultural vandalism. Leader, 15 January.

The Guardian (2006) Eyewitness. Mecca, Saudi Arabia. 3 January, p. 14.

Tomkins, R. (2000) *Derbyshire Churches and Chapels Open to Visitors.* Scarthin Books, Cromford, UK.

Tremlett, G. (2006) Spain tries to stop sale of Córdoba beams. *The Guardian*, 10 March, p. 16.

Tresidder, R. (1999) Tourism and sacred landscapes. In: Crouch, D. (ed.) *Leisure/Tourism Geographies.* Routledge, London, pp. 137–163.

Urquhart, C. (2006) Plans for Holy Land theme park on Galilee shore where Jesus fed the 5000. *The Guardian*, 4 January, p. 3.

Wallis, R.J. (2003) Shamans/Neo-Shamans. *Ecstasy, Alternative Archaeologies and Contemporary Pagans.* Routledge, London.

Woodward, S.C. (2003) Faith and tourism: accommodating visitor and worshipper in the historic city. In: *6th US/ICOMOS International Symposium, 'Managing Conflict and Conservation in Historic Cities'*, 24–27 April 2003, Annapolis, Maryland (http://www.icomos.org/usicomos/Symposium/SYMP03/Woodward.htm).

6 Sacred Pilgrimage and Tourism as Secular Pilgrimage

Vitor Ambrósio

Escola Superior de Hotelaria e Turismo do Estoril, Estoril, Portugal;
e-mail: vitor.ambrosio@eshte.pt

Introduction

This chapter provides insights into the pilgrim's experiential perspective of the spiritual fundamentals of pilgrimage, in which the author articulates emic insights into the emotions of the tradition of Christian pilgrimage. This is compared with different academic discourses of the characteristics of pilgrimage. For the author, independently of the academic and analytical perspectives of pilgrimage, it is viewed as a significant event in the believer's life, one which should enrich them with a cognitive and aesthetic experience.

The Spiritual Fundamentals of Pilgrimage: the Pilgrim's Experiential Perspective

The pilgrimage concept based on spirituality is essentially defined as an encounter between Man and God. Mattoso (2000, p. 4) writes that, through pilgrimage Man has been trying to contact the occult forces that enrich his existence. Pilgrimage exists in all or in most civilizations, being almost always integrated within religious practices and it is directed to concrete points, with marked itineraries, rituals and preferential dates.

The Papal Council for the Pastoral of the Migrants and Itinerants (1999, pp. 3–4) reinforces this idea, underlining that evangelization is the main reason for the Church to propose and to encourage pilgrimage, and to sanction it as a deep and matured experience of faith. For example, throughout the centuries, Christians have walked towards the places that resonate to 'the memory of God', or to those that represent important moments in the history of the Church. They have approached Marian shrines to worship the Virgin and venerate ' the saints', to engage in a conversion process in an intimacy of longing for the Divine.

Lived as a celebration of their faith, pilgrimage is for Christians a cultural event to be accomplished with fidelity to tradition, with deep religious feeling and as a performance of their paschal existence. Its dynamics reveals clearly distinct stages that are reached by pilgrims: the departure symbolizes a decision to 'move forward' on a 'path', in order to reach the spiritual goals of their baptismal vocation; the 'path' leading them to solidarity with others and preparing them for the encounter with God. The visit to the shrine invites them to listen to the 'word of God' and sacramental celebration, and the return reminds them of their mission in the world as 'witnesses of the salvation' and builders of peace.

Pilgrimage drives Christians towards a spiritual encounter and a renewal of their baptismal pledge. At the shrine, when they confess their sins, their conscience is challenged, they are forgiven and they forgive, and they become new creatures through the sacrament of the reconciliation, feeling the 'divine grace' and the 'divine mercy'. According to this enunciation, Chélini and Branthomme (1982, p. 429) observe that, although the Church has not created the pilgrimage, it is nevertheless authenticated by the religious institution and organizes it in order to afford the pilgrims a larger spiritual elevation.

This spiritual elevation includes pilgrims' 're-finding themselves' through silence, reflection, meditation and prayer, and in an examination of conscience. In this sense, Aucourt (1990, p. 19) agrees with the characteristics of pilgrimage articulated by the Association Nationale de Directeurs Diocésains des Pèlerinages (ANDDP), which include moments of freedom and the capacity to see, to hear, remind, find, testify, celebrate and pray, in order to become 'different'.

Also, Giuriati and Gioia (1992, p. 9) suggest that, through pilgrimage, pilgrims seek conversion and salvation in their everyday life, which represents a symbolic path where pilgrims 'cross the border' of the superfluous, to enter in a field of authentic values.

In consideration of what pilgrimages should include, the Papal Council for the Pastoral of the Migrants and Itinerants (1999, p. 36) considers that the Episcopal Conference of each country should have the responsibility of ensuring the effective management of shrines to ensure that pilgrims have the opportunity to express the blooming of their faith, and should also intensify, through prayer, a communion with God. Guerra (1989, pp. 276–277) observes that a shrine is a place where one comes back with a sense of both pleasure and lingering absence.

In reality, the theology of a pilgrimage centre is based on three pillars, or three dimensions of time: memory, presence and prophecy of God with men. Guerra suggests that:

> In relation to the only and definitive past of the redemption event, the shrine offers itself as the memory of the origin of God; related to the present, it is delineated as a sign of the divinity, place of the alliance, where the Christian community regenerates and expresses itself; as far as future is concerned, it becomes the prophecy of the tomorrow in God.
>
> (Guerra, 1989, p. 59)

The shrine is not simply the 'fruit' of human construction, steeped in cosmological or anthropological symbolism, but it testifies, above all, to the initiative of God in communicating to Man, with the goal of establishing with him the pact of salvation. In short, pilgrims go to shrines to invoke and to welcome the Holy Spirit, transferring it, later on, in terms of everyday actions. This includes the celebration of the sacraments at the shrine, expressions of prayer and the importance of the Eucharist as 'the centre of the life' in a sacred place.

The Papal Council for the Pastoral of the Migrants and Itinerants (1999, pp. 56, 79) still observes that, at the shrine, pilgrims learn how to 'open their hearts to all', in particular to the 'different': the guest, the foreigner, the immigrant, the refugee, those who profess other religions and the non-believer. These authors also contend that the shrine is the bearer of a precise message linked to 'the here and now', but connected to the lineage of the past.

Academic Perceptions of Pilgrimage

Academics regard pilgrimages as a social science phenomenon. They base their analyses on empirical data related to individuals who take part in them. The research insights of Vukoni'c (1996, p. 117) observe that, since the time of the old mythologies and the emergence of religions, a believer's faith has been reinforced through visits to sacred places that will relieve them of their problems, either spiritual or materialistic.

In this process, depending on the degree of the pilgrim's faith, they are prepared to begin shorter or longer trips and to satisfy their religious needs (which may accomplish an obligatory act of their religion). Doctrinaire Christian teachings try to explain pilgrimage as one of the expressions of spirituality in a context not only transcendental, but also with terrestrial characteristics. In particular, the Catholic faith envisage pilgrimage to be part of a worldly Diaspora, dispersed to sacred places to learn about the lives of the saints or Maria, about Jesus' terrestrial experience or about the revelation of 'His truth'.

In this sense, Mattoso (2000, p. 5) considers that pilgrimage is incompatible with scientific rationality because pilgrimage encourages a dislocation in space and in time, with the obligation to follow the ritual of celebration within a group. Furthermore, it is viewed as more than 'a simple trip': it is a state of mind that is the result of a set of conditions that are determined by different societies. According to Mattoso, the visit to privileged places of pilgrimage reinforces the rituals and the conditions created by the nature and the distance from everyday and 'artificial' life.

For Voyé (1996, p. 52), pilgrimages possess – besides the capacity to reconcile body and spirit – the capacity to implement national, regional and local identities, particularly in a world that 'suffers' from globalization. In terms of division into categories, pilgrimages for Chélini and Branthomme (1982, p. 417) are classified according to the motivations that determine the departure: pilgrims' sense of devotion, spiritual improvement and, in its 'purest form', the perfection of the soul and the search for eternal salvation. The penitential pilgrimage, frequently imposed in medieval times by either the priest, the ecclesiastical court or the lay judge, constitutes a more or less severe form of punishment for serious mistakes/crimes.

The request pilgrimage brings to the shrines, among others, the sick and infirm. Russell (1999, p. 46) adds to this categorization that pilgrimage is a religious commandment: to attend a 'prayer encounter' with a religious leader, to testify or to participate in a religious ceremony or to go to a place where it is speculated that, in the future, miracles will take place.

In a more pragmatic perspective, Ambrósio (2000, p. 1) observes that pilgrimage is not linked to a certain mark of civilization or to a certain form of thinking, or even to a socio-economic status. It contended that it is an act latent in each human being and comprises two aspects: a spiritual order and a practical order (of travel to a shrine, increasingly viewed as religious tourism).

Kaszowski (2000, p. 75) suggests that pilgrimage has complex and interdisciplinary charactereristics in its essence, in that it is a religious act and that its study belongs to the research field of theology and other disciplines that deal with religion. Furthermore, as human activity it should be observed under social, historical, geographical, psychological, cultural, economical and legal perspectives, with its spatial and temporal concentrations.

Kaszowski (2000) emphasizes the matrix of interdisciplinary elements of pilgrimage in which culturally modified natural and geographical landscapes are transformed into sacred landscapes, altering, in this process, behaviours, habits and the mentality of local communities driven by regional differentiation. The mobility and migration of large groups of pilgrims has stimulated the development of destinations supported by technical infrastructures and services and legal regulation. Furthermore, Kaszowski (2000) divides pilgrimage into two categories: (i) theoretical and cognitive; and (ii) practical.

1. Theoretical/cognitive factors

- Ability to identify – to recognize the pilgrimage phenomenon and to distinguish it from other similar phenomena.
- Ability to describe – to characterize the pilgrimage phenomenon and to specify its attributive and secondary features.
- Ability to determine the context of the phenomenon – the background and conditions of pilgriming, as well as the diverse, anticipated consequences.

2. Practical factors

- Ability to think over – to plan a pilgrimage, prepare and organize it, fulfil the plan and the programme, conduct the pilgrimage – to be its guide.
- Ability to use the pilgrimage for educational purposes (development of Man).

The first is category related to the identification, description, perception and determination of the object in study; the second is linked to its organization and the application of its purposes.

Another aspect of the study of pilgrimage is to understand the point of view of the pilgrim. According to Branthomme (1982, p. 18), the pilgrim has to create the perception of walking a physical and moral path, i.e. not the one of everyday life; that this path, separated from everyday life will create unexpected risks and sacrifices, with the possibility of a vision beyond the routine of everyday life, a lucidity inspired by the sacred place of visitation, which provides a spiritual wealth.

Ostrowski (2000, p. 55) suggests that pilgrimage and the fulfilment of religious acts require pauses, because these experiences are very intense. The suggestion is that the 'overcharging' of pilgrimage can result in the opposite of what is intended: the drive for psychic and spiritual 'hygiene' is necessarily entwined with the drives of the mundane, of human curiosity, of seeing new places, of meeting new people and even of the search for entertainment.

In his novel, Lodge (1997, p. 257) suggests that it is possible to look at a pilgrim according to three phases of personal development, initially proposed by Kierkegaard: the aesthetic, the ethical and the religious. The aesthetic phase is typified by interest in the amusement and in the fruition of the picturesque and cultural pleasures that he/she can achieve along the 'path'. The ethical phase that confronts the pilgrim is, above all, a test of their psychic force and self-discipline, of the possibility of secumbing to temptation, and incorporates a very competitive attitude towards other pilgrims.

The 'true' or 'religious' pilgrim is viewed as acting 'naturally' as a pilgrim, knowing instinctively how to engage in pilgrimage (it is worth noting that this categorization is not without its contradictions in that, in the Kierkegaardian sense, Christianity was 'absurd' because, if it were entirely rational, there would not be any merit in being a believer).

Finally, pilgrimage can also be viewed as a form of social grouping. Hitrec (1991, p. 14) paraphrasing Jukic (1988), observes that this phenomenon is essentially a collective act during which, from a sociological perspective, pilgrims subscribe to the idea of unification inside the same religion. Reinforcing this idea, Boisvert (1997, pp. 5–6) affirms that there is also a shared social experience during pilgrimage in which pilgrims are able collectively, through a tradition of 'shared community', to enter a mythical realm outwith the temporal and spatial context of the pilgrimage.

In this sense, Fortuna and Ferreira (1993, p. 60), basing their ideas on Victor Turner (1969), explain that when pilgrimage assumes a character of unification, it generates a spirit of communitas spirit and a departure from social conditions, which enables a suspension of class and cultural inequalities. This action promotes an effect of exorcism, or a temporary suspension of society, conferring on the experience a peculiar sense of involvement, of a figuration of nature, tantamount to the dynamics of sports groups described by Elias and Dunning (1971).

Pilgrimage versus Tourism

Both church and lay scholars often make use of tourism and pilgrimage definitions: the former to distinguish the different phenomena, the latter in order to combine them. During the 1970s, with the increasing development of tourist activity, some church scholars felt that it was necessary to establish differences between these two forms of travelling.

For Gendron (1972, p. 81), the tourist tries to 'find him/herself' when he/she becomes free from the pressures that everyday life imposes, while the pilgrim departs to be close to God. In this division, the author considers that the religious tourist – as any other tourist – travels to free him/herself from everyday life; although their 'convergence centre' is the divine place. In other words, the pilgrim is attracted by the shrine, by the proximity with the divine, but does not go exclusively to worship God. In this sense, Roussel (1972) verifies that a visit considered as a pilgrimage should be done with a devotional intention, it not being enough to be a simple curiosity stop or a tourist trip to a sacred place: it requires some form of adoration.

In opposition to this view is the one that there are no major differences between pilgrimage and tourism. Cohen (1974) sustains the theory that tourism is a kind of modern pilgrimage, although the reasons for undertaking the trip are more substantial than simply pure recreation and entertainment. According to the author, tourists move towards a destination that is a type of symbol of their desires and needs, just like a pilgrim does when he goes to a shrine looking for the satisfaction of his/her religious and spiritual aspirations.

In this sense, MacCannell (1976) defines tourism as a 'ritual of the modern society', considering the tourist a pilgrim who has to see the places where extraordinary powers are embodied (for example, in Europe he/she has to go to Paris, and in this city it is obligatory to visit Notre-Dame, the Eiffel Tower and the Louvre).

Turner and Turner (1978) also conclude that a tourist can be considered a semi-pilgrim if the pilgrim is considered a semi-tourist, adding that, when a person mixes themselves in an anonymous crowd of a beach, or in an agglomeration of believers, he/she is looking for a symbolic form of company, which 'removes' them from their daily life.

In 1981, Cohen reformulated his opinion, observing that although pilgrimage and tourism have similarities, they are different phenomenon: the elements in common consist of the temporary change of residence, in the departure to a chosen destination and in the search for other ideals. However, they differ in their characteristics, in the activities performed during the trip and/or during the stay.

In the ecclesiastical field, Guerra (1988, pp. 43–49) analyses visitors by considering the evangelistic function of the shrine, granting the most honourable term of pilgrim to those who know sufficiently the nature of the sacred place and obtain the inherent spiritual advantage from their trip. A second category is constituted by those who go to a pilgrimage centre, exclusive or mainly to engage in religious pilgrimage. The third and final category of visitors is the one constituted by tourists in which Guerra (1989, pp. 276–278) distinguishes pilgrimage from 'vulgar' tourism, arguing that the element that separates them is faith.

In the last decade of the 20th century, although some authors continued to insist on the demarcation between pilgrimage and tourism, many scholars (either ecclesiastic or lay) attempted to establish connections between the two phenomena. Bauer (1993, p. 26) persists in the conviction that the image of tourism is linked to banality, frivolity and consumption, and conversely he considers pilgrimage to be associated with seriousness and commitment. This author reinforces his point of view by paraphrasing the opinion of Jan Pach

(1992), who defends the premise that pilgrimage is not a tourist trip, but a spiritual retreat that demands 'sacrifice' and religious motivation, and perhaps viewed as a transcendental experience.

Bauer (1993) concurs with Robi Ronza (1992), who retains the term pilgrimage, (excluding the term religious tourism) because tourism and pilgrimage are two opposite conceptions of the world. Consistent with this view, Vukoni'c (1996, p. 135) articulated the position of the Church during the International Christian Conference of Asia (Manila, 1981), where it was confirmed that modern tourism is not pilgrimage, because pilgrims 'step the sacred soil smoothly' with humility and patience, while tourists 'trample these places, photographing them, travelling with arrogance and in a hurry'.

A transitional approach articulated by Hitrec (1991, p. 5) – and supported by the authors Hunziker and Krapf (1942) – is that the characteristics of some human migration are rooted in religious motivations; this approach tries to connect and even integrate them into the definitions of tourism. Having in mind the spiritual framing and the religious conceptions of tourism, Hitrec (1991) paraphrases MacCannell (1976), advocating that while sacred places and objects are losing their sacredness, this can be offset by tourist trips that provide an opportunity to look for the authentic reality and the meaning of human existence.

In this sense, theologians declare that tourism is a way of connecting with the world of the 'divine creation', and that leisure time can be used for the spiritual enrichment and even for a moral rebirth. Furthermore, pilgrims will be interested in the natural and built environments (enjoying them as tourists). Smith (1992, pp. 1–2) still observes that tourism and pilgrimage have both been defined as activities rooted in three operative elements (income, free time and social permission to travel); the social sanctions, or what society thinks is correct behaviour, as well as the prevalent philosophy based on socio-economics and policies also influence the conditions of free time and vacations.

In terms of shrines as the locus for 'believers' and religious tourists, Vukoni'c (1996, p. 129) concurs with Cohen (1992, pp. 33–37) that these 'centres' are typically 'out there' – in other words, eccentric to population agglomerations and to mundane socio-political axes and, consequently, they tend to be peripheral and remote. In this context, the concentricity of pilgrimage 'centres' means that pilgrims travel towards the sociocultural nucleus of their society, while tourists travel from it to the periphery.

When the pilgrimage centre is eccentric (located in the sociocultural and geographical periphery of the pilgrim's society). the pilgrimage will be characterized by touristic aspects: the longer the distance of the shrine from population agglomeration, the stronger will be the tourist components of the trip. In this sense, Boisvert (1997, p. 7) posits that pilgrims and tourists create a distance in relation to their places of residence, an estrangement that allows them to reflect on their own existence. Nevertheless, what characterizes pilgrims is their capacity to interpret their experiences as a form of personal transformation.

The burgeoning tourism literature has attempted to focus on the management and administration of pilgrimage sites as distinct from spiritual analysis, opting for a more pragmatic perspective. For example, Murray and Graham's (1997) article on Santiago de Compostela, in Galacia, Spain, verifies that pilgrimage to the Spanish city – the Camino de Santiago – relies on a complex dialectic of apparent contradictions and tensions with visits from different market segments (pilgrims, tourists, motorized travellers and walkers). They highlight the conflicts that appear because of the varying types of tourist activity within a sacred pilgrimage destination (see Table 6.1).

In spite of differences, Murray and Graham (1997) agree with Nolan and Nolan (1992, p. 77) when they observe that tourism and pilgrimage are not incompatible activities; consequently, the changes introduced in the meanings should not be connoted as negative, because it was tourism that reinvented the Santiago Trail, augmenting an ancient pilgrimage path with tourist resource within contemporary society. Although some authors continue to highlight a division between pilgrimage and tourism, the concern of most specialists is to establish an intermediate category between the two phenomena.

In relation to the first group, one may observe that the authors who choose the division are, above all, the ones without connection to the tourism phenomenon, as in the case of Mattoso (2000, pp. 4–5): he persists in his view of the journey/pilgrimage as being distinct from tourism, an act of travel undertaken in a superficial way. Conversely, authors such as Liszewski (2000, pp. 49–50), when comparing pilgrimage with religious tourism, integrate the first phenomenon into the second one, although defending the maintenance of the traditional term (pilgrimage), since this has existed for many centuries.

Finally, Santos (2003, p. 32), aware of the complexity of these phenomena, agrees with the scheme proposed by Stoddard (see Table 6.2), where the latter author conjugates the types of travellers with the motives, relating both with two kinds of travelling, recreational and religious.

Table 6.1. Some touristic and religious interpretations of religious product and its meaning (from Murray and Graham, 1997).

Religious product	Religious interpretation	Touristic interpretation
Shrines and ceremonies		
Santiago de Compostela	Pilgrimage destination	City of culture
Cathedral of Santiago	Prayer, worship	Heritage attraction
Feast Day of St James and Botafumeiro	Ritual	Special event tourism
Holy Years	Prayer	Themed tourism
Relic touching	Devotion	Good luck/the 'wishing well'
The routes		
Camino de Compostela	Expiation	Certificate of achievement
Pilgrim ways	Penance, punishment	Self-renewal, off-road adventure trails
Pilgrim shrines	Prayer, expiation	Architectural heritage
Pilgrim hospice	Sanctuary	Parador
Scallop shell	Pilgrim	Product-branding logo

Table 6.2. Recreational versus recreational travel: types of traveller and motives (from Santos, 2003).

Travel category	Tourist category	Motives
Recreational	Secular Tourist	Profane
	Religious Tourist	
Religious	Pilgrim	Sacred

In this table, one finds a consensus in a perspective based on the creation of three types of traveller: one at each end of the spectrum (secular tourists and pilgrims) and a transitional one (religious tourists).

Summary

In comparing the different perspectives on the spiritual fundamentals of pilgrimage as a sacred and secular activity, this chapter has provided a range of insights on what it means to be both a pilgrim and tourist in contemporary society. It has been acknowledged that pilgrimage within the Christian tradition (and indeed in other religious traditions) is a celebration of faith, with the characterization of distinct stages of a journey both physical and symbolic in its composition.

The departure symbolizes a 'path' towards spiritual goals that not only enables pilgrims to establish solidarity with others but also, crucially, to prepare them for an encounter with God. In listening to the 'word of God' at a religious shrine, pilgrims return home spiritually transformed, with the renewal of a baptismal pledge.

In providing these insights into the sacred and pious qualities of pilgrimage, it was acknowledged that the wider insight to emerge from this analysis of pilgrimage is this: whilst the concept of pilgrimage might have distinct features within different civilizations, its common element is the spiritual foundation of an encounter between man and God.

Therefore, in addition to exploring the different components or stages of pilgrimage while travelling on a symbolic path to reach spiritual goals, this chapter also reviewed different academic perceptions of pilgrimage, emphasizing that pilgrimage has emerging secular qualities. In reviewing academic perceptions of pilgrimage, it was acknowledged that there are both theoretical and cognitive elements of pilgrimage, with a matrix of interdisciplinary elements incorporating the transformation of natural and geographical areas into 'sacred landscapes'. Further perspectives include aesthetic, ethical and religious elements of pilgrimage, which inform the actions of the individual, with sociological perspectives explaining the shared experience or communitas experienced by groups of pilgrims.

There are contrasting interpretations of potential dichotomies between pilgrimage and tourism, with one interpretation being that, in contrast to the tourist, the pious pilgrim needs to engage in some form of adoration at a religious shrine. However, differing interpretations suggest that whilst the pilgrim is attracted by a shrine and a 'proximity with the divine', the visit is not exclusively for the purposes of worshipping God. Cohen's (1992) analysis contrasted the concentricity of pilgrimage 'centres' with the peripherality of tourist 'centres'.

Whilst Guerra (1989) contrasted 'vulgar tourism' with pilgrimage, and Bauer (1993) characterized the image of tourism underpinned by frivolity, banality and consumption with pilgrimage, concerned with commitment and seriousness, other authors acknowledged the merging of the sacred and secular qualities of pilgrimage and tourism.

Indeed, in this respect, MacCannell (1976) characterized tourism as the 'ritual of the modern society', while Turner and Turner (1978) labelled contemporary pilgrims as 'semi-tourists'. The example of El Camino and the path to Santiago de Compostela in Spain provides an example of the augmentation of the ancient qualities of pilgrimage with a tourism resource in contemporary society.

In considering a range of academic perspectives on these concepts, it is possible to theorize about the unification of tourism and pilgrimage as concepts, and also about the distinctiveness of pilgrimage, which retains an ancient lineage as a sacred and spiritual form of travel.

References

Ambrósio, V. (2000) *Fátima: Território Especializado na Recepção de Turismo Religioso*. Instituto Nacional de Formação Turística, Lisbon.

Aucourt, R. (1990) Pélèrins, Touristes ou touristes religieux. *Espaces* 102, 19–21.

Bauer, M. (1993) Tourisme religieux ou touristes en milieu religieux. *Les Cahiers Espaces* 30, 24–37.

Boisvert, M. (1997) Le pélèrinage. *Teoros* 16 (2), 5–9.

Branthomme, H. (1982) Introduction. In: Chélini, J. and Branthomme, H. (eds) *Les Chemins de Dieu: Histoire des Pèlerinages Chrétiens, des Origines a nos Jours*. Hachette, Paris.

Chélini, J. and Branthomme, H. (1982) *Les Chemins de Dieu: Histoire des Pèlerinages Chrétiens, des Origines à nos Jours*. Hachette, Paris.

Cohen, E. (1974) Who is a tourist? A conceptual clarification. *Sociological Review* 22 (4), 527–555.

Cohen, E. (1992) Pilgrimage centers: concentric and excentric. *Annals of Tourism Research* 19 (1), 33–50.

Fortuna, C. and Ferreira, C. (1993) Estradas e santuários. *Revista Crítica de Ciências Sociais* 36, 55–79.

Gendron, H. (1972) Le tourisme religieux. In: *Le Tourisme: Le Fait, les Virtualités Chrétiennes, Ebauche d'une Pastorale, La Pastorale du Tourisme de la Conférence Catholique Canadienne*, Montreal, Canada. Fides, Montreal, Canada, pp. 80–82.

Giuriati, P. and Arzenton, G. (1992) *Les Sens du Chemin, les Pèlerinages Marials: Analyse Comparative de l'Éxperiences des Pèlerins de Lourdes, Fátima, Medjugorje, Lorette et Our Lady of the Snows-Belleville (USA)*. CRSR, Padua, Italy.

Guerra, L. (1988) Peregrinação e aprofundamento da fé, peregrinação e devoção popular. In: Cardoso, A.P. (ed.) *Peregrinação e Piedade Popular*. Secretariado Geral do Episcopado, Lisbon, pp. 35–69.

Guerra, L. (ed.) (1989) O turismo religioso no mundo de amanhã. In: *Tourism Education for the Early 21st Century*. INP, Lisbon, pp. 275–288.

Hitrec, T. (1991) *Religious Tourism: Development, Characteristics, Perspectives.* Cahiers du Tourisme Série C, No. 164.

Kaszowski, L. (2000) Methodology of pilgrimage. *Peregrinus Cracoviensis* 10, 75–82.

Liszewski, S. (2000) Pilgrimages or religious tourism? *Peregrinus Cracoviensis* 10, 47–51.

Lodge, D. (1997) *Terapia.* Gradiva, Lisbon.

MacCannell, D. (1976) *The Tourist: a New Theory of Leisure Class.* Schoken, New York.

Mattoso, J. (2000) Peregrinar. In: da Silva, H.V. (ed.) *Caminho do Tejo.* Selecções Reader's Digest and Centro Nacional de Cultura, Lisbon, pp. 4–5.

Murray, M. and Graham, B. (1997) Exploring the dialectics of route-based tourism: the Camino de Santiago. *Tourism Management* 18 (8), 513–524.

Nolan, M.L. and Nolan, S. (1992) Religious sites as tourism attractions. *Annals of Tourism Research* 19 (1), 68–78.

Ostrowski, M. (2000) Pilgrimages or religious tourism? *Peregrinus Cracoviensis* 10, 53–61.

Papal Council for the Pastoral of Migrants and Itinerants (Conselho Pontifício para a Pastoral dos Migrantes e Itinerantes) (1999) *A Peregrinação (no Grande Jubileu do Ano 2000). O Santuário (Memória, Presença e Profecia do Deus Vivo).* Paulinas, Lisbon.

Roussel, R. (1972) *Les Pèlerinages.* PUF, Paris.

Russell, P. (1999) Religious travel in the new millennium. *Travel and Tourism Analyst* 5, 39–68.

Santos, M. da G. (2003) Religious tourism contributions towards a clarification of concepts. In: Fernandes, C., McGettigan, F. and Edwards, J. (eds) *Religious Tourism and Pilgrimage – Atlas: Special Interest Group* (1st Expert Meeting). Tourism Board of Leiria/Fátima, Fátima, Portugal, pp. 27–42.

Smith, V. (1992) Introduction – the quest in guest. *Annals of Tourism Research* 19 (1), 1–17.

Turner, V. and Turner, E. (1978) *Image and Pilgrimage in Christian Culture.* Columbia University, New York.

Voyé, L. (1996) Les pèlerinages aujourd'hui en Europe Occidentale: une quête des sens et d'identité. In: *1st International Meeting of the Sanctuary and Pilgrimage Towns*, Azienda Promozione Turistica di Loreto. ATTI, Loreto, Italy, pp. 41–57.

Vukoni'c, B. (1996) *Tourism and Religion.* Pergamon Press, Oxford, UK.

7 Religion, Pilgrimage, Mobility and Immobility

ALEXANDRA ARELLANO

School of Human Kinetics, University of Ottawa, Ottawa, Ontario, Canada; e-mail: alexa 37@hotmail.com

Introduction

New, alternative ways of experiencing the archaeological complex of Machu Picchu in Peru are now reconfiguring its meaning towards the 'sacred'. The recent wave of New Age travellers is expanding, as several mystical pilgrimages to the lost city invite a mystic tourist clientele to recover lost wisdom and accelerate spiritual growth.

Beyond Incaness, Machu Picchu is constantly reconfigured as a 'power place' that is said to enable pilgrims to get in touch with their creative energies, return to basics, reconnect with nature and with the sustaining power of the ancient Inca civilization. These emerging forms of touring sacred places as a transformational pilgrimage have elevated Machu Picchu into a global network of 'power places', where ancient and prehistoric civilizations 'join up' by means of linked energy spots such as Stonehenge, Egypt's pyramids, Mount Everest and mystical temples such as the Taj Mahal.

More than simply seeking to gaze at an authentic culture–people–landscape, the 'post-tourist' (Urry, 1990) wants to live an 'experience'. These newly developing tourist quests are centred towards self-transformation and constitute the new ground for the 'authentic'.

This chapter draws on Hanegraaff 's (1999) discussion on the 'religious' and presents two trends towards the 'religions of the self'. On the one hand, the New Age travellers perform a renewed spirituality, while on the other, and intertwiningly, they 'worship nature' as a religious experience through performances that enable the transformation of the self and body.

As expressions of the secularization of religion and its transformation, these tourist mobilities are depicted as new manifestations of 'spiritualities' that draw on a symbolism embedded in secular culture (Hanegraaff, 1998). The self, the body, the nature and spirits of the ancient civilization are here combined to offer a so-called 'transformational pilgrimage', where the stiff urban body and over-socialized self of contemporary Western life are replaced by a 'return to basics'. Is this a new, middle-class market niche, a social movement or the only 'true way' of experiencing the 'power place'? While being sold as 'sustainable' or 'green' and differentiated from mass tourism, the Inca trail pilgrimage to Machu Picchu is an expression of contemporary quests that require the rebranding of the pilgrimage as a 'transformational' as well as a 'responsible' experience.

This chapter is based on the author's in-depth research on the Inca heritage revivals (Arellano, 2003, 2004), drawing on extensive fieldwork on the Inca trail, including: (i) participant observation; (ii) structured and semi-structured interviews to travellers, local tourism agents and tourist guides; and (iii) World Wide Web research on travelogue and travel agencies' websites. These tourism-related narratives and symbols are here conceptualized as 'New Age spiritualities' and 'worship of nature', two trends that are shaping the new reconfiguration of tourism and travel.

New Age Spiritualities

The 'alternative' way to experience Machu Picchu is often expressed by Cuzco inhabitants in reference to what they call 'esoteric tourists'. Even if these performances seem always to have existed on the margins of an 'institutionalized' and mass tourism, these seekers of spirituality are increasingly visible in the region as local people involved in developing 'mystic tours' are making successful businesses.

This 'transformational' way of experiencing Machu Picchu and the region of Cuzco is expanding, as several 'mystical journeys' and 'healing conferences' invite tourists to recover lost wisdom and accelerate spiritual growth. The 'mystic' tourist clientele, typically middle class and from Protestant countries, is likely to spend more than average tourists in order to experience a transformational journey. Today, several international tour operators promote Machu Picchu as a 'power place', bringing thousands of visitors to get in touch with 'their creative energies' to return to 'basics' and reconnect with the sustaining power of the ancient civilization.

Several authors have associated this phenomenon with the New Age move-ment, which is seen as the continuation of the counter-culture movement of the late 1960s (see Bellah, 1991; Bloom, 1991; Heelas, 1996; Hetherington, 2000):

> 'Meditation, shamanic activities, wilderness events, spiritual therapies and forms of positive thinking' are all key ideas and practices related to the movement. We saw that the adventurers or ecotravellers constructed their performances based on a differentiation from 'mass tourists'. Here, 'New Age' travellers seem to reject most of the official performances and discourses of the Inca citadel. From the 'mystic gaze', culture and nature are combined in the 'sacred', where Machu Picchu is more than a place to play: it is a 'power place' where the 'trainee' performs a self-declared 'quest' in order to receive a local teaching.
>
> (Heelas, 1996)

Machu Picchu is not only a 'symbolic' global place, it is a therapeutic centre that provides the required energy and indigenous spiritualities required for reaching a 'liminal' state (Turner, 1969) or a transformational experience with the 'beyond'. These 'self-authoring' practices elevate Machu Picchu into a global network of 'power places', where ancient and prehistoric civilizations and specific 'energy' spots link up Stonehenge, Egypt's pyramids, Mount Everest, 'mystical' temples like the Taj Mahal and the like on a 'global' pagan path.

Machu Picchu is located among 'powerful' nature and landscapes where the ancient civilization is seen as the 'spiritual heritage' of a people that 'worshipped' nature, 'the beyond', the stars and healing energy. As it is commonly known, the Incas claimed to be the 'Children of the Sun' and to have descended from celestial realms. The fact that popular ideas claim that Machu Picchu was an Incan 'astrological centre' or 'astronomy observatory' have also suggested to New Agers that the Incas were in contact with extraterrestrial life.

The mystery of the meaning of the architectural geometry of the citadel (Temple of the Sun, the 'solar clock' that measures time according to the position and shadow of the sun), its location, height and position in the middle of Andean mountains are some of the features transforming the Inca archaeological site into a sacred sanctuary and one of the greatest 'power places' in the world.

The 'mystic gaze' can be undertaken by a series of performances and quests that are not always easy to grasp. The 'spiritual guides' working with tourists are often local shamans who teach and 'inspirit' the 'disciples' towards the awareness and control of the inner powers as the Inca way. As a 'conference' mode of promoting New Age tours advertises, 'many speakers offer opportunities for one-to-one consultation that can be truly transformational'. Touring, learning and improving one's self and relationships with others by learning how to magnetize energies are among the basic ideas that motivate 'the quest'.

These New Agers perform not only in uncommon grounds but also in prohibited spaces, in order to avoid crowds and experience the very essence of energy. Entering Machu Picchu by night, for example, is to take advantage of solitude, silence, starlight and sunrise. Aluna Joy Yaxkin, a spiritual guide who leads and organizes several pilgrimages to Machu Picchu and has travelled to several sacred sites, prefers to enter these power places at night to meditate and pray. A night of meditation in these sites proved to be 'a profound way to tune in and receive sacred mystery schoolteaching', and she stated that:

> On my last day in Machu Picchu I was ready to enter the site at night. I waited until 1:00 am to make sure the guards were asleep. I climbed over a cliff beside the ticket gate to enter the site. I ascended up part of the Inca trail to a special carved rock where I could see the entire site laid out before me. Machu Picchu was exquisite, lit up by starlight and the silence was profound.
>
> (Yaxkin, 2001)

Spiritual pilgrims experience Machu Picchu differently from the 'adventurers' or the 'regular' day-return-train tourists. This alternative way of gazing with the whole body and spirit favours the learning experience. As an experienced 'spiritual guide' explains:

> We do not learn solely with our mind as we have been taught in the modern world. We learn with our entire being, and our entire being will shift because of this

learning. We understand that the living library locked within our DNA is in every single cell of our body. This is whole-body activation and is exactly as the ancients intended us to learn.

(Kachina, 2002)

Here, the use of the body is different, as the New Agers do not usually drive their bodies to extreme physical challenges, but still praise a certain 'embodied sacrifice'. Enlightenment and the 'liminal' phase do not come after a simple 'unusual' gaze like 'gazing at night'; there is hard work to do to reach the 'anti-structure' (Turner, 1969) that uses the body and the senses differently.

New Agers seek personal enlightenment, teachings manifested by signs from 'another dimension'. They see the Inca ruins in the middle of nature but they 'force' the gaze in order to detect particular lights, stars, angel shapes and any sign that comes from 'the beyond'. New Age travellers are 'students' who learn how to see these mystical signs and how to read them properly in order to understand the teachings.

How to read signs, how to hear messages, how to 'forget' the body pain in order to feel the beyond, and how to look at the landscape in order to transgress into another dimension are different and increasingly popular ways of sensing Machu Picchu and its mysterious power. Through meditation, New Agers are looking for enlightening 'visions', where the gaze seems to be primordial but at the same time is intended to be (totally) subordinated to the authority of the self.

The search for visions and for spectacular spots full of energy is not led by 'the gaze' as simply the vision as a sense, but 'the gaze' is commanded by the inner self through meditation. Here, the 'turn within', or what Bellah (1991) called the 'internalization of authority' is motivated by the loss of faith in the authority of institutions. In other words, the self becomes the only truth, where the Incas act as models, as ideal healers and as 'voices' towards an authority that has not been 'contaminated' by modern institutions like family, education or work – as imposed by society.

Modernity generates uncertainties and quests for 'authentic experience as a means of revitalizing fragmented personal identity' that initiate a search for authentic essential nature (Heelas, 1996, p. 148). Going further than MacCannell's (1976) search for authentic 'untouched' cultures, the New Agers locate their 'quest' in complex spatialities that do not simply gaze at 'indigenous authenticity' but are constantly in 'play' with different dimensional layers that engage the body, the senses and the spiritualities with the Incas, the stars and the beyond. The New Age 'experience' is aesthetic, kinaesthetic, but also self-transformational and healing.

The mystic gaze seeks a reality located inside the self rather than outside, the one that uses the vision as a medium to reach the inner self at the same time as it rejects the 'socialized gaze' and institutionalized self. Indeed, in the New Age philosophy, the senses are to be avoided in order to reach the path to interiority. As Bloom (1991, p. 33) comments: 'All life as we perceive it, with the five human senses or with scientific instruments, is only the outer veil of an invisible, inner and causal reality'.

Yaxkin's meditation consisted of forgetting about the cold stone, freezing temperatures and exhaustion. Transcending the body and the senses as 'infected' by the pre-given order of things is the path towards the authenticity of the 'within'.

More than searching beyond the body and the senses, Bellah (1991) goes even further by saying that the quest is 'beyond belief'. Accordingly, the healers, shamans, New Age teachers or charismatic leaders do not impose anything upon the 'students', but 'guide' them towards their own 'soul'. The 'within' in this case lies in inner voices and intuitions that force out the 'false personality'. Paraphrasing Heelas (1996), Machu Picchu is the stage and the made-up context that enables travellers to reach their own spirituality and authority.

Worshipping Nature

The other dimension of new spiritual activities seeks self-transformation through a close relationship of the body with nature. Nature goes hand in hand with 'responsible' performances, narratives of sustainability and environmentally friendly touring. In fact, on the margins of 'mass tourism', day return at the Inca ruins, the self-distanced and conscious 'post-tourists' (Urry, 2002) are guided to perform practical acts of conservation at the same time as supporting causes like the protection of endangered sites.

'Travellers' or the 'un-tourists' (see Birkett, 2002) are aware that tourism has to be compatible with preservation, and many of them follow the rules of preservation of the 'alternative' way of 'experiencing' Machu Picchu. The 4-day Inca trail leading to the citadel is promoted as 'ecotourism' for a responsible 'ecotraveller'. Several new lodges, hotels and travel agencies in Cuzco and Machu Picchu are now emphasizing their 'ecooperated' 'ecotechnologies'. Tourists are now 'environmentally aware' and opt for ecotravelling, a market that is set to flourish in the coming years.

The rebranded 'ecotraveller' differentiates him/herself from the (mass) 'tourist' who is constantly being 'condemned as anti-ethical' (Birkett, 2002). But more than promoting ecological performances based on sustainable tourism programmes that minimize impacts on a pristine area, ecotourism is here conceptualized as a more 'authentic' way of experiencing through fully corporeal practices that challenge the body and seek a full and revitalizing contact with nature.

It is interesting to speculate that if we all have an 'inner Indiana Jones' or something like a sense or desire for adventure – and perhaps this was manifested during the 1980s, with a growing interest in hiking the 'Inca trail' – this has helped to transform this citadel into a global place for adventure. The trek is imagined and performed as restoring and re-sensitizing a so-called 'metropolitan body' into a highly sensuous corporeal body. In his discussion on Simmel's perception of the 'modern individual' Lewis describes an 'irredeemable rupture for embodied experience', where 'there is an intensification of nervous stimulation as our senses become besieged by the information overload endemic to modern life' (Lewis, 2000, pp. 65–66). Therefore, in the world of the adventurer, automatic and passive metropolitan bodies are in search of enjoyment and momentary recovery of fully corporeal and highly sensuous activities.

A 'healthy' tourist who does not enter Machu Picchu by trekking the Inca trail has not 'experienced' or felt what it was like to live in the Inca era. The 4-day trek is essential to reaching this sensuous 'state', as the long-distance walk and camping among nature, beauty and ancient civilization allows the achievement of a reflexive awareness of the body and senses and, therefore, a fully corporeal experiencing of the sacred site.

Over the last 10 years, the Inca trail has become a tourist rite of passage that testifies to the 'real Inca experience'. To gaze at Machu Picchu, 'to be there', to take a picture of oneself in front of the Temple of the Sun as a proof of 'I was there' is no longer enough. The visit requires sacrifice, challenge, physical endurance and a wide range of multidimensional embodied performances that convert 'touring' into 'performing' and give way to a self-transforming experience.

The main physical activity involved in performing the Inca trail is obviously 'walking'. But more than walking as a leisure activity, how has '4 days of gruelling hiking in various conditions' become so attractive for travellers? Why does the tourist seek physical challenge, sacrifice, pain, tiredness, illness, *soroche* (altitude sickness), cold, stomach problems, sunburn and so on? Improving the over-socialized self by braving one's physical capacities and reaching the confines of sensuous experience are plausible answers. As Edensor comments: 'Beyond the trial of physical endurance and mental strength lies the promise of a more confident self and a return to a masculine (bodily) essence, replete with fantasies about getting back in touch with [one's] nature' (Edensor, 2001, p. 93).

The hike starts at an altitude of 9842 feet (2953 m), ascending to 13,779 feet (4200 m) at its highest point and ending at 7545 feet (2264 m) when reaching Machu Picchu. The second day of the trek is the most physically demanding, and many people have difficulty in reaching Warmihuanusca (Dead Woman Pass), the summit of the trail. This pass is reached after 3–5 hours of climbing a mountain with a temperature that ranges from below freezing to the semitropical climate of the rain forest.

Indeed, the whole route is tough, stony and is composed of many steep ascents and descents. The idea of carrying a heavy backpack, the fear in general, the blisters, the flies and other 'obstacles' formulate the trek as a physical challenge that has to be accomplished successfully. Walking here is not simply the embodied practice usually seen as central to tourism. It is rather an arduous journey made on foot, demanding a sense of adventure. Jen Cravens, a young traveller, calls the trek 'the Inca trial' and writes on how she 'survived the Inca trail':

> I was terrified of the hike, of the pain and strain and unknown obstacles. But I had come this far, and I would never forgive myself if I allowed fear to dictate my actions. So with bated breath and a knot of dread in my stomach, I agreed with my companion, William, that I would choose the adventure of the trail over the ease of the train. With a heart filled equally with hope and fear, I left Cuzco ... where we began our adventure.

The Inca trail requires physical and mental preparation, as most people who brave the Inca trail are not passionate or experienced hikers. In fact, the 'expert' hiker avoids that trail during the high season when novices seem to be 'queuing up' in the mountains. Therefore, the trail is a challenging rite of passage and a unique experience that requires physical and mental conditioning.

Tourists hike towards Machu Picchu by confronting their body capacities and undertaking a battle against nature. But in addition to walking, there is another very interesting and surprising way of 'performing' the Inca trail. A Peruvian native now living in Los Angeles, Devy, defines himself as a 'multi-day ultra-wilderness running freak' who has been guiding runners in the Andes for the past 3 years. During a trip to Cuzco in 1995, Devy, decided to 'run' the Inca trail in a single day. This experience gave birth to an increasingly popular 'tour' that he now leads several times a year.

Running the Inca trail is a much more formidable challenge. Confronting wilderness, altitude and the unknown is the best way to 'gaze with the whole body'. As one runner expressed upon his arrival at the Gateway of the Sun (where one catches the first glimpse of Machu Picchu at the end of the run): 'Wispy clouds cling to the dilute air, adding a sublime stillness to the scene. I am at once exhausted and awestruck as I make my way to the ruins.'

Running in high altitude is certainly a great challenge, as the run reaches 13,779 feet (4200 m). This runner added that: 'The air is thin and diffused, and it feels like I am sucking air through a straw. The sheer steepness is horrifying to a flatlander like me' (*Timberland Magazine*, 2002).

Many people regard taking the train to Machu Picchu as a great experience. Walking and camping for 4 days on the Inca trail and finally to reach the most magnificent view is certainly more taxing and better valued on a modern scale of achievements. But without doubt, running the Inca trail in 10 hours 43 minutes instead of in the course of a 4-day walk is an exploit that can hardly be surpassed.

Modern people need some challenge, and another runner encapsulated this challenge by stating that: 'I was turning 50. I had seen so many lives turned upside down by the "mid-life crisis" thing that I decided I'd better do something to hit it head-on to be sure the "fall-out" wasn't too devastating. Thus Peru.' As Edensor stresses: 'Fulfilment takes the rhetoric of individual achievement counterposed to the regulations and fetters of everyday family and work life, connected to a "can do" philosophy of personal growth and reflection' (Edensor, 2001, p. 95).

From 'I was there' to 'I did it [the Inca trail]' and from 'I hiked there' to 'I ran there' indicates the increasing importance of claiming status through physical achievement where pleasure and competition, athletic performance and touring are new and flourishing ways of sensing the Incas. These experiences push the body to extremes and achieve a reflexive awareness of the body.

A site with such qualities is becoming more appealing for world travellers and for people who cherish everything related to 'nature'. One of the issues that Macnaghten and Urry (1998, 2001) have explored is the emergence of a 'culture of nature' in most Western countries. According to them, this phenomenon is 'a culture that emphasizes valuing the natural, purchasing natural products, employing images of nature in marketing, supporting organizations concerned with conserving nature, being in the natural environment and engaging in practices that enhances the "naturalness of one's body"' (Mcnaghten and Urry, 2001, p. 1).

In the adventurer's imagination, it could be said that beauty is evaluated in terms of environment, ecology, fauna and landscape in relation to the sensuous contact of the body 'subject with nature. The Inca trail to Machu Picchu reflects the very performance of 'sensing' the Incas, as the traveller experiences a grandiose representation of nature and the mystery of the past.

The Incas are always depicted as a people who were very close to nature, and Machu Picchu is a monumental demonstration of intimacy, with its terraces and buildings constructed in perfect harmony with nature and the mountains. As every tourist knows, the Incas praised the Sun, the mountains, *pachamama* (Mother Earth) and all forces of nature. As they had neither horses nor wheeled transport, the Incas relied upon walking. Therefore, entering Machu Picchu through the Inca trail is a way of experiencing the Inca nature by walking and reviving corporeal past performances.

While gazing with all of the body, the adventurer is alternatively in 'play' with the natural and the cultural through corporeal performances that are aimed at being more 'real' and authentic than those of the 'passive gazer' of the packaged tour. Within the choice of a challenged bodily 'experience' over the ease of the package tour lies a search for authenticity based in a 'sense of reality' that is achieved through re-enacting Incas' past performances.

Walking, being close to nature and recovering momentarily the fully corporeal and sensuous experience of the ancient civilization requires a sense of adventure and of sacrifice that braves the body fitness. The desire to exceed the 'passive' gaze of the 'archaeological site' by engaging the whole body and senses adds to the experience of touring and transforms the sanctuary into a re-enacted Inca civilization, wherein actors perform the past and get closer to the 'real Incaness'.

Summary

This chapter has explored how New Age travel provides alternative ways of configuring the sacred meaning of such archaeological sites as Machu Picchu in Peru. New Age travel emerges from counterculture movements that see a new generation of pilgrims in search of accelerated spiritual growth. This transformational form of pilgrimage and esoteric tourism is apposite to a range of sacred sites including Stonehenge, Egypt's pyramids, Mount Everest and the Taj Mahal.

Post-tourists are exploring experiences based on the search for the 'authentic' and 'religions of the self' (Hanegraff, 1999), spiritualities that draw on the symbolism embedded in secular culture. The extension of this thesis is that the secular pilgrim is trying to move beyond the over-socialized self and through transformational pilgrimage is trying to 'return to basics'.

This chapter has highlighted how this form of tourism might be characterized as alternative tourism, a contrast with mass tourism. However, this form of 'un-' or 'post-' tourism can be differentiated from adventure tourism in that this form of tourism characterized by New Age pilgrims, the latter are seeking personal enlightment and 'signs' from another dimension. A loss of faith in the authority of institutions has seen a quest for locations such as Machu Picchu with complex spiritualities that enable the 'over-socialized self' to move beyond the 'socialized gaze' of traditional tourism.

Tourist performances based on these newly emerging quests contribute to the process of sacralization of Machu Picchu as a 'power place'. But beyond traditional sightseeing travel, New Age travellers transform the tourist experience into a religious and spiritual journey that is embedded in secular symbolism but also maintain 'contact with a meta-empirical framework of meaning' (Hanegraaff, 1998, p. 147) is embedded in secular symbolism; nature, ancient civilization and the body are seen as new, autonomous expressions of spiritualities of the self.

These new alternative forms of travel are real 'transformational pilgrimage', differentiated from mainstream tourism practices and regarded as less 'authentic', superficial and anti-ecological. New performances at Machu Picchu have been rebranded as 'life-changing opportunities for you and the environment' (Birkett, 2002).

Self transformation through meaningful experiences improves the self – spiritually and bodily – at the same time as it is seen as being ecologically performed. Accordingly, we could say that these rebranded performances, based on spiritualities of the self, veil the ambiguity of conserving *and* commodifying heritage sites as travellers 'buy' more 'alternative', 'responsible' and 'religious' performances that are, in fact, quite staged. Thus, after the world heritagization of Machu Picchu, bodies, spirits and Incas are now haunting the spectre of temporary configurations reassembling the 'secret place' of the Incas into a global 'power place' for urban contemporary spiritualities.

References

Arellano, A. (2004) Bodies, spirits and Incas: performing Machu Picchu. In: Urry, J. and Sheller, M. (eds) *Tourism Mobilities, Places to Play, Places in Play*. Routledge, London.
Bellah, R. (1991) *Beyond Belief*. University of California Press, Berkeley, California.
Birkett, D. (2002) *Ethical Tourism*. Hodder & Stoughton, London.
Bloom, W. (1991) *The New Age. An Anthology of Essential Writings*. Rider, London.
Edensor, T. (2001) Walking in the British countryside: reflexivity, embodied practices and ways to escape. In: Macnaghten, P. and Urry, J. (eds) *Bodies of Nature*. Sage, London.
Hanegraaff, W. (1999) New Age spiritualities as secular religion: a historian's perspective. *Social Compass* 46 (2), 145–160.
Heelas, P. (1996) *The New Age Movement*. Blackwell, Oxford, UK.
Hetherington, K. (2000) *New Age Travellers, Vanloads of Uproarious Humanity*. Cassell, London and New York.
Lash, S. and Urry, J. (1994) *Economies of Signs and Space*. Sage Publications, London.
Lewis, N. (2000) The climbing body, nature and the experience of modernity. *Body & Society* 6, 58–80.
MacCannell, D. (1976) *The Tourist: a New Theory of the Leisure Class*. McGraw-Hill, New York.
Macnaghten, P. and Urry, J. (1998) *Contested Natures*. Sage, London.
Macnaghten, P. and Urry, J. (eds) (2001) *Bodies of Nature*. Sage, London.
Turner, V. (1969) *The Ritual Process*. Penguin, London.
Urry, J. (1990) *The Tourist Gaze*. Sage, London.

8 Religious Tourism and Cultural Pilgrimage: a Chinese Perspective

ZHANG MU, HUANG LI, WANG JIAN-HONG, LIU JI, JIE YAN-GENG AND LAI XITING

Department of Tourism Management, Shenzhen Tourism College of Jinan University, Shenzhen, Guangdong, China; e-mail: szzm2005@hotmail.com

Introduction

This chapter initially analyses and discusses the origins of religious tourism, exploring existing definitions that incorporate historical and cultural traditions and people's beliefs regarding cultural pilgrimage and religion. The second part of the chapter considers the incentives and geographical characteristics of religious tourism in China and, in the process, highlighting differences in traditional culture between eastern and western China and the incentives for religious tourism. Finally, this chapter considers the development issues as applied to Chinese religious tourism and cultural pilgrimage.

The Historical Perspective

The emergence of religious tourism and pilgrimage in China

As a cultural phenomenon, religion has a close relationship with tourism, and is a special tourist attraction based on distinctive traditions and cultural backgrounds, resulting in different forms of religious tourism. Tracing back this route of religious history or the history of tourism of the world, major religions globally have stimulated forms of 'tourism' as a foundation for spreading their own religious beliefs.

The founder of Buddhism, Sakyamuni, the Islamic Prophet Mohammed and Jesus Christ in Christianity have inspired acts of pilgrimage as part of their establishment as three major religions in the world today. Indeed in the historical process of development for all of the countries in the world, religious pilgrimages have always been one of the major factors for motivating people to travel. A great number of pilgrims have travelled to their particular sacred places to pay their tributes and missionaries have accomplished their religious missions through travelling.

Religious tourism refers not only to the form of tourism with strong or single-minded religious motivation of pilgrimage, but also to those non-pilgrimage tourist activities, such as travelling to the religious sites for sightseeing, cultivation and recreation. The history of pilgrimage travel has a long historical lineage. Although the degree of this connection in the spread of religion is somewhat weakened as a result of the appearance of other modern means, the momentum to develop tourism through religiously related events or activities seems to be growing and increasing.

According to the statistics of UNESCO, about 60% of the world population is religious. The numbers of followers of the world's major religions have been estimated (see Table 8.1). Such a large number of religious believers are indeed an incredible driving force for the development of religious tourism.

Many countries put great emphasis on the development and utilization of their religious cultural resources. The combination of pious religious beliefs and great quest for knowledge can easily be transformed into motivation for tourism at any time and in any place. Some famous religious/sacred sites have all become internationally developed destinations for pilgrimage, such as: (i) Mecca in Saudi Arabia: the Sacred Hall of Islam where the prophet Mohammad is believed to have ascended to heaven; (ii) Jerusalem: the Church of the Holy Sepulchre, the Islamic Aqsa Mosque and the Sacred Solomon Hall of Judaism; (iii) Bethlehem: home of King David of Ancient Israel for Judaism and Church of the Nativity; and (iv) the Vatican: the centre of the Catholic religion.

Bygone tourist activities were usually oriented around religious pilgrimages, explorations with few sightseeing activities. The Chinese Temple Fairs, for example, traditionally in spring, involved the burning of joss sticks and contained more or less religious elements. For thousands of years, Chinese Buddhist followers have travelled west to seek doctrines, travelled around to pursue truth and travelled to famous mountains and religious sites to do pilgrimage, all of which have promoted the growth and development of Chinese folk tourism.

In the mid-Donghan dynasty, Chinese and Indian Buddhism factions began to make contact with each other. The spreading eastward of Buddhism led to a

Table 8.1. Demography of followers of the world's major religions.

Religion	Adherents (million)	Proportion of world population (%)
Christianity	1955	33.70
Islam	1127	19.40
Hinduism	739	14.30
Buddhism	311	6.00
Sikhism	17	0.33
Judaism	14	0.28
Others[a]	123	2.37

[a] Mostly newly established religions.

large-scale development of folk tourist activities. Such high-level Buddhas as Faxian, Xuanzhuang and Yijing brought back with them the exotic, colourful arts of different cultures. They wrote travel books, such as *Notes on the Land of Buddhism*, *Account of Travelling West in Tang Dynasty* and *The Internal Doctrines of the South Sea Return*, which are still important historical reference books for the study of ancient Indian and South East Asian history, geography, culture and religion (Bao and Chen, 1996).

For Western peoples, religious tourism has always been their strong driver for travel to religious/sacred place for pilgrimage. Most Western religions have prospered through religious travels. Religion, as a particular view of the world and a value system, will certainly create a strong tendency for the extension of an internal driver, motivating people to travel to sacred places for pilgrimage and to the temples, in order to accomplish sacred religious rituals. Indeed, tourism and religion have always been connected with each other from ancient times to today, and they both have promoted each other's growth and development and, in a sense, they are naturally inseparable.

The tourism academic field usually refers to tourist activities related to religion and culture as 'religious tourism' or 'religious, cultural tourism'. Religious tourism, therefore, has always taken the spread of religion and religious beliefs as its main purpose. It is a kind of special tourism with preaching, following of preachers, seeking scriptures and as an act of pilgrimage where one starts by leaving one's permanent residence for a 'journey'.

It can be divided into two stages, the 'journey of the spread of religion' and the 'journey of religious travel'. In bygone times, this kind of journey was full of hardship and difficulties, and enjoyment of the journey was not on these travellers' agenda. Gradually, as religion became more established, the element for tourism was promoted and developed into a journey of both religion and tourism, with the former as the main purpose.

People involved in this gradual process of development were, initially, professional religious followers, but in later times lay religious followers also participated. Regarding this trend, a Chinese tourist geographer, Chen Chuang-kang, pointed out that: 'Traditionally, religious tourism refers to how to develop religious tourist sites to attract religious followers for pilgrimage, so that non-religious followers can also be attracted for sightseeing and business, trade and the economy can be indirectly promoted' (Chen, 2003).

Viewed as a special level of activity for tourism, religious tourism, however, is not fit only for religious followers, but also attractive for lay tourists because of its unique history, architecture and cultural tradition. Every year, almost 1 million Muslims travel to Mecca in Saudi Arabia for pilgrimage, and this event has already developed into the largest religious event in the world; moreover, it also attracts more than 3 million tourists to travel to this sacred city to see the scene for themselves.

Statistics show that more than 3 billion people are followers of the three major religions in the world, and many have a deep-seated need for this kind of religious tourism as pilgrimage. Therefore, modern religious tourism has already attracted non-religious followers as well as religious followers to travel to the religious and cultural relics and tourist sites for the various purposes of pilgrimage, sightseeing, etc., and also purely for the purpose of 'religious travel'. Du (2004), therefore, proposes that it is more accurate to call this 'religious tourism' rather than 'religious and cultural tourism'.

There is no single confirmed definition for religious tourism (Cui *et al.*, 1998; Yan, 2000; Chen and Zhou, 2001; Fang, 2001; Lin, 2002). Generally speaking, there are two views: the first is based on the fact that religious followers conduct touristic activities for the purpose of religion, including pilgrimage, worshipping, 'roaming around', doctrine-spreading, etc; the second focuses on the various touristic activities performed around resources of religious tourism. From this, we can see the full extent of the meaning of religious tourism: it is different from other general forms of tourism based on sightseeing and cultural tourism; it focuses on religious culture and possesses the qualities of piety, belief and seriousness.

Conversely, however, it can include non-religious travel to religious attractions, tourist sites, festival-sightseeing tourism and exploration of the cultural tourism of religious culture. Therefore, we provide the following definition for religious tourism: it is a special tourist activity orientated by religious culture, with the help of specific eco-cultural environment, and it refers to such special tourist activities as worshipping, research, sightseeing and culture carried out by religious followers and lay tourists.

The impact of different cultural backgrounds on the development of religious tourism

The concepts of religious tourism in the West and in the East are different and, although religious tourism is a kind of tourism of world events, oriental continental civilization and Western oceanic civilization demonstrate great differences in the characteristics of tourism as far as religious tourism is concerned.

Western peoples close to the sea are familiar with travel and fond of tourism, whereas the inland Chinese have no culture of travelling far, and are comparatively less outgoing and by no means adventurous. Western missionaries have spread their Christian doctrines to every corner of the world for a long time and have implemented a policy of active religious expansion. Under these circumstances, these missionaries' travels have shown more of a kind of religious spread and expansion.

In China, because of its geographical parameters, there were only a few Buddhas who went to India and Nepal for scriptures and doctrines. What the Chinese religious leaders did had more to do with the spread of religious practices to temples all around the country. Their brand of religious tourism has shown more of the characteristics of academic exchange with, generally, no purposeful intention of religious expansion.

In Western tradition, religious tourism is considered more of a process of self-reflection, and the hardships suffered along the journey are considered as a test of character. People have shown attitudes of deep respect and penitence concerning religious/sacred places. The early Western religious tourists (represented by missionaries) had a strong sense of obligation, and they travelled around the world with the main purpose of spreading Christianity or Islam.

As the world developed, people increasingly became religious, with important and significant architectural sites and regions having become sacred places for religious followers. They had no fear of hardship and travelled far to engage in a kind of spiritual ordeal and repentance. It is this kind of hope of returning to the 'spiritual home' that has promoted the development of modern Western religious tourism.

For example, the city of Jerusalem lies on the Judean Hill and is a world-famous ancient city with more than 5000 years of history. Jerusalem has always been considered as the 'Permanent Capital' of Israel. It is divided into western and eastern parts, with the main tourist attractions in the western part being the Knesset, the Supreme Court, the Children's Memorial, the Historical Museum and Israeli National Museum.

The eastern part, also called the Old City, has eight gates, in which there are four residential areas where Muslims, Christians, Armenians and Jewish people live. The Old City is the sacred place where Jewish, Islamic and Christian people from all over the world come to worship. Every day, pilgrims from all corners of the world come to worship at the Islamic sacred place, the Dome of the Rock, the Islamic Aqsa Mosque, the site of Christ's crucifixion, Christ's cemetery and the room for 'the Last Supper'.

The 'Western Wall' is the sacred place for the Jewish religion and attracts many followers each day for worship. The Mount of Olives is close to the Old City and is one of the most important sacred places for the Christian religion. It is said that Jesus Christ once preached here, but was betrayed by heretics and crucified here.

The Church of All Nations is situated just at the foot of the mountain. Pilgrims who come here choose their own way of vacationing according to their religion, including the following of 'tours of religious events', consisting of all kinds of religious festivals, visiting the various historical and religious relics and staying in the city temporarily for vacations of religious tourism.

To a Christian, this is the place where Jesus lived, preached, died and resurrected. To a Muslim, this is the place to which the prophet Mohammed was miraculously sent and ascended to heaven. Jerusalem is second only in importance to the sacred cities of Mecca and Madinah. To a Jewish person, this is the centre for their beliefs and the site of the sacred place. It is the city mentioned the most in the prophets' prophesies. Pilgrimage here becomes a kind of return, a comfort, a respectful place to worship and repent.

Although, for various historical and political reasons, Jerusalem has been constantly troubled by religious conflicts, this does affects its sacred status as a holy city, with its religious tourism continuing to prosper. So using the example of Jerusalem, we can see the momentous changes brought about by Western religious followers' inner religious drive and their absolute worship for their religions. It is clear that religious tourism in Western countries is deeply rooted in the depths of their people's religious beliefs. It possesses a distinct religious characteristic and is the basis for the sustainable development of religious tourism in Western countries.

The development of Buddhist culture and tourism in Tibet, China

Tibet, China, is situated on the 'Roof of the World', with a lofty topography and attractive scenery. The mysterious religion of Tibetan Buddhism in this mystical land came originally from India, but later formed its own characteristics in combination with some local religions. It reflects the original religious ideas, as well as its regional characteristics and ethnic features.

Tibetan Buddhism has spread for almost 1000 years, and so such Buddhist ideas as the 'cycle of life and death' and 'cause and effect retribution', etc. and the ecological viewpoints of 'people and nature are one' and 'peaceful coexistence' have all contributed to the seminal Tibetan ethnic qualities such as generosity, kindness, pureness and simplicity and affability.

Tibetan Buddhism has also had certain influences on the inhabitants of Tibet's surrounding ethnic regions, such as Mongolians, Tu, Yugu, Naxi, Menba and Luoba, who are still pious adherents of Tibetan Buddhism. It may be said that Tibetan Buddhism is not only an important part of China's Buddhism, but has also become one of the most extensive and influential religions in China.

Tibet has attracted tourists from all over the world because of its rich plateau views and religious features, and religious tourism has become the most important tourist activity in Tibet. According to researchers on the development of Tibetan Buddhism (Lin, 1993; Nan, 2000; Bai, 2004), the main religious tourist areas currently number seven: Lhasa, Changdu, Linzhi, Shannan, Rikaze, Ali and Naqu, the area of Lhasa being the richest with regard to concentration of religious elements.

Lhasa is not only the political and cultural centre of Tibet and the gathering place for all the major schools of Tibetan Buddhism, but it contains many important religious relics. Potala Palace lies in the centre of Lhasa City and is the symbol of the 'snow land' and the whole Tibetan Plateau. This highest, loftiest palace in the world is the symbol of the most wonderful part of Tibetan culture. Potala, a phonetic translation from Sanskrit, is also translated as 'Putuoluo' or 'Putuo', and its original meaning is the island of Bodhisattva, so Potala is also called the second Mount Putuo, Gandan Monastery.

During the course of over 1300 years, from the Tibetan King, Songtsan Gampo, to the 14th Dalai Lama, nine kings and ten Dalai Lamas have ruled and preached here. Dazhao Temple, beside Potala Palace, was the first temple built in Tibet, also called 'Zulakang' or 'Juekang' (Buddha's palace in Tibetan). It was built by Songstan Gampo in the 21st year of Zhenguan (AD 647) in the Tang Dynasty, in memory of Princess Wencheng coming into Tibet.

Additionally, there are three other large, sacred temples in Lhasa: Gandan, Zhebang and Sera, all of which are sacred sites for Tibetan Buddhism. Every year, thousands of religious followers are attracted to these sacred sites, which are also the main tourist attractions. Tibetan Buddhism attributes mystic spiritual meaning to all the mountains and lakes in Tibet. Mountains symbolize the male, representing men, husbands and fathers. Lakes symbolize the female, representing women, wives and mothers. Tibetan people strenuously protect these sacred mountains and lakes.

Up till now, such sacred mountains as Ganrenboqi, Namunani, Luozifeng, and the sacred lakes of Yangzhuoyong, Namucuo and Qinghai have all become famous Tibetan religious tourist areas. According to Wang Yaxin's study (Wang, 2005), Tibetan Buddhism has already infiltrated into every aspect of Tibetan life, such as politics, economy, ideology and culture. It not only influences deeply the Tibetan peoples' view of life, value, morals and beauty, it is also objectified in such artistic forms as architecture, painting, sculpture, drama, music, dancing, etc., contributing greatly to the culture and humanities of Tibetan tourist resources. The characteristics of Tibetan Buddhism and Tibetan culture create a foundation for the promotion of the social, economic and cultural elements of the tourist industry.

In China, apart from Tibetan Buddhism, the Islamic religion is also popular and has experienced three stages of development: starting first in the Tang/Song dynasties, spreading rapidly in the Yuan dynasty and gradually transforming into Chinese Islam. Islam in China has spread with distinct ethnic features, its believers coming mainly from the ethnic minority residential areas in north-western China, such as Xinjiang, Inner Mongolia, Gansu, Ningxia and Qinghai provinces.

Because these minority groups live closely together, they commit themselves to Islam, and Islam is worshipped widely. As a result, most folk celebrations and festivals there are religious, local and ethnic and attract many foreign tourists. Religious tourism in other provinces in western China has also developed rapidly (Yang and Cao, 2004; Cao and Huang, 2005; Li, 2005), such as Shangri-La in Yunnan province (Cao and Cao, 2005). All the provinces in the vast area of western China are therefore suitable for the development of tourist destinations with abundant and colourful religious features.

The development of religious tourism in eastern China

In contrast to western China – mainly composed of ethnic minorities – the majority of the eastern areas in China are populated by Han Chinese. Compared with their western counterparts, Han people are less enthusiastic about religion, but their adoration of traditional culture has been greatly influenced by religious tourism.

Confucius' instrumental idea – that tourism was certain to be fruitful and good for the promotion of one's virtues – infiltrated early thinking on religious tourism in China. Confucius expressed a philosophy towards life that: 'The wise enjoy water, the benign enjoy mountains.' As mainland China's important political and economic reforms develop, the driving force for religious tourism has also changed tremendously. Many tourists attending religious activities hope to cast off loneliness, acquire release from pressure and find inner peace through attending or watching religious activities.

Whilst Chinese culture is rich and colourful, with a 'deep' oriental culture, tourists' thoughts and sentiments are various and manifold. Some pilgrims come to burn incense for the simple reason that they have lost faith in the worldly life and desire to find comfort from here. After touring those famous mountains and temples, they expect their 'agony' to be abolished and their spirit purified.

Statistics show that, in China, there are 100 million believers in various kinds of religion, 85,000 sites for religious activities, 300,000 religious workers and more than 3000 religious groups (Ren and Yang, 1989; Ma, 1997). Han people live mainly in eastern China and the Han's attitude towards religion is more or less 'none-of-my-business'. Before Buddhism came to China, there already existed a developed civilization, so the development of Buddhism in China can be seen as a process of Buddhism with Chinese features, which has integrated many of the ideas of Confucius.

Many religious tourist centres are not only religious/sacred places, but also cultural destinations. Throughout China, there are more than 13,000 monasteries and temples, with more than 200,000 monks and nuns. Furthermore, there are 219 famous Buddhist mountains, among which the most famous are Mount Emei in Sichuan province, Mount Wutai in Shanxi province, Mount Jiuhua in Anhui province and Mount Putuo in Zhejiang province. There are 736 Buddhist temples, the most famous being the Shaolin Temple in Henan province, Baima Tample and the temples of Taer and Famen in Shaanxi province. There are 690 main grottoes and pagodas in the country: Dayan Pagoda in Xian city, Dunhuang Pagoda in Gansu province and Maijishan and Longmen Grottoes in Henan province are the best known.

The native Chinese religion, Taoism, was established formally in the late Donghan dynasty, and it has a history of more than 1800 years. Today, there are more than 1500 temples, accommodating more than 25,000 Taoists. There are 107 famous Taoist mountains, such as Mount Wudang in Hubei province, Mount Qingcheng in Sichuan province, Mount Longhu in Jiangxi province and Mount Qiyun in Anhui province. There are 143 famous Taoist temples, with 92 major stone inscriptions and relics. In addition, there are 20,000 mosques. Within the designation of 180 nationally preserved cultural heritage sites, 80 of them are religious tourist destinations. In the first and second classes of 84 national-level tourist sites, 63 of them are related to religion.

It is clear that religious tourist sites in China are an important part of Chinese historical and cultural heritage, which is an indispensable part of tourist resources in the Chinese tourism industry. Although there are not many religious followers in the eastern Han residential area, non-religious believers are now increasingly willing to travel to religious tourist destinations. Under the influence of Confucius' culture, Han tourists in the eastern part of China are seeking traditional and cultural elements at religious tourist sites and they 'sense their cultural depth' in these famous religious mountains within an establishing market of cultural pilgrimage.

The study of tourists' psychology shows that the main elements affecting a person's touristic behaviour are psychological and social. People are members of a society and their psychological elements tend to be confined and affected by social factors (political, economic, ideological, cultural, educational, ethnic, etc.). Although China carries out a policy of religious freedom, the religious population on the whole is not large, apart from some ethnic minorities (such as Tibetan, Mongolian, Dai Buddhists, and Hui, Uygur and ten other ethnic minorities who follow Islam). Many people show a great interest in religion, but fall short of being really converted to it. Whilst sectors of the population are indifferent to religion, they nevertheless accept the existence of religious activities.

In China, the famous religious tourist sites are often the popular tourist destinations for both tourists at home and abroad and those whose charm derives not only from religion itself. As many scholars have pointed out: 'Tourists nowadays are less pious, but more sensible. They are more interested in the wonderful, charming Chinese religious and cultural heritage' (Zhang, 2002).

The various kinds of religious and cultural touristic activities planned by tourist agents – at home or abroad – include those for non-religious groups, organizations and lay people, who enhance their cultural life from this kind of tourism rather than by believing in a certain religion. The development of such religious tourism can satisfy the tourists' primary needs of connecting tourism with some kind of religious culture.

At the same time, the pure religious content in religious tourism can also meet the requirements of religious workers and followers. In eastern China, the majority of tourists are non-religious followers, which means that the majority of Chinese tourists are strongly motivated to be cultural pilgrims. The fact that they travel to religious destinations or attend religious activities shows that they are equally influenced by Chinese culture and tradition, so the eastern area of China is suitable for the development of tourist activities incorporating cultural pilgrimages.

The Modern Perspective

Imbalance in development patterns

Buddhism and Taoism in China are both in a relatively strong position and they have spread widely, almost all over the country. Islam and Christianity, however, are both relatively weak in regard to the numbers of followers and the scope of their spread. Taoism and Buddhism, especially the latter, have spread very widely, from the coastal areas in the east to the north-western inland areas and, even to the barren and deserted Gobi, there is evidence of many religious relics.

Islam and Christianity have spread in a different way. The former has spread mainly to the large and medium-sized cities in coastal areas, closely connected to communication with foreign countries in Chinese history. Besides, Islam has also spread in the minority inland residential areas. These people are Arabian descendents of Islam who moved to China in the Tang and Yuan Dynasties. Christianity is in evidence mainly in large cities in the coastal eastern areas, with maritime cities having opened to foreign trade in the period following the Opium War (1839–1842).

Distinctive resources for religious tourism

Buddhist and Taoist followers are from all walks of life and from different classes, ethnic groups and regions. These two religions are both popular in China. Islam in China is concentrated mainly within such ethnic groups as Uygur and Hui, and Christianity attracts mainly embassy staff, foreign nationals and a small number of local followers. Buddhism and Taoism have spread not only to the larger and medium-sized cities but are also popular in the countryside, and even in some very thinly populated areas. Islam and Christianity have spread in cities that have historical links, and this is another reason for the differences in distribution of the varying religions.

Buddhism and Taoism have inseparable relations with mountains, the pursuit of tranquillity, freedom from desire and the adoration of gods and fairies. The existence of the holy Buddha is closely linked with a fantastic environment, so Buddhist and Taoist religious tourist resources are to be found mainly in the mountains and in the less-populated and beautiful scenic areas. Islam and Christianity tend to be symbolized by gatherings such as worshipping and fasting, and so are more widespread in densely populated areas.

Religious architecture

All the old temples and monasteries were built with wood, stone, brick and tile, combining technology and art and integrating spirit and material together, symbolizing fullness, perfection and the fruitful achievement of the ancient Chinese civilization.

It is especially worth mentioning the old Indian pagoda-style architecture, where monks' ashes were formerly kept; this has been transformed into the Chinese style of Buddha pagoda, which is really unique to Buddhist architecture, examples of which are the Dayan Pagoda in Xian City, the Liuhe Pagoda in Hangzhou City, the Zhenguo Pagoda in Quanzhou City and the Three Pagodas in Dali, Yunan province. The lofty architecture in Mount Wutai and the ordinary vernacular houses in Mount Jiuhua are all unique in their own way.

Painting, sculpture and readings

No matter whether a tourist is religious or not, he or she can inspect, purify and comfort his or her soul in front of the sculpture of Budhisattva. Here lies the charm of these religious sculptures, because not only are they extraordinary, artistically speaking, but also infused with a 'broad heart' and spiritual force of the salvation of all lives. Many murals and painted eaves in the temples strengthen this kind of atmosphere. China is vast, so different cultures, traditions and customs in different regions have different styles. For example, the stone sculpture in Yungang Grotto in Shanxi province and the earthen sculpture and statues in Maijishan, Gansu province, show two quite different artistic skills.

Religious tourists visiting temples can read and appreciate column inscriptions that not only enlighten one's wisdom and view of life, but also help them understand those difficult religious doctrines, which incorporate both spiritual and worldly life in general. Of course, many inscriptions are descriptions of the history of the temple, but many are the poems and words of famous people and craftsmen.

Economic benefits of religious tourism

Religious tourism has economic benefits for the tourism industry in that it benefits local economic and social development. For example, Dengfeng City, Henan province, has a Shaolin Temple on Mount Song, famous for its religious and cultural tourism, promotion of religious culture academically, internationalization of Shaolin martial arts and promotion of Shaolin culture, which increases the attraction and influence of Mount Song. Now there is a steady tourist market in Dengfeng City, with about 3.2 million tourists every year, of whom around 81% come to either the Shaolin Temple or the one other sacred Taoist site, Zhongyue Temple.

Quanzhou City is famous for its 'world religious museum', whose wide variety of religions exhibited is unique within China. Buddhism, as represented by Kaiyuan Temple in Quanzhou City, is most influential, making Quanzhou the so-called city of the 'Buddhist Land'. Qingjing Mosque is the oldest Islamic mosque in China, the Grass Temple being a unique relic of Manicheism, and the Laojun Rock is the biggest existing stone sculpture of Taoism. In addition, the city also has precious cultural relics of Hinduism and Brahmanism. All of these religious, cultural relics have enabled Quanzhou City to be listed as one of the 24 historical and cultural cities by the State Council of China.

For more than 10 years, Quanzhou City has developed these religious resources, and the tourism industry has become the main sector in local industry. Tourists from home and abroad alike have been attracted, with both religious believers and scholars engaged in research with the outside world. For example, in recent years, Quanzhou has hosted seminars, such as the international seminar concerning the inspection of religious relics. The unique features of religious tourism resources and stable tourist markets have all contributed to the sustainability of religious tourist sites.

Religious tourism and environmental protection

Religious doctrines pursue solitude, a return to nature and also, historically and ideologically, religion has been positioned diametrically opposite to political centres and 'world life', so religious/sacred sites are built mostly in the mountains. For example, Taoism considers high mountains to be the home of fairies and gods, and an ideal place for solitude and longevity (Yuan, 2004; Kong, 2005). Buddhist meditation also requires an environment with the fresh air and tranquillity of the mountains.

Sacred Buddhist sites especially evidence this kind of environment, such as Mount Wutai, Mount Jiuhua, Mount Putuo and Mount Emei. The four biggest Taoist mountains – Mount Longhu, Mount Qiyun, Mount Qingcheng and Mount Wudang – are also beautiful and tranquil.

Apart from the unique advantages noted already, many religious/sacred sites also have some man-made environmental features consciously designed to raise tourists' awareness of the environment and to suggest ways in which they might help to protect it. For example, most temples have created wildlife ponds to educate tourists not to kill any creatures and to maintain the balance of the ecosystem.

This kind of religious guidance is a good way to teach people to treat their material desires sensibly, to purify their soul and also to maintain the environment, all of which may lead to their idealogical purification and enable a re-examination of their material desires. By so doing, they have reached the stage of recognizing the importance of environment and ecosystem. Religion here plays a positive role, as an American scholar, R. Brown once highlighted: 'As the source and guardian of values, religion plays an important role in the transition to a sustainable society.'

The economist, E.F. Schumacher, proposed a new view based on Buddhist economics, which advocated simplicity and non-violence. These ideas were intended to free people from an 'addiction' to wealth and desires for comfort, enabling people to obtain high levels of satisfaction with low consumption. In doing so it was anticipated that it would create the conditions for sustainable development for both Man and nature.

From the analysis of the main tourist attractions of China (Zheng *et al.*, 2004; Yuan, 2005), the areas of protected natural scenery include ecotourist routes to temples and religious tourist sites. Almost half of the important national scenic spots contain religious sights, excluding those religious sites in the less well-known tourist scenic spots, which reflects the positive role that religious culture plays in the protection of the eco-environment.

A cautionary note should be raised regarding the rapid increase in the number of tourists at religious tourist sites and their impact on local environments. Through the commercial pressures exerted at these sites, some unique religious canons and rituals have gradually lost their mystic characteristics, and some have even been orientated by pure commercial recreational activities. It is not unknown for some tourists to destroy and pollute the environment with litter, graffiti and rowdy behaviour, which jeopardizes the unique tranquillity and holy atmosphere of the religious relics.

For example, the world-famous Dunhuang Murals of the Buddhist Grotto have been affected by the huge influx of tourists. The internal temperature of the grotto is so high that it has already caused great damage to the murals. Another statistic shows that some of the 112 cultural tourist sites of the famous Taoist mountain, Mount Wudang, have been damaged in varying degrees, including the Taihe and Zixiao Palaces.

In the quiet valley of the Taizi Slope, the local government has even built a small concrete dam, which looks odd in the cultural and natural environment of Mount Wudang. It is said that the purpose of the dam was to raise the water table so as to develop such tourist activities as drifting and swimming. As far as the sustainable development of religious tourism is concerned, overdevelopment will weaken its religious significance, and this means that these short-term developments for the needs of tourists will potentially create more damage to these religious tourist destinations.

External cultural intrusion on religious tourist sites

The eastern part of China is a developed area for the tourist industry, which attracts many tourists for religious purposes, but most of these are not devout religious followers: they travel to the religious destination simply out of curiosity or for the beautiful mountain scenery. In this area it is rare to have dedicated religious tourist routes, but because there is a proliferation of religious tourist resources, many tourist routes also include some religious tourist sites. For example, Mount Tai in Shandong province is a tourist site, with both natural and cultural elements and an established attraction.

On the Mount Tai tourist route, many tourist agencies now also include Confucius Temple in Qufu. Tourists are not as interested in Confucius Temple as in Mount Tai but, if time permits, it is 'OK' for them to see one more cultural heritage attraction. However, in adding the Confucius Temple to their Mount Tai itinerary, they are interacting with religious relics that have the features of being special, rare and vulnerable. Therefore, its future development and utilization must be preconditioned with protection, as overdevelopment will lead to the commercialization of such scenic 'spots' and eventually to the destruction of the genuineness and integrity of the religious/sacred relics.

At present, many religious tourist sites in China already have specific rules of protection. For example, within religious tourist sites, it is forbidden to litter, smear, inscribe, barbecue or cook in the open, cut trees, set off firecrackers or fireworks or take photographs of murals. The number of tourists is restricted and these measures have been quite effective.

In a word, we must not profit from tourism at the cost of losing the original meaning of religious culture. All successful practices worldwide have proved this one tenet: the inheritance, protection and spread of religious culture can not be separated from the development of tourism, and the development of a tourism industry also depends on the precious resources of religious culture.

Summary

This chapter initially reviewed the different perspectives on the global origins of religious tourism and, in doing so, revealed not only the main motivations for travel but also identified the cultural differences in China, which have led to divergent perspectives on religious tourism. These cultural differences are important in defining the way in which religions have prospered and stimulated growth in travel and tourism in China.

We argued initially that there are potentially two main facets to religious tourism: (i) there are religious followers who conduct tourist activities for the purpose of religious worship and veneration; and (ii) various tourist activities are 'performed' around resources for religious tourism. We posited that religious tourism is a special tourist activity orientated by religious culture, with the help of specific, ecocultural environments, and it refers to such special touristic activities as worshipping, research, sightseeing and culture, which stimulate travel by both religious followers and lay tourists.

We then identified the regional variations in religious worship throughout China, with reviews of the proliferation of Buddhism, Toaism, Christianity and Islam throughout different regions of China. What emerged as part of this review were the range of religious–cultural resources in existence for religious travel in China, and also the growing secularization of pilgrimage travel in China.

In this respect, for contemporary Chinese society, religious tourism is an expanding economic, social and cultural phenomenon that is highly significant to the development of the tourism industry and the utilization of touristic resources. Furthermore, the promotion of new tourist markets has increasingly attracted pilgrims and the visiting of religious tourist sites, all of which are effectively spreading, communicating and developing religious culture.

This chapter has highlighted the fact that religious culture and the tourism industry have a close, interactive relationship. Clearly, the protection and development of religious culture is significant to the sustainable development of the tourism industry, and the cultural wealth handed down through religious activities has already become a precious resource for the current tourist industry in China. The challenge for China is to be able to manage and develop these resources by adopting the principles of sustainable development to retain a vital cultural resource for future generations.

References

Bai, M.-C. (2004) A survey and analysis on a case of temple-based tourism. *Social Sciences in Yunnan* (5), 102–106.

Bao, J.-G. and Chen, Y.-M. (1996) Research on religious tourism. *Tropical Geography* 16 (1), 89–96.

Cao, H. and Huang, S.-M. (2005) Studies on development of religion tourism in western areas: present condition and countermeasures. *Guizhou Ethnic Studies* 25 (1), 43–45.

Cao, J. and Cao, M. (2005) From a religious and cultural belief of minority to a cultural symbol of global tourism: a case study of Shangri-la. *Journal of Thought Realm* 31 (1), 102–105.

Chen, C.-K. (2003) Tourism research collections, Qingdao. *Qingdao Press*, p. 194.

Chen, R.-F. and Zhou, M. (2001) Modern religious tourism development in China. *Social Sciences in Jiangxi* (1), 217–219.

Cui, F.-J. *et al.* (1998) Research on the religious tourism development of Mount Tai. *Journal of Central China University* 32 (3), 377–382.

Du, D.-S. (2004) A comment on religious culture tourism. *Journal of South-central University for Nationalities (Humanities and Social Sciences)* 24 (6),112–116.

Fang, B.-S. (2001) The ecological trend of religious tourism. *Journal of Social Science* 16 (1), 68–71.

Kong, L.-H. (2005) On Taoism tour culture. *Journal of Zhejiang University (Humanities and Social Sciences)* 35 (6), 27–33.

Li, L. (2005) An initial probe into the development of religious cultural tourism in Guizhou. *Journal of Guizhou University* (Social Sciences edn) 23 (3), 109–113.

Lin, J.-F. (1993) Festival culture of Tibetans. Lhasa. *Tibet People Press*, pp. 25–29.

Lin, M.-T. (2002) The religious tourism development in Putian city. *Journal of Putian University* 9 (4), 68–72.

Ma, J.-F. (1997) Study on religious tourism resources and its development. *Journal of Shanxi University* 25 (1), 107–112.

Nan, W.-Y. (2000) Preliminary discussion on Tibetan worship of mountains. *Research on Tibet* (2), 107–112.

Ren, B.-G. and Yang, W.-G. (1989) The religious resort of China. Chengdu. *Sichuan Peoples' Press.*

Wang, Y.-X. (2005) Development of the tourism value of Tibetan Buddhist culture. *Journal of Qinhai Nationalities Institute* (Social science edn) 31 (1), 15–19.

Yan, Y.-Y. (2000) Study on religious tourism. *Journal of Xiamen University* 143 (3), 69–73.

Yang, J.-R. and Cao, H. (2004) Research on the development of religion tourism in western areas of China. *Journal of Religious Study* 3, 126–128.

Yuan, Y.-Z. (2004) On the tourist resources of Taoist culture and the value of developing them. *Journal of Yibing University* (3), 29–31.

Yuang, G.-Y. (2005) The eco-protection implications in religious belief and culture of the minority nationality: cases and analysis. *Academic Exploration* (2), 105–111.

Zhang, C.-l. (2002) The distinctive tourism of Chinese religion. Nanjing. *Jiangsu Peoples' Press* p. 2.

Zheng, S.-T., Lu, L. and Yang, Z. (2004) Sustainable development of religious tourism. *Journal of Anhui University (Humanities and Social Sciences)* 32 (5), 536–540.

9 Centring the Visitor: Promoting a Sense of Spirituality in the Caribbean

JACKIE MULLIGAN

UK Centre for Events Management, Tourism, Hospitality and Events School, Leslie Silver International Faculty, Leeds Metropolitan University, Leeds, UK; e-mail: j.mulligan@leedsmet.ac.uk

Introduction

As communities become increasingly fragmented and decentred, and social frameworks more determined by 'interest' or 'lifestyle' rather than geography, events, cultural 'spectacles' and experiences can all play a key role in helping destinations to market seemingly meaningful associations to prospective visitors. Increasingly, destination managers are looking beyond the inherent natural environment to create new cultural forms based on former, forgotten and sometimes alien events and practices in order to meet the needs of visitors to 'escape the everyday' and 'reconnect with the true life' they are seemingly convinced is being 'lived' elsewhere.

In this process, destination managers treat culture like a new religion, transforming cultural places into sacred spaces and making cultural practices worthy of worship. By engaging in this process, destination mangers are tapping into a niche market of New Age faith tourists seeking new types of pilgrimage. In the Caribbean, more spiritual connections for 'disconnected' Westerners are creating a proliferation of arguably 'constructed ethnic' displays, transplanted faith experiences and endless imagery depicting the region as an 'unspoilt paradise'. All promise enrichment of the soul, but are making – through the process of illusion – any actual access to the 'soul' of the place ever more challenging for visitors.

The actual faith practices by communities within the region, for the time being at least, are being ignored by the marketers, and some might argue therefore remain unscathed by the trespasses of 'others'. However, as nostalgia begins to fade in the light of the growing popularity of New Age and new eclectic faith systems, encroachment on actual sacred sites and rituals within the Caribbean may not be too far away.

Cultural Connections and Reconstructed Ethnicity

'Cultural dimensions are very dynamic in society, but religious tenets form a stable and static pillar in society' (Fam *et al.*, 2004). This quotation emphasizes the impact of religious beliefs on behaviours and encapsulates how culture in tourism could manifest itself more as a quasi-religious experience. As communities become globalized, technology, cultures and communications in the developed world accelerate and change rapidly. In this constant churn, where nothing is stable, many Westerners do not appear to turn solely to religion for stability. Instead, it has been argued that they turn to the past (Hewison, 1987; Hughes, 1992).

It is interesting to speculate whether 'nostalgia' is always such a key motivation. Perhaps postmodern tourists are seeking a 'constant' rather than an 'authentic past'. The question for these New Age pilgrims is whether this constant is a new system to have faith in, or indeed a new faith system? This constant, stable, 'unspoiled' culture has become an ideal for 'pilgrims' from the developed world. With so much change, the 'stable and static pillar' (Hughes, 1992) they seek could be 'the unspoiled beach', 'the unchanged community', 'the undeveloped' rather than simply 'the past'.

Nevertheless, the constant is by its nature a freeze-framed moment or perception that shapes the 'geography of the imagination' (Hughes, 1992, p. 40). Indeed, it has been argued that host communities are being maintained in a weaker economic condition due to the desires of their guests (Britton, 1982; Urry, 1990; MacCannell, 1992).

With illusions of culture so prevalent in the Caribbean region, it is perhaps no surprise that when an inadvertent positive cultural interaction occurs when a visitor feels that they have stepped 'behind the scenes' – the impact of even the most simple encounter can have profound consequences. In fact, some have argued that the event can result in a healing experience. The following anecdote is purely illustrative of such an encounter, where a *Washington Times* journalist wrote about her experience at St Lucia's Jump-up party, which happens every Friday night in a settlement called Gros Islet:

> Makeshift grills are set up in the streets with people grilling meats and fish, and selling them straight off the grill as the meat turns up ready. Card tables covered with bottles of beer and other drinks are also scattered throughout the streets. Reggae and soca blare from some of the bars as people churn to and fro, in and out of the doors, hopping from one bar or beer stand to the next. And if the entertainment of the evening is a steel drum band, you should watch. Sure, the music sounds great from a distance, too, but the 'full experience' comes from watching amid the rest of a crowd gathered. Typically, the band of nearly 20 members or more starts the performance by carefully tapping out the steel beat, concentrating on their song. But, as the crowd gets riled, so does the band. Or maybe it's the band that gets riled, and the crowd follows its lead. Soon, all of Gros Islet is gyrating to the steel band music that is no longer a careful, tapping rhythm. Suddenly, tapping out the beat isn't an issue of concentration; it's just a matter of keeping up, because now the band is feeling the music, and the music is fast. Watch one drummer. He and his drum seem to be dancing with one another. And somehow the music magnifies the heartbeats of the

two dancers, the drummer and his drum. The hearts of this couple beat in synchrony with one another, but out of sync with the others in the band. The others, of course, are dancing to their own beats, to create the harmony of the song. So multiply the one beat shared by the drummer and his drum by 20 to feel the other 19 heartbeats in the band. Now feel all 20 or more musicians, coupled with their instruments, and dancing to their own beats. The musicians in this band are all dressed in the classic thrown-together uniform of matching coloured T-shirts and pants. Their uniform is not a costume meant to disguise a group of so-called musicians without talent, and it is refreshing.

(Washington Times, 2000)

Whilst tourists can experience this on a weekly basis, the standard fare for cultural display usually takes place in more controlled environments, where those very same 'thrown together' bands perform 'tropicalized' Western ballads in uniform matching 'tropical shirt' fashion in the resort hotels. In these contexts, these bands that can transform crowds into congregations often seemingly vanish into the tropical print wallpaper of the hotel foyers.

The former performance is what is often promised in some form or other to tourists. The pretty and tropical wallpaper print is unfortunately what is often received in its place. Tourists are promised the 'real thing', but receive passing scenery, a two-dimensional version of truth. But even though the former experience 'feels real', some would argue it is an illusion as well (Hewison, 1987; MacCannell, 1992; Baudrillard, 1994).

However, irrespective of its truth or authenticity, the excitement that arises from such gatherings supports the Durkheim school of thought that intense emotions can be produced when people escape the reality of their largely individualistic everyday activities (Durkheim, 1965; MacCannell, 1992). The collective gathering thus takes on an importance that may exceed its intrinsic value. In fact, some have argued further that beyond the 'escape' motivation, such experiences can have healing properties: 'At spectacles ... some of the felt forms of alienation may wither away or be cured, leaving the individuals in the audience feeling satisfied or ... filled all the way up with a single intense emotion' (MacCannell, 1992, p. 238). It is interesting to speculate whether this is the kind of healing process that the journalist in St Lucia described as 'refreshing' in her piece about the jump-up party.

Carnival Spirit

If we accept that some kind of 'healing' occurs through such gatherings or during cultural spectacles, then carnival is perhaps one of the most apparent forms of such gathering in the Caribbean and beyond. Carnival in mediaeval times parodied the official pageantry of the State and Church. Bakhtin (1984) describes the cultural form as one that countered the hierarchies and distinctions, returning religion to the people for them to refashion. The events succeeded in breaking down barriers between actors and audiences. Bakhtin claims that such celebrations were 'free of dogmatism', bringing together communities as a contrast to the hierarchies and support of inequality officially sanctioned by Church and State:

> On the contrary, all were considered equal during carnival. Here in the town square, a special form of free and familiar contact reigned among people who were usually divided by barriers of caste, property, profession and age ... Such free, familiar contacts were deeply felt and formed an essential element of the carnival spirit. People were, so to speak, reborn for new, purely human relations.
>
> (Bakhtin, 1984, p. 10)

The continued significance of such collectivity and desire to be 'reborn' can be evidenced by the continued growth of carnival celebrations and the increasing number of people wishing to be baptized into the tradition, suggesting that carnival followers might actually be a form of faith tourists. The roots of Caribbean Carnival are complex and borne out of European and African tradition, cultures, slavery and emancipation. The timing of carnivals links to religious calendars, and they are traditionally celebrated before Lent. According to the Definitive Caribbean website, Caribbean carnival is:

> the greatest show on earth: thousands of revellers shuffling and dancing in time in a mesmerizing sea of shifting colour. ... It is one of great Caribbean experiences. ... Many carnivals are still staged at the start of Lent, culminating on Mardi Gras or on Mercredi des Cendres (Ash Wednesday), but some are held to celebrate the end of the cane-cutting season, Crop Over in Barbados, or the zafra in Cuba. Others are staged at convenient moments in the calendar, for example Easter in Jamaica.

In spite of its roots, in the 21st century, carnival is almost exclusively viewed as essentially 'Caribbean' and often described as 'a model of ethnic harmony' (Scher, 2005, p. 46). In these Caribbean cultural forms that move and change according to demand and 'convenient moments', the spectacle that is carnival becomes what Baudrillard (1994) would describe as simulacra. Essentially, carnival is now assessed according to visitor numbers attending the event and the touristic experience and, in this way, as with many other events, the very essence is lost, as highlighted by Brown:

> Event managers have sacrificed the ritual element ... They have put aside ... the very heart and soul, the *raison d'etre* of any truly great event – in favour of artificially manufacturing events that try to meet the needs of clients and stakeholders. Such events alienate the very community that makes up part of their target market and from which many events have evolved.
>
> (Brown, 2004, p. 53)

Undoubtedly, the collective gathering for visitors can at least bring on the emotional intensity that MacCannell describes. The carnival simultaneously brings spectators and performers into a collective form of ritualistic pageantry and into a mythologized world of illusions (MacCannell, 1992; Baudrillard, 1994). The audience are both inside the spectacle and outside it, the barriers between performers and audience are broken and thus all 'join the parade'.

It could be the iconic representation that results from this 'performance' that enhances the impact of this kind of experience to 'higher levels' for participants. The carnival is the ultimate in Urry's (1990) 'otherness', where tourists view such spectacles and cultural manifestations as above their own culture. In the words of Butcher: 'The tourist gaze fixes upon sites that appear to offer an unmodern existence; an existence from which the tourist feels they have much to learn ...' This is no longer a 'tourist gaze' – this becomes 'a gaze in awe' (Butcher, 2003, p. 80).

However, like Baudrillard's depictions of 'Disneyland' as 'a deterrence machine set up in order to rejuvenate the fiction of the real in the opposite camp' (Baudrillard, 1994, p. 13). It is interesting to speculate whether carnival is actually 'hyper-real' and that the concept is now devoid of meaning, having lost connection with its origins. Carnival has been imported and exported around the globe. Indeed, in any one year up to 50 'Caribbean carnivals' take place in North America and Europe (Scher, 2005, p. 45). In this new globalized form, participants are experiencing a 'reconstructed ethnicity' (MacCannell, 1992, p. 160). Within this reconstruction: 'The notion of conflict, where it exists, is emphasized in relation to the white power structure ... against which "ethnicity" is made, reified, celebrated and maintained in Carnival' (Scher, 2005, p. 47).

Nevertheless, even if one accepts that what is produced is a pure simulation, it still affects the audience and the performers. According to Scher, the carnival serves to create a 'social alchemy – transforming workers to peoples and peoples to people' (Scher, 2005). It is seemingly the magical powers of carnival and collective interactions that may help to heal the alienation we feel through 'the monotony of the daily routine, the cold rationality of factories, offices, apartment blocks, shrinking human contact, the repression of feelings, the loss of nature and naturalness' (Krippendorf, 1987, p. xiv).

However, what renders the reconstructed ethnicity that produces these alchemic, spiritual impacts so false is the fact that the reconstruction is shaped by extrinsic demands and motives. By shaping experiences to suit the perceptions of 'others', culture's dynamic form becomes petrified. When culture is written in stone, it becomes its antithesis: it becomes a generally agreed set of beliefs and behaviours that cannot be questioned or transformed. Culture becomes dogma. Culture becomes exiled where, instead of being a part of 'the everyday', it is displayed to give meaning to life and to contextualize our existence. Such a belief in culture could be interpreted as a new faith system. It certainly echoes Jung's explanation of the functionality of religion:

> For Jung, religion could play a positive role in human life: 'Man positively needs general ideas and convictions that will give meaning to his life and enable him to find a place for himself in the universe'. Religion thus acts as a form of therapy, explaining and reconciling human beings to the pains and suffering of the world.
> (Jung, 1938; Momen, 1999, p. 64)

Excavating Culture like a Static Pillar

The reification and reconstruction of ethnicity through events and in carnival forms is one way in which countries and communities are seeking to conserve and protect their cultures from the external forces of change, globalized economies and tourism (Hewison, 1987; Hughes, 1992; MacCannell, 1992).

None the less, in the case of the Turks and Caicos Islands, in 2001 externalities created an impetus to excavate and entrench cultural forms, behaviours and beliefs for both the host community and guests. The result of the work produced new rituals, dress codes, cultural displays, products and music forms based on an elective and illusory time period: a period perhaps designed to give a sense of a particular meaning or a set of meanings to its own and to other communities.

The Turks and Caicos Islands has an identity crisis. It is a British Overseas Territory, politically the Caribbean but geographically the West Indies and often perceived to be 'The Bahamas'. It is known primarily by its stamps – which collectors around the world value – and for its diving, thanks to its situation on the third largest coral reef system in the world.

It is nowadays becoming more closely associated with upmarket resorts such as Parrot Cay – a resort defined more by Hollywood celebrities and spa retreats. The Tourist Board perceived that the culture of the Turks and Caicos Islands was being undervalued, leading to an increase in an Americanized culture and a lack of national pride amongst residents.

The Turks and Caicos Islands is not unique in the challenges it has sought to overcome in being a part of the Caribbean. In this region in particular, in addition to the globalization and Americanization, countries are suffering from what might be characterized as 'Jamaicanization'. The images used to promote the many all-inclusive resorts, the big brands like Sandals, the proliferation of reggae music and images of Rastafarians, dreadlocks and red, gold and green emblazoned on TV commercials, brochures, posters, websites and T-shirts all help to instil images of a single Caribbean with a single belief system in 'one love'.

The Jamaicanization of the Caribbean concurs with the geography of the imagination (Hughes, 1992) of the majority of visitors, but makes it increasingly difficult for other countries to meet the expectations of disembarking passengers looking for reggae bands or Bob Marley posters and also makes it near impossible to promote a country's uniqueness against this homogenous perception of the region, a perception largely created by the holiday brochures that promote the region and fail 'to distinguish between one island and the next, building on the impression of nothing but sand, sea and sun from the Bahamas to Bonaire' (Patullo, 1996, p. 144).

In 2001, the Tourist Board appointed a Cultural Director, David Bowen, a native of the Islands who worked hard to counter the impacts of tourism development and to restore 'cultural pride'. His first step was to visit the National Museum. The two factors that are important to note here is that the culture provision was situated within tourism and that historic authenticity was perceived by David Bowen as the only starting point.

For his work to be successful, the activities, events and products created had to have been rooted at one time in the community, a time he defines as a starting point. However, to be accepted by the community and to increase the sense of national pride, the cultural activities would need to attract the eyes of a visiting audience. David Bowen was effectively being asked to reconstruct ethnicity: not to define the identity of Turks and Caicos Islanders, but more to define 'ethnic difference' between the Islanders and the visitors (MacCannell, 1992).

In 2003, The Turks and Caicos Tourist Board launched the first cultural calendar. The aim of the calendar was to promote national events, from sports days to church bazaars, from beach festivals to carnival pageants. The objective was to raise the profile of these events, alert the populace to the volume of activities and to encourage a view of the Turks and Caicos as a country with a unique culture and a unique programme of cultural events for tourists.

Ink drawings depicted aspects of life such as basket weaving, fishermen, dancing, ripsaw music and conch horn blowing from a forgotten and mythologized multigenerational time frame. The illustrations were not entirely alien inventions; the community recognized some of them, especially the older generations, but some of the practices had been forgotten thanks to the placement of these cultural practices on the periphery of tourism development rather than centre stage.

It is striking to think that tourism in the Caribbean has developed so much and so far without focusing on its unique cultures and heritages, when over 30 years ago De Kadt described 'a growing sense of outrage about development that puts authenticity, environment, cultural, social questions at the periphery rather than the heart' (De Kadt, 1979, p. 47).

Two of the principal areas of focus for the Tourism Board and Cultural Director were to promote the uniqueness of the destination through its history and culture, and also to emphasize the uniqueness of the individual islands that make up the Turks and Caicos Islands. Semiological associations of the nation and individual islands were devised to create clear identification points for visitors and communities. The choice of a national tree, national flower and the development of the national costume signified a major development in the quest for a sense of identity.

The national costume borne out of David Bowen's research was based on the salt-raking costume of the Turks Bank and the straw hats of the Caicos Bank. The costume, produced in neighbouring Haiti, was launched during the Golden Jubilee and gained such wide appeal that hundreds were immediately ordered by institutions, schools and individuals.

Students at the Community College and at schools were offered a TCI Studies course, focusing on local history on the syllabus and, for those less than enchanted about the idea of learning history, they were in turn invited to engage in the newly excavated TCI's culture through modern interpretations such as 'salt-raking dances', which fused African rhythms that alluded to slavery and the salt-rakers. David Bowen had created a heritage product which, following Ashworth's definition was 'chosen not because it is valuable, but because it has valued effects' (Ashworth, 1996, p. 181).

The Tourist Board's attempt to excavate culture in providing something more meaningful to visitors resulted not in a staged authenticity (Hewison, 1987) but in a 'staged ethnicity'. Here emerges a paradoxical tension: as the Islanders seek to make the visitors less alienated by connecting them with a 'real' culture, they alienate themselves by becoming actors simply performing rituals (Goffman, cited in MacCannell, 1992). Indeed, irrespective of whether a culture is reinvented or commoditized, once the work or output is valued only as to whether it can be sold to tourists, the essential essence of the form is lost (Turner and Ash, 1975).

Once again, culture is reduced to a static form. This example is one of reconstructed ethnicity that ultimately 'represents an end point in dialogue, a final freezing of ethnic imagery which is artificial and deterministic' (MacCannell, 1992, p. 168).

In spite of the loss of intrinsic value created in this process, Turner and Ash (1975) believe that even if cultural forms are staged, they still maintain the power to educate because tourists can become enlightened about their own history and place in the world by visiting and experiencing other cultures.

From this, it could be argued that, when the tourist is looking outward, their subconscious 'tourist gaze' is inward – a quest for understanding themselves and a quest for enlightenment. Such inward revelations do not rely on any essential truth, and can be derived as easily from a theatrical play, a long journey, a good book or a church sermon as from an authentic cultural display. Increasingly, the transformative power of destinations to reveal our 'souls' to us is being demonstrated not by the cultural forms of the host communities, but through transplanted faith experiences that bear no relation to their sociogeographic locations.

Recentring the Tourist, Decentring the Place

In 2001, the Caribbean Tourism Organization adopted a new slogan to promote the region: 'Everything you want it to be.' A few tourism directors at the World Travel Market presentation – where the new slogan was launched – seemed hesitant about accepting such a generic description. One tourism director suggested at the meeting that the line be changed to 'Everything you want to be'. His suggestion alluded to the sense that this study could well support, that rather than the visitor transforming the region by their own perceptions, values, needs and desires, the region had the power to transform the lives and value systems of its visitors.

Such a quest to transform ourselves through our travel has resulted in a growing interest in cultural and ethical tourism, described as New Moral Tourism (Butcher, 2003). In this interpretation, the New Moral Tourist has sought to address the 'widespread disillusionment with modernity' though 'temporary immersion in a culture they perceive to be less sullied by modern society' (Butcher, 2003, p. 78).

However, increasingly, the immersion that is occurring is beyond the realms of the host culture and community and is taking on a more spiritual dimension. Whilst the importance of physical location diminishes in the face of globalization, the significance of 'place' in mental, emotional and spiritual terms is enhanced. Such a shift in balance between image and location has created an excellent opportunity for the region to exploit its physical assets in metaphysical terms.

The spiritual retreats of the Parrot Cay Resort in the Turks and Caicos Islands form a key part of business. Guests stay at the resort and pay 'top dollar' to revive their souls with beach-based yoga, pilates, massage and new guidance in living their everyday lives the 'Como Shambhala' way. These packages are by no means unique: the proliferation of spa-style vacations that bring ancient beliefs and wisdoms, from China to the Caribbean and other foreign shores, is a relatively new, yet fast-growing phenomenon.

Such 'spiritual' New Age-faith experiences are based on a series of convergent and divergent cultural and faith systems that are transplanted onto destinations. As 'stressed' executives attempt to levitate in yogic positions above the sand at sunrise in order to 'centre' their souls and reconnect, they are doing so in a transplanted zone with no actual connection to a physical place. This need to connect with a generic 'natural environment', to commune with nature and centre our soul has been explained thus: 'Due to the complexity of modern life and our separation from our natural environment, the individual will be faced with a variety of perceived needs to establish a state of physical and mental wellbeing' (Burns and Holden, 1995, p. 39).

The yearning has led to an increase in a wide range of resorts offering a combination of New Age spirituality and ancient wisdoms. The promotional materials for Como Shambhala Spa at Parrot Cay in the Turks and Caicos Islands resemble an invitation to a religious temple. Online, virtual visitors can explore Como Shambhala's philosophy:

> Parrot Cay's Como Shambhala retreat is the perfect refuge for those seeking a balance of spiritual and physical renewal. Shambhala translates as 'centre of peace and harmony'. Como Shambhala is Parrot Cay's ultimate point of stillness, a sanctuary dedicated to renewing the body and rebalancing its energies. It combines the spiritually based healing traditions of Asia with natural therapies from the sea and earth, offering an holistic approach to the wellbeing of the mind and body.
>
> (Como Shambhala Spa website)

On the home page, the Spa introduces its belief system: 'At Como Shambhala, we believe in balance – of mind, body and spirit – and the inspiration of the soul, afforded by a place of beauty.' Such retreat experiences are an increasingly important phenomenon for destinations, and offer a source of comfort and solace to 'spiritual tourists' seeking something in addition to or as an alternative to religion as a 'symptom of collective uncertainty' (Brown, 2003, p. 79).

This 'search for selfhood' goes beyond traditional religious belief systems: it is a search for a more New Age spirituality that is 'something personal and specific to individuals, not part of any system. New Age spirituality as opposed to religion is not a single moral framework but is a fluid phenomenon' (Butcher, 2003). The fluidity of the spirituality and spiritual experiences being demanded by tourists who no longer seek to avoid the 'uncertainty of the future' by looking back (Hewison, 1987) – but rather, by looking up – is an important factor that could change the very nature of destinations and 'cultural tourism' in the future.

Pilgrimages to Paradise

Whilst destinations may be slower to transform according to consumer demands and the wants of postmodern Western communities, promotional literature casts and recasts the imagery of destinations to lure us in rapid fashion. Ironically, the imagery used in brochures, websites and TV commercials often reveals more about ourselves that the 'other' we are seeking to visit. Studies have focused on what motivates people to choose certain destinations and, indeed, what motivates people to travel for pleasure.

However, the reason we need to 'escape' and what we are actually escaping from and to at a subconscious level is often left open to interpretation. Research measures extrinisic motivations, but 'Such conditioned motivations are induced by social pressures, and there is a danger that the real, deep-rooted, personal needs of the individual are neglected. The latter are the real inspirations for holiday-making' (Goodall, cited in Burns and Holden, 1995, p. 133).

The homogeneous imagery of the Caribbean and the developing world as a 'paradise' is not a new phenomenon. Britton (1979) believed such picturesque depictions were a distortion. Developing countries become a nirvana, something that should not and cannot be changed. The environment is precious and fragile and any kind of development is seen as an attack, a 'spoiling' of a culture or even a country (Butcher, 2003, p. 80).

It is within this presentation that the Caribbean has been able to maintain its position and 'reputation as a Garden of Eden before the Fall' (Patullo, 1996, p. 141). It is only through this suppression of 'development' that an alternative to the developed world is made available and true 'difference' can be observed. Tourists seek to 'admire poor people whose lives seem richer than their own' (Patullo, 1996). Such a demand for meaning beyond material possessions ensures that the host culture can continue to be 'held to possess something that the tourist culture has lost – a sense of community, of spirituality, of being closer to nature' (Patullo, 1996).

The advertisements for destinations show idyllic scenes to Westernized eyes. Miles of white, sandy beaches, lone footprints on the beach, men holding their children above the sea, women looking out to the horizon or raising their faces to the sun. The biblical and religious allusions are not coincidental. Here, men, women and children are baptized in clear, turquoise waters and enter a new world of simple rituals afforded and deserved by them thanks to their individualistic pursuits 'back home'. Such a quest for personal salvation echoes the philosopher Hume's beliefs on Christianity – simply 'an egotistical concern for personal salvation in another world' (Humes, cited in Shaughnessy, 2002).

The questionable status of religion in modern society could be one reason why people appear to seek a 'mortal paradise' or could be a consequence of our ever more rapid lives, where people may not want to literally wait a lifetime to experience the 'other world'. Brooks (2000), as cited in Butcher (2003), claims that bourgeois, bohemian tourists (Bobos) in particular reject their own wealth in order to attain new levels of spirituality: 'The Bobo ... is looking for stillness, for a place where people set down roots and repeat the simple rituals.'

They are generally seeking 'to get away from their affluent ascending selves into a spiritually superior world'. Of course, as Bobos they will actually need to use their resources to enter this superior world promised in the brochures. Examples of how this superior world is promoted are as follows: 'Think of it in simple terms: a place to rediscover those forgotten rhythms of long days, easy nights, and the salve of peace' (Parrot Cay website).

Certainly, the trend towards emphasizing the 'other worldly' charms of destinations would support this theory. The advertising and the travelogues repeatedly use terms like 'spirit', 'soul', 'eternal', 'magic', 'miraculous', 'paradise', 'heaven' and 'blessed', all illustrating the fact that in a 'Godless' Western society – or at least in a Western world seeking something more than 'God' to comfort them – a holiday has become a kind of pilgrimage to a 'heaven on earth'.

The word 'pilgrimage' is not far-fetched when exploring the phenomenon of tourism in this light. Tourists plan their trips in advance of the event, deciding when and where to go (Pearce, 1993). They leave with a purpose of finding something, even if that something is simply 'to get back in touch with life' (Cousineau, 1998, p. 18) or to 'engage in a search for selfhood' (Butcher, 2003, p. 78). Cousineau (1998) described pilgrimage as 'a transformative journey to a sacred center – a spiritual exercise, an act of devotion to find a source of healing, a journey to a holy site associated with gods, saints or heroes or to a natural setting imbued with spiritual power' (Cousineau, 1998, p. xxiii).

The postmodern pilgrims consult advertising materials, brochures and guidebooks to formulate their plans. One of the best-selling books used by backpacking tourists in particular is the *Lonely Planet Guide*. In Alex Garland's *The Beach*, which follows a backpacker's quest for adventure in Thailand, he repeatedly refers to the *Lonely Planet Guide* as 'The Book'. The main protagonist, Richard, follows the recommendations of 'The Book', believing in its 'higher authority' – 'Traveling where The Book decrees and generally acting as a disciple of the new religion of travel' (Butcher, 2003, p. 45; *Lonely Planet Guide* website).

In 'The Book', as in the colourful tourism brochures, destinations have clear religious – indeed Eden-like – connotations; St Lucia's nuggetized description in the *Lonely Planet Guide* is of 'a tropical Eden at the end of the rainbow'.

The holy sites that we visit may be natural settings that have been imbued with spiritual power thanks to the promotional imagery. However, in the Caribbean, the holy sites may be associated with heroes such as authors like Ian Fleming, whose shrine – his former estate, 'Golden Eye' – can be found on a 15-acre hideaway in Jamaica and is described as 'a magical place; a retreat nestled among tropical forests and lush gardens on a seaside bluff overlooking the Caribbean' (Villas of Distinction website).

Alternatively, pilgrims may seek to visit the sacred sites associated with the Caribbean icon Bob Marley. In the 'Jamaicanized' Caribbean where Marley imagery and sounds pervade, alongside museums and Marley tours in Jamaica, more concrete shrines to the icon are being constructed elsewhere. Marley Resort and Spa in the Bahamas promises visitors:

> a place where the needs and desires of all guests are met through a multitude of quality services. ... This former Marley home embodies the life, legend and inspiration of the Marley family and the true essence of freedom. Come embrace the feeling of 'one love' and 'one heart' in only 'one place'.
>
> (Marley Resort and Spa website)

Summary

The cultures, cultural events, ethnicity and actual geography of the Caribbean are being used, adapted, modified and commoditized to meet the needs and demands of Western tourists seeking to find their own 'spiritual centres' in the various destinations (Butcher, 2003). Cultures and ethnicities have been constructed and reconstructed to provide illusions of another world, a world that is constant and unspoilt. Events like carnival support and restore our faith in the exotic, affording us a chance to look upwards 'in awe' at another world and, in doing so through our own participation, to be healed – or at least to gain some respite from our everyday alienation.

The geography of the Caribbean has been transformed from a region rich in African and colonial history into a place of spiritual contemplation and enlightenment, achieved through the borrowing of an eclectic range of faith systems and ancient wisdoms transplanted onto its shores. The entire region has then been re-presented to the world as an earthly paradise. Nevertheless – unlike the definition of 'paradise' (*Oxford English Dictionary*) as the 'ultimate abode of the just' – this heaven on earth has become the 'ultimate abode' only for those who can afford to enter it. Such a hyper-real depiction of the spirituality of the region appears to have safeguarded the faith practised by the host communities.

Tourism developers are now seeking to cross further boundaries in the areas of moral, cultural and religious tourism. In the quest to bring wider experiences to tourists, some are arguing for tourism to include the faith practices found in the region. Former CNN anchorwoman and author Andria Hall spoke about faith in the Caribbean at the Caribbean Media Exchange on Sustainable Tourism (CMEx) conference in Nassau, Bahamas in 2006. She claimed that 'faith tourism' was an overlooked market for the Caribbean Tourism industry and that faith tourism was worth US$1.1 billion in the USA alone (Cmex website).

'The lines between culture and religion are thus growing ever more blurred. Whilst culture becomes a construct, static and dogmatic, religion takes a more dynamic form to reach "new demographics".'

The original premise of this chapter began with a question as to whether culture was the new religion for destination managers – in the sense that it has become a static pillar providing visitors with an unchanging vision, and thus an understanding of their own roles in the world. In the light of the dynamism of religion and faith in the Caribbean, perhaps the question should be changed: Is religion the new culture for destination managers?

References

Ashworth, G.J. (1996) Elements of planning and managing heritage sites. In: *Planning, Managing and Marketing Heritage, International Conference on Tourism and Heritage Management (ICCT), 1996*. Yogakarta, Indonesia.

Bakhtin, M. (1984) *Rabelais and his World*. Indiana University Press, Bloomington, Indiana.

Baudrillard, J. (1994) *Simulacra and Simulation*. University of Michigan Press, Ann Arbor, Michigan.

Britton, R. (1979) The image of Third World in marketing. *Annals of Tourism Research* 6 (3), 313–329.

Britton, S. (1982) The political economy of tourism in the Third World. *Annals of Tourism Research* 9, 331–358.

Brooks, D. (2000) *Bobos in Paradise: the New Upperclass and How they Got There.* Simon and Schuster, New York.

Brown, J. (2004) In: Yeoman, Robertson, *et al.* (eds) *Managing the Arts, Culture and Leisure Experience: Event Design and Management in Festival and Events Management.* McMahon-Beattie, London.

Brown, M. (1998) *The Spiritual Tourist.* Bloomsbury, London.

Burns, P. and Holden, A. (1995) *Tourism: a New Perspective.* Prentice Hall, New York.

Butcher, J. (2003) *The Moralisation of Tourism.* Routledge, London.

Cousineau, P. (1998) *The Art of Pilgrimage.* Element Books, London.

De Kadt, E. (1979) Social planning for tourism in developing countries. *Annals of Tourism Research* 6 (1), 36–48.

Durkheim, E. (1965) *The Elementary Forms of Religious Life.* Free Press, New York.

Fam, K.S., Waller, D.S. and Erdogan, B.Z. (2004) The influence of religion on attitudes towards the advertising of controversial products. *European Journal of Marketing* 38 (5/6).

Hewison, R. (1987) *The Heritage Industry.* Methuen, London.

Hughes, G. (1992) *Tourism and the Geographical Imagination.* E. & F.N. Spon, London.

Jung, C.G. (1938) *Psychology and Religion.* Yale University Press, New Haven, Connecticut.

Krippendorf, J. (1987) *The Holiday-makers: Understanding the Impact of Travel and Tourism.* Butterworth-Heinemann, Oxford, UK.

MacCannell, D. (1992) *Empty Meeting Grounds.* Routledge, New York.

Momen, M. (1999) *The Phenomenon of Religion: a Thematic Approach.* One World Publications, London.

O'Shaughnessy, N.J. (2002) Marketing the consumer society and hedonism. *European Journal of Marketing* 36 (5/6), 524–547.

Pattullo, P. (1996) *Last Resorts.* Ian Randle, Jamaica.

Pearce, P. (1993) In: Pearce, D. and Buteler, W. (eds) *Fundamentals of Tourism Motivation in Tourism and Research: Critiques and Challenge.* Routledge, London.

Scher, P. (2005) From the Metropole to the Equator. In: Ho, C.G.T. and Nurse, K. (eds) *Globalisation, Diaspora and Caribbean Popular Culture.* Ian Randle, Jamaica.

Turner, L. and Ash, J. (1975) *The Golden Hordes: International Tourism and the Pleasure Periphery.* Constable, London.

Urry, J. (1990) *The Tourist Gaze: Leisure and Travel in Contemporary Society.* Sage, London.

Washington Times (2000) Special report prepared by the advertising department. 25 January (http://www.internationalspecialreports.com/archives/00/stlucia/14.html, accessed 22 March 2006).

Websites

CMex http://www.mediaexchange.info/ (accessed 8 March 2006).

Como Shambhala Spa http://comoshambhala.bz/default.asp?section=332 (accessed 9 March 2006).

Definitive Caribbean http://www.definitivecaribbean.com/specialinterest_carnivals.aspx# (accessed 9 March 2006).

Dominica http://www.dominica.dm/index.php (accessed 5 March 2006).

Fun in the Son http://www.funinthesonjm.com/history.html (accessed 9 March 2006).

Jamaican Tourist Board http://www.visitjamaica.com/planning_your_trip/features_general.aspx?
    guid=de4b2176–79d1–4cf4–8f88-d7abac8a008a (accessed 7 March 2006).
Lonely Planet Guide http://www.lonelyplanet.com/worldguide/destinations/caribbean (accessed
    9 March 2006).
Marley Resort and Spa http://www.marleyresort.com (accessed 9 March 2006).
Parrot Cay http://parrotcay.como.bz/default.asp (accessed 7 March 2006).
Villas of Distinction http://www.villasofdistinction.com/villas/Specialty-Properties-Goldeneye—
    The-Ian-Fleming-Estate,-Jamaica.htm (accessed 2 March 2006).

10 Case Study 1: the Festival of Sacrifice and Travellers to the City of Heaven (Makkah)

RAZAQ RAJ

UK Centre for Events Management, Leeds Metropolitan University, Leeds, UK; e-mail: r.raj@leedsmet.ac.uk

Introduction

Events and festivals have played an important part in human life since the days of Adam. Events and festivals provide humans with an opportunity to assert their identities, both for themselves and to share with other people in our modern society which, by definition is increasingly secular and culturally motivated.

The hajj is considered as the culmination of each Muslim's religious duties and aspiration. It is stated in the Holy Qur'an that every physically and financially able Muslim should make the hajj to the Holy City of Makkah once in his or her lifetime. In Islamic belief, the hajj honours a number of events in the life of prophet Abraham and his family in Makkah. Prophet Abraham is the figurehead for Christianity, Judaism and Islam.

Several leading authors – Lefeuvre (1980), Nolan and Nolan (1992) and Richards (2001) have often wondered what Muslims do during their pilgrimage. Pilgrims come for hajj from all parts of the globe – from the Middle East, South East Asia, Africa, Europe, America and Australia. Hajj is a pilgrimage to Makkah in Saudi Arabia, which constitutes the fifth and last of the acts of worship prescribed by Islam. The hajj is one of the Five Pillars of Islam: at least once in a lifetime, any Muslim who is able, financially and physically, to complete this journey must do so.

Hajj takes place during the first days of the lunar month of Dhul-Hajjah, the 12th month of the Islamic year, and lasts for as long as 6 days. Makkah marks the spot where, according to tradition, the prophet Abraham first built a shrine to worship God. It was a caravan crossroads through rocky outcroppings in the desert, which grew into a modern, noisy, bustling centre for the Muslim pilgrimage.

The hajj is obligatory once in a lifetime for those Muslims who can afford it, provided that adequate arrangements have been made for the journey and for the welfare of those remaining at home.

The hajj constitutes a form of worship with the whole of the Muslim's being: with his body, mind and soul, with his time, possessions and the temporary sacrifice of all ordinary comforts and conveniences the person normally enjoys. The person should assume for few days the condition of a pilgrim wholly at God's service and disposal.

This chapter will explore how people perform hajj and what the experience of hajj is for the individual participant. It will discuss the principal rites and experiences of hajj and their meaning to an individual. Finally, the chapter will offer discussions on the topic of pilgrims engaging in religious ritual at the hajj but will suggest that it is inappropriate to confuse pilgrimage with tourist activity and to equate the hajj with religious touristic events.

The Hajj

Performing the rituals of hajj

Hajj is pilgrimage to Makkah in Saudi Arabia, which constitutes the fifth and last of the acts of worship prescribed by Islam. The hajj is obligatory once in a lifetime for those Muslims who can afford it, provided that travel and security arrangements are in place and that provision has been made for any dependent family while the pilgrim is away from home performing the hajj. The hajj constitutes a form of worship involving the whole of the Muslim's being: body, mind and soul, involving time, possessions and the temporary sacrifice of all ordinary comforts and conveniences that a person normally enjoys. The person should assume for a few days the condition of a pilgrim, wholly at God's service and disposal.

The hajj is one the major forms of worship, and it is the fifth pillar of Islam that Allah sent Muhammad.

The hajj is considered the culmination of each Muslim's religious duties and aspiration. It is stated in the Holy Qur'an that every physically and financially able Muslim should make the Hajj to the Holy City of Makkah once in his or her lifetime.

> And (remember) when we prepared for Abraham the site of the (scared) House, (saying): 'Do not ascribe anything as associate with me, and sanctify My House for those who circumambulate it and those who stand and those who bow and those who prostrate themselves (there).
>
> (Qur'an, Chapter 22, verse 26)

> And proclaim the hajj to men; they will come to thee on foot and (mounted) on every camel, lean on account of Journeys through deep and distant mountain highways.
>
> (Qur'an, Chapter 22, verse 27)

> Abu Hurairah reports that Muhammad said:

> Whoever performs hajj for the sake of pleasing Allah and therein utters no word of evil, nor commits any evil deed, he returns from it as free from sin as the day on which his mother gave birth to him.
>
> (Hadith[1])

---

[1] The Hadith is a collection of traditions containing sayings of the prophet Muhammad which, with accounts of his daily practice (the Sunna), constitute the major source of guidance for Muslims apart from the Qur'an.

In the Hadith, many important edicts about the hajj appear:

1. Hajj should be for God's sake, and that there should be no worldly object and no ulterior motive prompting this holy deed, neither should it be for the show of things, nor for personal fame. Prophet Muhammad once said:

> Near the time of Judgement day the rich ones from amongst my people will perform hajj for the sake of travel and holidays; (like having a holiday in Saudia Arabia instead of one in London or Paris). The middle class will perform hajj for commercial purposes, thereby transporting goods from here to there while bringing commercial goods from there to here. The scholars will perform hajj for the sake of show and fame. The poor will perform hajj for the purpose of begging.

(Hadith)

2. In another hadith it is mentioned: 'Perform hajj and become rich, travel and become healthy.' In other words, the change of air, places and weather often bring about better health. This has been experienced time and again.

3. In a third hadith it is stated that: 'Continuous hajj and ummah[2] keeps away poverty and sin in the same way that fire removes rust from iron.'

Principal rites of hajj

As the pilgrims reach Makkah, they enter into a state of consecration known as Ihram. One takes on Ihram by expressing one's intention of entering into that state, and putting on the pilgrim's dress (which is called Ihram). The dress for male pilgrims is a garment unique to hajj, which consists of two pieces of white, unsewn cloth covering the lower and upper parts of the body; because no specific garment is prescribed for women, they enter into Ihram wearing normal garments.

Types of pilgrimage

Al-Uthaimeen (1999, p. 2) states that there are three forms of hajj, which are all mentioned in the Hadith.

Tamattu'

A pilgrim wears Ihram for Ummah only during the months of hajj, which means that when he reaches Makkah, he makes Tawaf and Sa'yi for Umrah. He then shaves or clips his hair. On the day of Tarwiya, which is the eighth of Dhul-Hijja, he puts on his Ihram for hajj only and carries out all of its requirements.

Ifraad

A pilgrim wears Ihram for hajj only. When he reaches Makkah, he performs Tawaf for his arrival and Sa'yi for hajj. He doesn't shave or clip his hair as he

---

[2] Ummah represents the religious ties that bind all Muslims together.

doesn't disengage from Ihram. Instead, he remains in Ihram till after he stones Jamrah Al-Aqaba on the Eid day. It is permissible for him to postpone his Sa'yi for hajj until after his Tawaf for hajj.

Qiran

A pilgrim either wears Ihram for both Umrah and hajj or wears Ihram first for Umrah, then makes intentions for hajj before his Tawaf for hajj. The obligations on one performing Ifraad are the same as those on one performing Qiran, except that the latter must slaughter whereas the former is not obligated to do so. The best of the three forms is Tamattu', which is the form that the prophet encouraged his followers to perform.

Even if a pilgrim makes intentions to perform Qiran or Ifraad, he/she is allowed to change his intentions to Tamattu'; he/she can do this even Tawaf and Sa'yi have been performed. Moreover, pilgrims need to have a clear understanding of the following obligations stated by Islam:

1. Hajj is obligatory on every adult Muslim who can afford to go to Makkah during the hajj season, whether on foot or by any other means of transport.
2. If a person can travel to Makkah to perform hajj, but cannot travel to Al Madinah (Westernized: Madinah), hajj is obligatory on him/her also. One can perform hajj without visiting Al Madinah, the resting place of Muhammad.
3. A Muslim woman cannot travel for hajj unless she is accompanied by a mahram (i.e. husband or relative, such as son, father, brother, etc.). If she can not find any mahram to accompany her, hajj is not obligatory on her until she finds one. However, she must make a will stating that, in case she dies before performing hajj, her heirs should arrange for her hajj-e-badal from her estate.
4. Hajj is obligated only once in one's lifetime. After performing the obligatory hajj, one is not required to perform it again. However, one can perform the nafl (optional hajj) as many times as one wishes.

In 632 CE[3] the prophet Muhammad, on his return to Makkah from exile in Al Madinah. The prophet Muhammad started his journey from Al Madinah towards Makkah with thousands of his followers, then took over Makkah with little resistance. He then visited and destroyed the idols there and restored the principle of hajj rites to their original status: purity and devotion to one God alone.

In the same year (632 CE) the prophet Muhammad with 200,000 followers made the journey to hajj. The year 632 CE saw the farewell by hajj for the prophet Muhammad, when he delivered the last sermon to his followers on Mount Arafat. He stated that it was essential for pilgrims to be present at Arafat, and that those who had been present at Arafat would have performed the hajj. In addition, he stated that, in the event of a pilgrim arriving too late to perform the initial rites at the Grand Mosque in Makkah, as long as he or she had taken part in the assembly at Arafat, the hajj would have been accepted by God.

---

[3] CE, Common Era, another term for Christian Era.

The Ka'aba

As pilgrims reach Makkah, after having found suitable accommodation and taken care of the physical necessities, their first obligation is to visit the Ka'aba and perform certain prescribed acts of worship, following the example of the prophet Muhammad. Figure 10.1 shows the Ka'aba, an oblong stone building located approximately in the centre of the quadrangle of the Grand Mosque in the Holy City of Makkah. The front and back walls are 40 feet (12.0 m) in length, the side walls are 35 feet (10.5 m) and the height 50 feet (15.0 m). The story of the building of the Ka'aba is told in the Holy Qur'an:

> And remember Abraham and Ishmael raised the foundations of [the] (sacred) House, (saying): 'Our Lord, accept it from us, for Thou art the All-Hearing, the All-Knowing. Our Lord, make us those who submit to thee and of our descendants a people who submit to thee. And show us our rites, and forgive us. Indeed, thou art the forgiving, the mercy-giving'.
>
> (Qur'an, Chapter 2, verses 127–128)

And again:

> Remember We made the House a place of gathering for men, and of security. And you take the station of Abraham as place for prayer. And We covenanted with Abraham and Ishmael that they should sanctify My House for those who circumambulate it or use it as a retreat, or bow prostrate themselves (there in worship).
>
> (Qur'an, Chapter 2, verse 125)

Fig. 10.1. Ka'aba, in Makkah.

Set in a silver surround in the east corner of the Ka'aba, some 4 feet (1.2 m) above ground level, is the Black Stone. This sacred stone, the focal point of the hajj, is the only remnant of the shrine that Abraham built when it was given to Abraham by the angel Gabriel. The stone (which may be of meteoric origin) is believed to date from even earlier times – to that of the first man, Adam. Figure 10.2 illustrates the position of the Black Stone and the area around the Ka'aba where pilgrims undertake Tawaf.

The pilgrimage route

To perform hajj, the pilgrims have to go through a number of stages during the 6 days of hajj. The climax of the hajj occurs on the 9th day of the Dhul-Hajjah (the 12th month of the Islamic year) the Arafah. Pilgrims perform the following duties during the 6 days of the Dhul-Hajjah. On the first day of hajj, they pour out of Makkah towards Mina, a small, uninhabited village east of the city. During the second day (the 9th of Dul-Hajjah), they leave Mina, via Muzdalifah, for the plain of Arafat for the Wuqoof (the 'standing'), the central rite of hajj (see Fig. 10.3).

Plain of Arafat

The 9th day of the Dhul-Hajjah is called Youmul, or Arafah (The Day of Arafah). This is the date when the hajj pilgrims assemble on the barren, treeless plain of Arafat, 6 miles away from Makkah, where they perform the most essential part

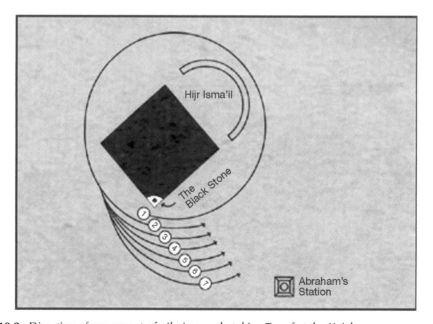

Fig. 10.2. Direction of movement of pilgrims undertaking Tawaf at the Ka'aba.

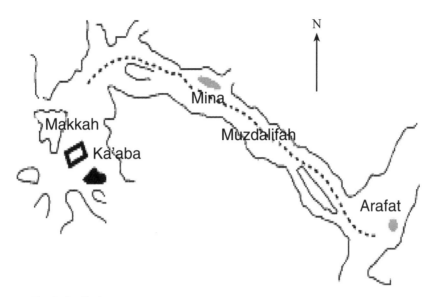

Fig. 10.3. The hajj pilgrimage route.

of the prescribed duties of hajj, namely, the Wuqoof of Arafat (the stay in Arafat). The prophet stressed the essential nature of this day's observance by saying that one who had been present at Arafat would have performed hajj.

It is the most important day for the pilgrims: every person who is performing the hajj has to take part in the assembly at Arafat, and their hajj would be accepted by God. The pilgrims spend this day of the Dhul-Hajjah on the plain of Arafat until sunset, after which they retrace their steps to their next station, Muzdalifah.

Plain of Muzdalifah

The pilgrims will spend the night at Muzdalifah. Here, they will gather 49 pebbles that they will use for stoning the three stone columns representing Satan (the devil), which have stood since ancient times in the village of Mina. These stone pillars stand at sites in the remote Plain of Mina, where Satan appeared to Abraham and Ishmael, tempting them to disobey God when Abraham was taking his son to be sacrificed at God's command.

Village of Mina

Pilgrims will then spend the next 3 days at the village of Mina, after their brief stop at Muzdalifah, to complete their pilgrims' rites and then disperse. On each of the 3 days of their stay in Mina, pilgrims go to the columns, stoning them with the pebbles they have collected in order to symbolize their rejection of Satan, in the same way that Abraham once rejected Satan. After the first day's stoning, most of the restrictions applicable to the pilgrim in the state of Ihram are now lifted.

The principles and rules of sacrifice of an animal (qurbani)

The sacrifice of an animal has always been treated as a recognized form of worship in all religious orders originating from a divine book. Even in pagan societies, the sacrifice of an animal is recognized as a form of worship, but it is done in the name of various idols and not in the name of Allah, a practice totally rejected by Islam.

Mohammad stated that sacrifice of an animal has been recognized as a form of worship only during 3 days of Dul-Hajjah, namely, the 10th, 11th and 12th of that month.

Qurbani is a demonstration of total submission to Allah and a proof of complete obedience to Allah's will or command. This practice is to commemorate the unparalleled sacrifice offered by the prophet Abraham when he, in pursuance of a command from Allah conveyed to him in a dream, prepared himself to slaughter his beloved son, Ishmael, and actually did so. However, Allah Almighty, after testing his submission, sent down a sheep and saved his son from the fate of slaughter. It is from that time onwards that the sacrifice of an animal became an obligatory duty to be performed by every well-to-do Muslim.

Sacrifice of an Animal (Qurbani) is a demonstration of total submission to Allah and a proof of complete obedience to Allah's will or command. When a Muslim offers a *Qurbani*, this is exactly what he/she intends to prove.

Thus, the Qurbani offered by a Muslim signifies that he/she is a slave of Allah at best and that he/she would not hesitate, even for a moment, once he/she receives an absolute command from his Creator, to surrender before it, and to obey it willingly, even if it be at the price of his/her life and possessions.

When a true and perfect Muslim receives a command from Allah, he/she does not make his/her obedience dependent upon the command's reason-ableness, as perceived through his/her limited understanding. He/she knows that Allah is all-knowing, all-wise and that his/her own reason cannot encompass the knowledge and wisdom underlying the divine command. He/she, therefore, submits to the divine command, even if he/she cannot grasp the reason or wisdom behind it.

This is exactly what the prophet Abraham did. Apparently, there was no reason why a father should slaughter his innocent son. But, when came the command from Allah, he never asked about the reason for that command, nor did he hesitate to follow it. Even his son, when asked by his father about the dream he had seen, never questioned the legitimacy of the command, nor did he pine or whine about it, nor did he ask for one good reason why he was being slaughtered. The one and only response he made was: 'Father, do what you have been ordered to do. You shall find me, God willing, among the patient' (Qur'an).

The present-day Qurbani is offered in memory of this great model of submission set before us by the great father and the great son. So Qurbani must be offered in our time, emulating the same ideal and attitude of submission.

Sacrifice of an animal can only be performed during the 3 days of Eid, namely the 10th, 11th and 12th of Dul-Hajjah. It is only during those days that slaughtering of an animal is recognized as an act of worship. No sacrifice can be performed on any other days of the year. Although sacrifice is permissible on each of the 3 aforesaid days, it is preferable to perform it on the first day, i.e. the 10th, of Dul-Hajjah.

No sacrifice is allowed before the Eid prayer is over. However, in small villages where the Eid prayer is not to be performed, sacrifice can be offered any time after the break of dawn on the 10th of Dul-Hajjah. Sacrifice can also be performed in the two nights following the Eid day, but it is more advisable to perform it during daytime.

Those required to perform Qurbani

Every adult Muslim, male or female, who owns 614 grammes of silver – or its equivalent in money, personal ornaments, stock-in-trade or any other form of wealth that is surplus to basic needs – is under an obligation to offer a Qurbani. Each adult member of a family who owns the above-mentioned amount must perform their own Qurbani separately. If the husband owns the required quantity, but the wife does not, the Qurbani is obligatory on the husband only, and vice versa. If both of them have the prescribed amount of wealth, both should perform the Qurbani separately.

If adult children live with their parents, Qurbani is obligatory on each one of them possessing the prescribed amount. The Qurbani offered by a husband for himself does not fulfil the obligation of his wife, nor can the Qurbani offered by a father discharge his son or daughter from their obligation. Each one of them is responsible for their own.

However, if a husband or a father – apart from offering his own Qurbani – gives another Qurbani on behalf of his wife or his son, he can do so with their permission.

During this period, pilgrims also return briefly to Makkah to perform their final act of worship of Ka'aba. This is another essential rite of hajj: the Tawaf, the sevenfold circling of the Ka'aba, with a prayer recited during each circuit. Their circumambulation of the Ka'aba, the symbol of God's oneness, implies that all human activity must have God at its centre. It also symbolizes the unity of God and man. The pilgrims leave the village of Mina before sundown on the third day or the following morning, and their pilgrimage is now complete. Finally, however, before leaving Makkah, pilgrims make a final Tawaf round the Ka'aba to bid farewell to the Holy City.

Pilgrims' experience of hajj

The pilgrims gain a number of benefits from hajj; every year, over 3 million Muslims from more than 70 countries make the journey by land, sea and air – to the holy city of Makkah for spiritual pilgrimage. Pilgrims share the unanimous view that nothing can quite prepare them for the sheer beauty of the experience and the overwhelming feeling of humbleness that overcomes them. They enjoy the sense of purification, repentance and spiritual renewal during the journey of hajj. Malcolm X (Malik el-Shabazz) stated in his autobiography:

Every one of the thousands at the airport, about to leave for Jeddah, was dressed this way. You could be a king or a peasant and no one would know. Some powerful personages, who were discreetly pointed out to me, had on the same thing I had on. Once thus dressed, we all had begun intermittently calling out 'Labbayka! (Allahumma) Labbayka!' (Here I come, O Lord!) Packed in the plane were white, black, brown, red, and yellow people, blue eyes and blond hair, and my kinky red hair – all together, brothers! All honoring the same God, all in turn giving equal honour to each other ...

Never have I witnessed such sincere hospitality and the overwhelming spirit of true brotherhood as is practised by people of all colors and races here in this ancient Holy Land, the House of Abraham, Muhammad, and all the other Prophets of the Holy Scriptures. For the past week, I have been utterly speechless and spellbound by the graciousness I see displayed all around me by people of all colors ...

(http://www.colostate.edu/Orgs/MSA/find_more/m_x.html)

Nazim Yunis, an information technology consultant from Leeds, UK, said:

I have enjoyed the experience of my lifetime during the journey of hajj. It made me realise that once you come to hajj, regardless of your profession, every body get to [sic] Ihram, wearing white piece of cloth. The whole community is praying together in front of Allah. For me it was a great experience to be involved and practice [sic] that I never felt in my whole life.

Serfraz Qayyum, from Middlesborough, UK, said:

When I first saw it, it was 1997 and I couldn't believe it. Now I believe in God's mercy in my own life and I've realised how lucky I am. I'm just beginning to recognize his mercy. All I could do was thank God for bringing me here once again. I thought that if I die right now, I really wouldn't be bothered. Nothing else matters to me. I just want to stay here forever. I can feel Allah all the time. All the time. You are always conscious of him and wherever you look around you can see him and feel him, the sky, the stones, the people, and the trees. It's a beautiful feeling that everyone is remembering and praying to God.

(http://www.channel4.com/community/showcards/H/Hajj.html)

Hajj is a unique spiritual event, bringing together people from every part of the world – such an immense diversity of human beings. These people represent such vast differences in culture and language, forming one community and performing the same faith, and all are devoted to the worship of their single creator. For this reason, Michael Majid Wolfe, an Islamic scholar, commented:

This is one of the images that sticks with me most powerfully about the hajj. The idea of praying five times a day all over the world is a very orderly idea. To see this idea enacted by almost 3 million people in one space at the same time is awesome. When the prayer takes place in Mecca with this many people it's so quiet you can hear clothing rustle as the people change their postures. It is a stunning event.

(http://edition.cnn.com/COMMUNITY/transcripts/2001/03/05/wolfe/)

Muhammad Sohail, a financial consultant from Bradford, UK, having undertaken hajj in January 2006 stated that:

The hajj was an opportunity for me to enhance an established belief and commitment to Islam. I now value differences much more than before, and appreciate the magnitude and magnificence of the religion; its diversity across all colours and races.

In a gathering of millions from across the Globe, I networked extensively, guaging the world view within a whisper. A fabulous experience which demonstrated to me how in today's troubled world we so need a uniting force which overlooks all differences as blessing. We need Islam.

For these reasons, individual experience shows how human beings treat one another during hajj. They also show kindness and consideration to their fellow pilgrims and without any barriers such as race, colour and social status shown by the individual pilgrim. As Wolfe has stated, above, it set the standards for the individual pilgrim to respect the values and cultural differences of every other pilgrim who has come to Makkah to perform hajj.

Hajj pilgrimage versus the Western view of pilgrimage

The Muslim performs hajj as part of his religious beliefs, and not as an escape for leisure and entertainment. The fifth and last Pillar of Islam is hajj, and that is the reason people travel to the holy city of Makkah. Moreover, every physically and financially able Muslim should – as stated in the holy Qur'an – perform hajj once in his or her lifetime and every physically and financially able muslim should make the hajj.

MacCannell (1976) states that pilgrimage used for secular activities provides the additional motivation of escape for leisure and entertainment. This secular viewpoint is not appropriate for hajj, which is an exclusively religious experience. In his view:

Traditional religious institutions are everywhere accommodating the movements of tourists. In 'The Holy Land', the tour has followed in the path of the religious pilgrimage and is replacing it. Throughout the world, churches, cathedrals, mosques, and temples are being converted from religious to touristic functions.
(MacCannell, 1976, p. 43)

He argues that 'sight sacrilization' is the process whereby tourist attractions take on iconoclastic qualities, and are venerated in the same manner as religious site festivals. Ancient pilgrimage routes linked to religious travel destinations in Europe include Fátima in Portugal, Montenero in Italy, Knock in Ireland, Medjugorje in Bosnia-Herzegovina, Lourdes in France and Santiago de Compostela in Spain. On a global level, the hajj and the holy places in Saudi Arabia have a sacred quality in the world of Islam, with this act of pilgrimage a defining moment in the life of pilgrims.

Hajj is an event that takes Muslims in the footsteps of Muhammad to the barren plain of Mina and the slopes of Mount Arafat; it is the biggest yearly mass movement of people on the planet. Hajj is not a tourist phenomenon for pilgrims – it is the journey of lifetime for the individual pilgrim to visit Makkah and perform hajj. In this respect, performing hajj is also an education, almost challenging convention.

Many verses in the holy Qur'an have been illustrated in connection with rules of hajj and its virtues. The books of Hadith are also filled with traditions of the Prophet Muhammad on the topics of hajj. The Muslim follows the rites of hajj to carry out the duties laid down by the Islamic faith and to follow in the footsteps of Abrahamic origin, as outlined in the following statement:

> The rites of the Hajj, which are of Abrahamic origin, include circling the Ka'aba seven times, and going seven times between the mountains of Safa and Marwa as did Hagar during her search for water. Then the pilgrims stand together on the wide plain of Arafat and join in prayers for God's forgiveness, in what is often thought of as a preview of the Last Judgment.
>
> (http://islamicity.com/mosque/pillars.shtml)

Moreover, the hajj is not a tourist phenomenon: it is the Islamic faith for Muslims to perform hajj as stated according to the Holy Qur'an and Hadith. It is not like any other pilgrimage in the world, where people visit sites of pilgrimage with overtones of tourism. The people who go on hajj feel unanimous in the view that nothing can quite prepare them for the sheer beauty of the experience and the overwhelming feeling of humbleness that overcomes them during the pilgrim of hajj. Kandhalvi (1980) and Al-Qahtaanee (1997a, b) stated that, for Muslims, hajj represents judgement day: a symbolic representation of what is to come to each of us.

The pilgrims are there to perform hajj as their main priority, although they can buy religious souvenirs once they have performed it. The two religious souvenirs pilgrims bring back with them most frequently are the water of Zam-Zam, which is provided free of charge, and dates. Pilgrims spend the majority of their time on pilgrimage in the act of worship of God during their stay in Makkah and Al Madinah: there are limited opportunities for cultural exchange.

Therefore, whilst other pilgrimages, such as those to Santiage de Compostela and St Peter's Basilica at The Vatican, are used for secular activities and provide additional motivations of escape for leisure and entertainment, from a Muslim perspective these comparisons are not appropriate for hajj, which is exclusively a religious experience.

It is clear from the above research that hajj is a very important element of the Muslim faith. The pilgrims who perform hajj are not tourists: they are individuals who are carrying out a religious act while showing great humbleness and devotion during the pilgrimage.

Summary

The finding of this research show us that hajj is an event that leads Muslims in the footsteps of Muhammed to the barren plain of Mina and the slopes of Mount Arafat and is the biggest yearly mass movement of people on the planet. The hajj contains unique spiritual aspects, and brings together people from an immense diversity of mankind.

Hajj is a pilgrimage to Makkah in Saudi Arabia, which constitutes the fifth and last of the acts of worship prescribed by Islam. The hajj is obligatory once in a lifetime for those Muslims who can afford it, provided that: (i) the practicalities of the journey have been addressed; and (ii) adequate provision has been made for all dependents left at home.

Hajj constitutes a form of worship with the whole of the Muslim's being: with his body, mind and soul, with his time, possessions and the temporary sacrifice of all ordinary comforts and conveniences a person normally enjoys. The person should assume, for those few days, the condition of a pilgrim wholly at God's service and disposal.

The hajj pilgrims feel unanimous in their view that nothing can quite prepare them for the sheer beauty of the experience and the overwhelming feeling of humbleness that overcomes one during the pilgrimage of hajj. Hajj is not a tourist phenomenon for pilgrims: it is the journey of lifetime for the individual pilgrim to visit Makkah to perform hajj.

Finally, let us now offer a prayer: May God in his infinite Mercy impart some of His humble blessing on the writer of these words and its publisher.

> And our last call shall be: Praise be to God the Sustainer of all the worlds. And may God's choicest blessings and peace be upon the most virtuous of all Prophets; and upon his family, and his Companions and his followers till the day of Judgement. We beg this O God, through your Mercy, O You Most Merciful one.

(Qur'an)

References

Al-Qahtaanee, S.S. (1997a) *A Manual on the Rites of Umrah*. Invitation to Islam Publishers, London.

Al-Qahtaanee, S.S. (1997b) *A Manual on the Rites of Hajj*. Invitation to Islam Publishers, London.

Al-Uthaimeen, M.A. (1999) *How to Perform the Rituals of Hajj and Umrah* (http://www.ind.org/books/HAJJ/html).

Danziger, N. (1996) *Danziger's Britain: a Journey to The Edge*. HarperCollins, London.

Eade, J. (1992) Pilgrimage and tourism at Lourdes, France. *Annals of Tourism Research* 19, 18–32.

Holloway, C. (1989) *The Business of Tourism*. Pitman, London.

Hunter-Jones, P. and Morpeth, N. (1996) Sustaining Spanish culture: El Camino Frances? In: Robinson, M., Evans, N. and Callaghan, P. (eds) *Tourism and Cultural Change*. Business Education Publishers, Sunderland, UK, pp. 109–128.

Kandhalvi, M.Z. (1980) *Virtues of Hajj*. Zam-Zam Publishers, Jedda, The Kingdom of Saudi Arabia.

MacCannell, D. (1976) *The Tourist: a New Theory of the Leisure Class*. McGraw-Hill, New York.

Nolan, M. and Nolan, S. (1992) Religious sites as tourism attractions in Europe. *Annals of Tourism Research* 19, 68–78.

Richards, G. (2001) (ed.) *Cultural Attractions and European Tourism*. CAB International, Wallingford, UK.

Shafi, M. (1998) *Maariful Qur'an*. Maktaba Darul-Uloom Publishers, Karachi, Pakistan.

Smith,V. (1992) The quest in guest. *Annals of Tourism Research* 19, 1–17.

Websites

http://www.bbc.co.uk/humber/features/seatrek/seatrek7.shtm (accessed 23 February 2006).

http://www.CNN.com (accessed 23 February 2006).

http://www.edition.cnn.com/COMMUNITY/transcripts/2001/03/05/wolfe/ (accessed 20 February 2006).

http://www.islamicity.com/mosque/pillars.shtml (accessed 20 February 2006).

http://www.princeton.edu/~humcomp/stages.html (accessed 20 February 2006).

11 Case Study 2: Christian/Catholic Pilgrimage – Studies and Analyses

VITOR AMBRÓSIO[1] AND MARGARIDA PEREIRA[2]

[1]Escola Superior de Hotelaria e Turismo do Estoril, Estoril, Portugal:
e-mail: vitor.ambrosio@eshte.pt; [2]e-Geo – Centro de Estudos de Geografia e
Planeamento Regional Faculdade de Ciências Sociais e Humanas,
Universidade Nova de Lisboa, Lisbon, Portugal; e-mail: ma.pereira@fcsh.unl.pt

Introduction

In this chapter, four Catholic sanctuary towns, founded after the apparitions of the Virgin Mary – Banneux in Belgium (1933), Fátima in Portugal (1917), Knock in Ireland (1879) and Lourdes in France (1858) – will be compared in terms of urban development. We will argue that these sanctuary towns represent two different evolutionary situations: one associated with successful development and the other with weaknesses in planning. Although their importance as pilgrimage destinations differs, Banneux and Knock are considered medium-sized sanctuary towns, while Fátima and Lourdes are considered large. A similar, summarized description will be applied to each destination.

Banneux

Banneux is a sanctuary town situated in eastern Belgium (a few kilometres away from Liège). Annually, it receives over 0.5 million visitors, mainly from European countries. The eight apparitions took place from 15 January to 2 March, 1933. The Church approved them in 1942 and more solemnly in 1949. The seer, Mariette Beco, was 11 years old and was the daughter of poor, non-churchgoing parents.

The Virgin Mary's message focused on the title she attributed to herself: 'I am the Virgin of the poor', thus revealing by that the simplicity of the gospel. During the apparitions she asked people to pray a lot and to have a chapel built in her honour, stressing the need for prayer. During the apparitions she showed the seer the site of a fountain whose waters would mitigate the sufferings of the sick of all nations.

After this divine manifestation there was a period of hesitation, but due to the considerable affluence of pilgrims, the local priest instigated the building of the chapel, which was inaugurated on 15 August 1933. It is the heart of Banneux even today, as the shrine does not have a proper church. In its stead, many open-air sites and altars exist, which are complemented by sacred itineraries and nursing homes for sick pilgrims (who have always been numerous at Banneux). To commemorate the 50th anniversary, a large pavilion was built for the winter season.

Fátima

This sanctuary town is situated in the heart of Portugal (a few kilometres away from Leiria). Annually, it welcomes over 4 million visitors, who come from all over the world.

The six apparitions here took place between 13 May and 13 October, 1919, and were finally approved by the Church in 1930. The seers, Lúcia, Francisco and Jacinta, were aged 10, 9 and 7, respectively, their parents being poor and churchgoers.

During the apparitions, the Virgin Mary introduced herself as 'Our Lady of the Rosary', and asked people to pray a lot and to have a chapel built in her honour, stressing the need to pray and to meditate on the rosary mysteries. She asked for the reparation of the sins committed against her Sacred Heart, as well as the consecration of Russia to It. No other apparition may, indeed, be so linked to historical events as this one. This is probably the reason why it gave origin to an intense spiritual movement, which is the source of inspiration for the preservation of peace on earth.

In 1919, after the above divine manifestation, a small chapel was built. Ten years later construction of the basilica was started, with consecration in 1953. Besides those constructions, one should also mention: (i) the esplanade (bigger than the one at St Peter's in Rome); (ii) the scarlet oak tree, under whose shadow the little shepherds and the pilgrims waited and prayed before the Virgin Mary's apparitions; (iii) the nursery home; (iv) the retreats' home; and (v) the pastoral centre, with a 2124-seat conference room. In the village of Aljustrel, where the shepherds were born, their houses are still to be seen, as well as the Valinhos Calvary.

Knock

This sanctuary town situated in north-western Ireland, a few kilometres away from Galway. Annually, it receives over 1 million visitors, who come mainly from the Anglo-Saxon nations.

The only apparition here took place on 21 August 1879. The Church approved it in 1879, and more solemnly in 1939. The group of seers was constituted by 15 people of varying ages. This is one of the few apparitions of the Virgin Mary, said to have occurred in Ireland. Our Lady appeared accompanied by St Joseph and St John the Baptist, and at their right-hand side there was an altar with angels hovering over a lamb and a cross.

Although there was no spoken message, the divine manifestation was interpreted as a sign of heavenly assistance, an appeal for the Irish to remain faithful to the Catholic Church, especially as regards the cults of the Eucharist and of the Virgin Mary – the temptation to resort to violence would then be eliminated. The event helped to reduce social tensions and anger towards the English, who were the ruling body in Ireland at that time.

Because the apparition occurred at the rear of the small local church, a new church was not built; instead, an addition to the existing building was constructed. The present-day basilica holds 10,000 people and is set on 32 pilasters, representing the number of Irish Counties; it was built in the 1970s, having been consecrated in 1979. Besides these buildings, there are others worth mentioning: the chapel of reconciliation, the prayer guidance centre, the nursing home, the esplanade and the Calvary.

Lourdes

This town, situated in south-western France (a few kilometres away from Tarbes), annually receives over 5 million visitors, who come from all over the world.

The 18 apparitions recorded here took place between 11 February and 16 July 1858, and were approved by the Church in 1862. The seer, Bernadette Soubirous, was 14 years old, her parents being poor and churchgoers.

When the apparitions occurred, the Virgin Mary presented Herself as 'Our Lady of the Immaculate Conception', and called on people to pray and to do penance. She also asked that a chapel be built and processions held. As a sign of her presence, she also pointed out a spring at Massabielle to the seer. A number of cures have been attributed to this spring, and it has become a special destination for the sick from all over the world. The simplicity of the message and the atmosphere of the place have turned this sanctuary into a spiritual centre for the entire Catholic world.

A few years after this divine manifestation, a basilica was added to the grotto, thus replacing the small chapel that had previously been built. A second basilica was built in 1889, and a third one was consecrated in 1958 (this time constructed underground), with a capacity 20,000. Besides these buildings, there are others worth mentioning: (i) the esplanade (where processions of the sacraments and of the candles are held daily); (ii) the pools where the pilgrims bathe; (iii) the Calvary; (iv) the retreats' home; and (v) the nursing homes for the sick. In the town, all the sites connected with the life of Bernadette are of special importance.

Considering the bibliography of these four sanctuary towns, one may observe that, for the medium-sized shrines (Banneux and Knock), the literature focuses on description and analysis of the spiritual components. Even when the focus is on the sanctuary towns' physical structures, most authors prefer to expound on their spiritual functions than to analyse the territorial impacts that may ensue. A possible justification for this fact is that the manifestations of religious tourism in these two sanctuary towns are not obvious – either in the landscape or socio-economically – and, consequently, they do not arouse enough interest among scholars for study.

With regard to the larger sanctuary towns (Fátima and Lourdes), one may observe two different kinds of academic approach: the first referring to the spiritual elements, the second to the physical structures and their functions. The first analyses the spiritual meanings of both buildings and atmosphere within the towns, while the second evaluates the impacts that religious tourism provokes, either physically or socio-economically.

The Retrospective Evaluation of the Evolutionary Cycles of Sanctuary Towns

Since the existing bibliography provides insufficient material with which to chart the development of these four sanctuary towns, it has been complemented by observations made *in situ*. Analysis of the information available has afforded identification of three variables that help understand the ways in which these towns have developed: (i) the seers' level of consecration; (ii) the construction of a basilica to celebrate the centenary of the apparitions; and (iii) the facilities for overnight visitors.

Consecration of seers

In spiritual terms, the fame of a shrine is closely linked to the consecration of the seers and their the testimonies of the Virginal apparitions. When considering these, one should take into account whether or not the seer is still alive, and what title was granted them by the Catholic Church.

In Lourdes the seer is dead, having been canonized in the 1930s. In Fátima, two of the seers have been dead for many years: they were beatified at the beginning of the new millennium; the third (the most important) died in 2005, and so it is too early to advance her canonical process. In Banneux, the seer is alive; in Knock, all 15 seers are dead, none of them having been beatified or canonized.

The situation for each of the four sanctuary towns is therefore different: in Lourdes, all goals have been achieved; in Fátima, partially so; in Banneux, canonization remains something for the future and, in Knock, the opportunities were wasted and cannot easily be recreated. Thus, the level of consecration has a direct bearing on the degree of development of each town.

The basilica

The basilica represents the physical aspect of development. There are usually three stages in the construction process here: (i) a chapel; (ii) a medium-sized basilica; and (iii) a large basilica.

Considering this logical sequence, it will be noted that Banneux did not reach the second phase, substituting the great pavilion (with capacity of about 2000) for the medium-sized basilica. Maybe in the distant future, the opportunity will arise to move directly to the third stage, by way of marking the centenary celebrations. Another option might be to develop the shrine into a reference/meeting point for the Catholic Belgian community, something that does not yet exist.

In Knock, the second stage was bypassed, for two main reasons: (i) the lack of interest shown in the earlier years; and (ii) the dynamism of its rector in the beginning of the 1970s. As far as development is concerned, this situation demonstrates that a shrine that has, for some time, not created a great deal of interest, can eventually be transformed into a major religious tourism destination.

In Fátima, all three stages have been witnessed, although construction of the third (a larger basilica) has yet to start; this is anticipated within the next 10 years. Two factors seem to be involved in the current situation: (i) the urgency of creating better conditions for the reception of large numbers of pilgrims (mainly on Sundays); and (ii) uncertainty about the dynamism and energy of the team that will manage the shrine in the next decennium.

In Lourdes, the reference model for every sanctuary town in the Western world (as much for the positives as for the negatives), these three stages have occurred. The building of the chapel was followed by the construction of a medium-sized basilica; a few years later saw the building of a second basilica (with a similar capacity). Soon afterwards, it was realized that the scope of the tourism and pilgrimage markets demanded the construction of a larger basilica, in order to celebrate the centenary of the apparitions.

Overnight stays

In the medium-sized sanctuary towns of Banneux and Knock, the scale of existing religious activities does not justify the provision of overnight facilities.

In Fátima, and above all in Lourdes, the opposite is the case. Over the years, religious and business leaders have worked closely together in the creation of overnight facilities for pilgrims. One important factor in creating overnight facilities is the popularity of candle-lit processions.

Schematization of developmental processes

Since the data utilized for the four sanctuary towns in this study are extensive, with countless interconnections, it is convenient to combine the information and to schematize the development processes involved. This allows observation of the developmental stages of each of the four towns, as shown in Fig. 11.1.

The innermost circle (A) includes those artefacts built by the Church for worship, from the first chapel to medium-sized basilica; the second circle (B) represents the infrastructure and structures supporting tourist activities: still very much a local presence with little regional impact. The innermost square (C) denotes an incipient development of the sanctuary town, capable of servicing the needs of visitors (with, as yet, little provision for overnight stays).

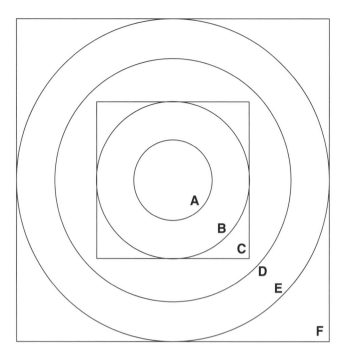

Fig. 11.1. Schematic representation of the evolutionary cycle of a sanctuary town. A–F, developmental stages.

Circle D indicates an increment in the level of religious activities, and in the building of more infrastructure to meet growing demands, i.e. from medium-sized to large basilica; circle E represents the efforts of local entrepreneurs and officials in the promotion of the site, now with strong socio-economic impact at regional level. Square F represents, therefore, the final aggregation of all previous development.

The adaptation of this scheme to each of the four sanctuary towns can now be illustrated.

Banneux

In Banneux (see Fig. 11.2), circle A is incomplete because the medium-sized basilica was not built (in its place is the winter pavilion). Circle B is also incomplete; although the necessary infrastructure is in place, the expected boom economic activity has not yet materialized (in 2002, the town could boast neither a bank nor an automatic cash machine). In this case, C is therefore also considered as incomplete.

Knock

In Knock (see Fig. 11.3), a medium-sized basilica has not even been planned, for reasons given above, with the resultant lack of infrastructure, so circles A and B are broken. As A and B are in an incipient phase, the square C is far away from

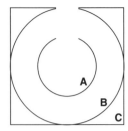

Fig. 11.2. Development of Banneux.

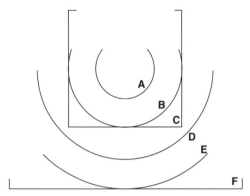

Fig. 11.3. Development of Knock.

being closed. This situation did not deter the ecclesiastical and some lay agents in advancing directly to the second development phase: the former promoting the construction of the large basilica, the latter investing in the construction of an international airport.

Fátima

In Fátima (see Fig. 11.4), the first conjugation framing (C) was complete by the time the medium-sized basilica was consecrated, coincident with the development of a regional infrastructure (largely under the control of central administration) in response to growing tourism demands. The second conjugation framing (F) is now almost complete, awaiting the inauguration of the large basilica (expected in 2007); this has been driven by the dynamic efforts of those responsible for the promotion of touristic activities.

Lourdes

In Lourdes (see Fig. 11.5), the closing of the first conjugation framing (C) took place over almost 100 years. Contributory factors for this were: (i) strong demand, both in France and abroad; (ii) a strong local entrepreneurial element; and (iii) the building of a railway link. With the tourist development of the post-

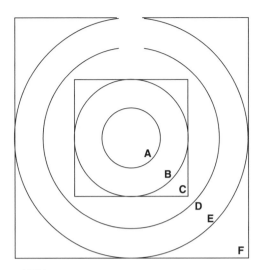

Fig. 11.4. Development of Fátima.

war period, the construction of the large basilica and the aforesaid entreprenurism, closure of conjugation framing F was soon achieved.

Nowadays, the main concern is to avoid any lessening of interest in Lourdes. To accomplish this, it is essential that attention is paid to the conservation and restoration of infrastructure (both religious and secular) and, above all, that maintenance of – or increase in – visitor numbers is achieved.

The Prospective Analysis of the Evolutionary Cycles of Sanctuary Towns

Another basis for analysis of the development of sanctuary towns is by the use of an adaptation of Richard Butler's model. This model covers the development of a tourist destination from exploration to rejuvenation or decline (see Fig. 11.6).

1. Exploration: the destination is visited by small numbers of adventurous tourists who tend to shun institutionalized travel. The natural beauty or cultural characteristics at the destination are the main attraction, but visitors are restricted by lack of access and facilities. At this stage, the attraction of the destination is that it remains as yet unchanged by tourism, and most tourists' contact will be with local people.

2. Involvement: at this stage, local initiatives – to provide for visitors and later to advertise the destination – result in increased and regular numbers of visitors. A tourist season and market area will emerge, and pressures may be placed on the public sector to provide infrastructure.

3. Development: once a destination moves into a developmental stage, large numbers of visitors arrive and the organization of tourism begins to change, as control is passed out of local hands and companies from outside the area move in to provide up-to-date facilities. Control in the public sector can also be affected, as regional and national planning may become necessary, in part to

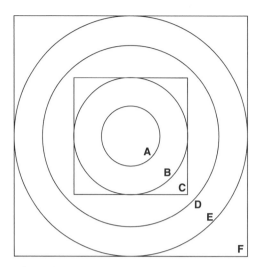

Fig. 11.5. Development of Lourdes.

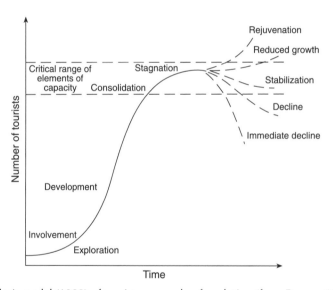

Fig. 11.6. Butler's model (1980) of tourist area cycle of evolution (from Pearce, 1989).

ameliorate problems but also in order to market to the international tourist-generating areas, as visitors become more dependent upon travel arrangements booked through the trade. This is a critical stage, as these facilities – and the changing nature of tourism – can alter the very nature of the destination. Failure may therefore be sown in the seeds of success: with the increasing numbers and popularity, the destination can suffer in quality through problems of overuse and deterioration.

4. Consolidation: by this stage, the rate of increase of visitors is declining, although total numbers are still increasing. The destination is now a fully fledged part of a tourism industry, with an identifiable recreational business district.

5. Stagnation: peak numbers have now been reached and the destination is no longer fashionable. Repeat visits from more conservative travellers dominate in this stage. Business use of the resort's extensive facilities is also sought but, generally, major efforts are now needed to maintain the number of visits. The destination may by now have environmental, social and economic problems.

6. Decline/Rejuvenation: visitors are now being lost to newer resorts and the destination becomes dependent on smaller geographical catchments for day trips and weekend visits. Alternatively, destination managers may recognize this stage and decide to rejuvenate, with the introduction of new types of facilities, or may extend the season and attract a new market.

In fact, this model and many others focus on three levels of development: (i) the spread of construction (mainly for lodging, restoration and commerce); (ii) the visitors' characteristics (based on evolution of the tourist area); and (iii) the demand for new places after saturation or rejuvenation of the older ones. They show how destinations evolve from discovery to decline, detaching the effects of their popularity.

Although the models are logical, we have come to the conclusion that it is not easy to apply them to all tourist destinations. The same is true of the development of sanctuary towns. While in seaside resorts it is easy to observe the life cycle phases, frequently with the transfer of the initial demand to another destination, in the case of religious destinations their substitution is problematic. The spiritualism associated with the foundation of such places is unique: for example, the place where Christ was born. Believers stop going to the Holy Land either for economic difficulties or for lack of security, but never because it has become unfashionable.

Also, for the religious tourism segment it is complicated to find a parallelism between the development of the destination and the gradual transfer from a wholly centric public (people who search for new destinations) to a psychocentric one (people who seek regular destinations). Not even during the so-called period of discovery are those who go there looking for adventure. Likewise, it is also difficult to talk of site diversification, since this could change the religious spirit of the place.

In addition, the fact that many destinations carry with them their own seeds of destruction does not apply to the sanctuary towns: these tend not to lose the qualities that attracted the visitors in the first place. Likewise, the sense of saturation and regret (for changes in their town) that the local populace usually feel with respect to the crowds of tourists do not take place in the sanctuary towns; one possible reason is that, in these towns there is not the decline in traditions and morals, as often happen in other tourism destinations (mainly in seaside resorts).

Considering building developments in the sanctuary towns, we have divided these into two groups: lay and religious. The analysis of the former fits quite well with the vision given in Butler's model; that of the latter applies more to the dynamics of the religious aspect, being possible to consider them as structures for the reception of the large numbers of believers. It must be underlined that in none of the four sanctuary towns studied did there occur any significant environmental changes, mainly because the religious authorities had bought the land, allowing its conservation. Although in Lourdes and Fátima some urban planning mistakes had been made, this led to the implementation of policies to correct them.

Realistically, one cannot predictively carry out accurate tourism forecasts for new sanctuary towns, since it is impossible to determine where and when the Virgin is going to appear. In addition, one cannot observe the consequences of less successful policies until the complete evolutionary cycle (A–F, Fig. 11.1) has been completed.

In spite of the differences in sanctuary towns when compared to other destinations, it is our belief that Butler's model is still the best basis from which to observe the development of religious tourism areas. In a proposed adaptation, besides the stipulated variables (time, number of visitors and phases of the evolutionary cycle), we find it is necessary to introduce two more categories: (i) construction of religious structures; and (ii) accommodation and commercial facilities (see Fig. 11.7).

In our adaptation, Butler's model is projected on the x-axis so as to allow the

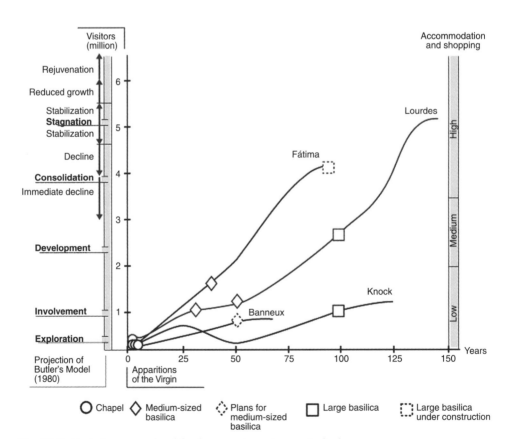

Fig. 11.7. Evolutionary cycle of the four sanctuary towns studied.

visualization of the evolution curve of the four sanctuary towns simultaneously. The variables considered are: (i) millions of visitors; (ii) time; (iii) temples; and (iv) accommodation and shopping facilities.

The construction of religious structures variable shows, on the one hand, the temporary progression and, on other, the response to the Eucharistic demands. Soon after the apparitions of the Virgin, the first believers go to these places and a small chapel is built; with the ecclesiastical approval of the apparitions, the first organized groups arrive, initially at a regional level and later at a national level. Simultaneously, it is possible to observe the involvement of the local population in the creation of facilities for the pilgrims. Pressure is also placed on the public sector to provide infrastructure.

With the growth in the number of pilgrims, the clergy decides to build a medium-sized basilica. Once the power of attraction of the shrine is acknowledged, a large-sized basilica is built, with seating for approximately 10,000.

As far as accommodation concerned, we have been able to determine that the number of rooms is not directly linked to the number of visitors. Most visitors stay for only a few hours, and consequently do not need accommodation. Only when there are a large number of visitors coming from afar is it possible to observe the development of this kind of industry. An analysis of the data shows that, for annual visitor numbers of up to 2 million, there are few accommodation facilities; 2–3.5 million, moderate; over 3.5 million visitors, the level of facilities is high.

The interaction between lay town and religious town is shown through the shape of the curves, each one demonstrating the extent to which both have worked together to augment the demand.

Looking at Fig. 11.7, the first impression gained is that the shape of the curves can be divided into two different groups: one associated with the medium-sized sanctuary towns (Banneux and Knock) and the other with the larger ones (Lourdes and Fátima).

In Banneux, the relatively few years of its existence do not allow us to extrapolate its evolutionary cycle; we can, however, conclude that a great opportunity has been lost through the lack of a large basilica.

In Knock, the initial period characterized by strong demand was followed by a major drop in the number of visitors to the sanctuary. This situation changed with the commemoration of the 50th anniversary of the apparition of the Virgin Mary, even though no basilica had been built for the occasion. The recovery of demand culminated in the construction of a large basilica to commemorate the centenary of the apparition. However, this recovery was not sufficient to eliminate the lack of past initiatives. As in the previous case (Banneux), one may note that there is either a continuous dynamism in the evolutionary process of a sanctuary town, or else it may be problematic to overcome original weaknesses.

Summary

Of the four sanctuary towns in our study, neither Banneux nor Knock has been able to move on to the advanced development stage. The towns of Fátima and Lourdes are successful in terms of both tourism and religion. However, in the context of the religious tourism market, it is important to underline the fact that visitor rates must not be allowed to drop.

The cases of Fátima and Lourdes confirm Butler's model in the sense that there has been a natural progression from exploration to stabilization. For this reason, it is possible to say that these two towns represent successful cases in terms of both tourism and religion.

Moreover, both in Banneux and Knock, after the exploration stage and some involvement of the local population, a set of conditions did not occur, so neither of these sanctuary towns was able to move on to the advanced development stage.

As regards Fátima, one may observe that this town is still going through its consolidation phase, although it is nearing a situation of stagnation. The bodies responsible for town planning, however, have not yet realized this. The most recent urban plan indicates that a large development is expected in the near future, suggesting that those responsible for the town's development have become dazzled by the economic growth of the recent past. In our opinion, solutions should be based on reliable alternatives that can guarantee the consolidation phase of this sanctuary town, as well as the preparation of its future phases.

In the context of Catholic sanctuary towns considered as religious tourism destinations, Lourdes is the precursor of them all. This French sanctuary has already reached the consolidation stage and is entering the next phase. Depending on both the authorities involved and the popularity of the shrine, three possible outcomes could arise: (i) rejuvenation; (ii) decline; or (iii) consolidation. However, its urban plan suggests to us that the authorities responsible for this area have chosen the later option. This decision reflects a strong awareness on their part that the area depends largely on religious tourism and that all efforts must be made to maintain the vitality of this sanctuary town.

However, it is important to underline the fact that the sustained development of these sanctuary towns depends, ultimately, on a willingness of all entrepreneurs and religious and lay authorities involved to constantly review and, if necessary, change their policies. Their actions must incorporate the valorization and promotion of the resources linked to the Virgin apparitions so as not to lose their share of visitors in the religious tourism market.

Further Reading

Pearce, D. (1989) *Tourist Development.* Longman, Harlow, UK.

12 Case Study 3: Ancient and Modern Pilgrimage: El Camino Frances

Nigel D. Morpeth

Centre for Tourism, Leeds Metropolitan University, Leeds, UK;
e-mail: n.morpeth@leedsmet.ac.uk

Introduction

The central aim of this chapter is to consider the implications of the diversification of one of the oldest journeys known to the Western World, El Camino Frances (El Camino) or the Way of St James, from primarily a focus for sacred pilgrimage, to increasingly a focus for secular forms of tourism. This chapter contends that El Camino, specifically the 709 km Spanish leg of the route from Ronscevalles in the Spanish foothills of the Pyrenees to Santiago de Compostela on the west coast of Spain, is the target for increased cultural and sporting usage stimulated through EU and Spanish Government initiatives (highlighted later within this chapter). In reviewing the work of Boorstin (1961), MacCannell (1976), Urry (1990) and Richards (2001), consideration is made of the dynamic characteristics of travel, tourism, and the emergence of an 'experience industry' and symbolic economy, as underpinning concepts to reviewing the changing nature of sacred and secular pilgrimage.

In Search of the Lost Art of Travel

The act of pilgrimage is a reminder of a slower form of travel than currently undertaken in the 'global village', with the emphasis on speed and immediacy of accessing destinations for pleasure. In the history of tourism studies authors such as Boorstin lamented this trend towards the immediate and the 'here and now' with his focus on the 'decline of the traveler and the rise of the tourist' (Boorstin, 1961, pp. 84–85) suggests that it provides the prospect of:

> The whole world being made a stage for pseudo-events. There has been no lack of honest and enterprising suppliers who try to give him what he wants, to help him inflate his expectations, and to gratify his insatiable appetite for the impossible.
>
> (Boorstin, 1961, p. 80)

In making reference to the male dominated *Grand Tour*, initiated in the seventeenth century, and the emergence of a tourist circuit of European travel for young aristocrats, he emphasizes the educative qualities of travel, suggesting that: 'unless one was a man of the world, he might not seem cultivated in his own country' (Boorstin, 1961, p. 82). Boorstin reminds us that until the twentieth century 'travel abroad was uncomfortable, difficult, and expensive' and that it was an experience that was 'laborious or troublesome' (Boorstin, 1961, p. 82) particularly in road-less landscapes. Furthermore, he argues that: 'foreign travel ceased to be an activity – an experience, an undertaking – and instead became a commodity' (Boorstin, 1961, p. 82).

In his review of the historical aspects of travel, Boorstin cites the work of John Ruskin (1865) who stated that: 'going by railroad, I do not consider as travelling at all; it is merely being "sent" to a place, and very little different from being a parcel' (Boorstin, 1961, p. 90). Whilst Boorstin notes that the early nineteenth century tours of Thomas Cook were promoted as 'agencies for the advancement of Human Progress', he recognized that with the massification of tourism: 'travel is no longer made to order but is an assembly-line, store-purchased commodity, (and) we have less to say about what goes into it' (Boorstin, 1961, p. 90). He viewed the role of travel agencies as 'insulating the tourist from the travel world'; and that: 'the tourist gets there without the experience of having gone. For him it is all the same: going to one place or another' (Boorstin, 1961, p. 90). Lamenting the trivialization of travel, he argues that: 'the tourist looks for caricature' and 'seldom likes the authentic' and that 'when the traveler's risks are insurable he becomes a tourist' (Boorstin, 1961, p. 90). The increasing homogenous qualities of travel destinations led Holloway (1989, p. 35) to dub them as 'cloned' destinations, with the tourist in search of ephemeral experiences.

Modern Rituals of 'Sightseeing'

It was Dean MacCannell (1976) who noted that 'sightseeing' is a ritual of the tourist who has the capacity to trivialize the sacredness of religious worship. In his view;

> Traditional religious institutions are everywhere accommodating the movements of tourists. In 'The Holy Land,' the tour has followed in the path of the religious pilgrimage and is replacing it. Throughout the world, churches, cathedrals, mosques, and temples are being converted from religious to touristic functions.
>
> (MacCannell, 1976, p. 43)

He argues that 'sight sacrilization' is the process whereby tourist attractions take on iconoclastic qualities, and are venerated in the same manner as religious sites. However, he contends that these 'attractions' are conduits for 'staged authenticity' which 'lends an aura of superficiality' to the tourist experience (MacCannell, 1976, p. 43). In his view there is; the use of a new kind of social space that is opening up everywhere in our society. It is a space for outsiders who are permitted to view the inner details of the inner operation of a commercial, domestic, industrial or public institution. Apparently, entry into this space allows adults to: 'recapture virginal sensations of discovery, or child-like feelings of being half-in and half-out of society, their faces pressed up against the glass' (MacCannell, 1976, p. 43). This imagery of the voyeuristic qualities of tourism is a central focus of the work of John Urry (1990).

The Tourist Gaze

Urry (1990) contends that the 'tourist gaze' is analogous' to the passivity of Boorstin's (1961) characterization of the tourist as a 'pleasure-seeker' and the traveller as 'active' (Urry, 1990). MacCannell highlights that the sightseer determines how 'sights' are 'meaningfully experienced' (MacCannell, 1976, p. 112) and that there is an 'empirical relationship' between the sightseer and the 'sight', in which personal meanings and experiences emerge. Nevertheless, the commercialization of 'sights' leads to commercial operators being involved in creating 'markers' for the sightseer. This raises the possibility that commercial operators and policy-makers might be the arbiters of ethical considerations in disseminating information to the tourist and the 'event-goer', and make more accessible the indiscriminate consumption of 'sights'.

The Historical Significance of Trails

Lane (1991) notes how the 'concept of the trail as a semi-formal cross country routeway', distinct from a formal highway, has an ancient lineage. He states how in Britain, by late medieval times, trails traversed the country from the salt mines of Cheshire, and through established drovers routes bringing cattle to London (Lane, 1999, p. 1). Within the context of the USA, he notes how trails such as the Sante Fe and Oregon Trails became significant with the 'opening up of the West' for settlers and traders, and have now been transformed for leisure and tourism use.

Lane identifies a typology of trails linked to users seeking 'escapism', leisure, and a multiplicity of other applications ranging from education, health and fitness, conservation and economic regeneration. Lane's references to trails and antiquity reveal the ancient qualities of trails as routes with spiritual significance. Nolan and Nolan (1992) highlight the significance of the formation of a network of European pilgrim routes, with established destinations containing religious shrines, which have become places of religious worship and festivals. Ancient pilgrimage routes linked to religious travel destinations in Europe described elsewhere within this book, include Fatima in Portugal, Montenero in Italy, Knock in Ireland, Medjugorje in Yugoslavia, Lourdes in France and Santiago de Compestela in Spain. On a global level the

Hajj and the Holy Places in Saudi Arabia have a sacred quality in the world of Islam, with this act of pilgrimage a defining moment in life of pilgrims.

The transformation of pilgrimage routes from sacred to the secular use

Whilst Chaucer's *Canterbury Tales* reveals the enjoyment of the worldly pleasures of pilgrims, in a contemporary context Nolan and Nolan (1992), Smith (1992) and Eade (1992) note how pilgrimage routes are increasingly becoming secularized, with the explicit promotion of routes for tourism, leisure and cultural engagement. In this respect Smith notes that: 'if a tourist is half a pilgrim then a pilgrim is half a tourist' (Smith, 1992, p. 1), suggesting a blurring of the boundaries between pilgrimage and tourism, with the basis for travel melding sacred and secular motivations. The inference from the work of Eade (1992) is that the secularization of pilgrimage is not limited to the wider utility of pilgrimage routes for cultural and tourism purposes, but that pilgrimage 'venues' such as Lourdes have succumbed to the pressures of commercialization and commodification. Eade (1992) highlights the 'tackiness' of the sale of religious trinkets (it is possible to purchase in Lourdes, a 'winking Christ', a Christ-like statue with flashing eyes) together with rowdiness between 'pilgrims', with the excess consumption of alcohol.

Perhaps representative of the changing nature of the sacred use of pilgrimage routes, is the secularization of El Camino or Way of St James to Santiago de Compestela, in Galicia, in Northern Spain.

Contemporary Tourism in Spain

Hunter-Jones and Morpeth (1996) noted how there was a considerable amount of literature reviewing the development of tourism in Spain (see for example Valenzuela, 1991; Barke, 1992). Traditionally Spain has been characterized as an established popular tourism destination at the forefront of post Second World War tourism development. This characterization included mass tourism, as the dominant model of tourism, largely synonymous with the all inclusive package holiday. The focus for much of the literature was that mass tourism holidays were concentrated within certain 'identikit' coastal resorts, and this remains the dominant narrative in the recent evolution of Spanish tourism. Turner and Ash (1975) suggest that the invasion of 'Golden Hordes' to 'identikit' destinations is popularized by the notion of the erosion of cultural heritage to a monolithic industry, generating mass consumption of a homogenized product. Hunter-Jones and Morpeth (1996) noted how beach tourism of the Spanish Costas, offered a homogenized and re-invented form of commodified culture. Prat characterized this in her study of tourism and culture on the Costa Brava stating that negative impacts of tourism had caused:

> the virtual disappearance of local agricultural activity, the abandonment of fishing activity and the dismantling of local industries, to the point of tourism becoming

almost the sole activity of the area to have prompted a radical change in lifestyle and customs of the local population ... a socio-cultural shock for the traditional and puritanical society of Franquist Spain.

(Prat, 1996, p. 12)

Tourism in Spain from the mid-point of the twentieth century and beyond was driven by economic development needs and repairing the image of a Civil War and a continuing political economy directed without a working democracy. Hunter-Jones *et al.* (1996) noted how there were a number of factors which caused 'fluctuations' in the demand for tourism including market maturity, image impediment, temporary, structural and environmental problems. This led to a questioning of the environmental problems and socio-cultural issues which degraded resources for tourism. Hunter-Jones and Morpeth (1996) cited the emergence of an institutional focus on Quality Tourism which not only considered included the regeneration of coastal tourism but a focus on tourism in the 'interior' which was designed to re-configure the spatial and temporal aspects of tourism.

The focus was to consider potential programmes of environmental improvements and a 'greening' of tourism in Spain.

Hunter-Jones and Morpeth (1996) noted that whilst the 1960s saw the apex of the development of mass-market package tours particularly in the form of coastal tourism development on the Spanish mainland and Balearic Islands, that in fact the origins of mass tourism in Spain can be located within the eleventh and twelfth centuries. Spain played host to the 'massification' of tourism through the continuing development of pilgrimage tourism along El Camino Frances.

El Camino Frances: from sacred to secular usage

Hunter-Jones and Morpeth (1996) noted how the history of pilgrimage tourism in Spain tended to become eclipsed by tourism development in Spain post Grand Tour (see Barke *et al.*, 1996).

The history of pilgrimage tourism in Spain included the discovery of the tomb of St James in Santiago de Compostela, and the emergence of El Camino (The Way of St James/The Road to Compostela/The Pilgrims Way). According to Hunter-Jones and Morpeth (1996) this long distance footpath is one of the oldest pilgrimage routes known to the western world. They noted that there are various 'starting' points to the route throughout Europe, and for example four roads beginning in Arles, Le Puy, Vezelay and Paris, are commonly recognized as leading into the Spanish leg of El Camino in the Basque country. They note how Santiago de Compostela, the end of the Route, symbolized not only the re-emergence of Christianity in Spain but became established as a commercial and cultural link for societies in medieval Europe.

The Route has 13 stages (*etapas*) which traverse diverse regions and cultural centres, with the eleventh and twelfth centuries seeing over half a million pilgrims a year making the journey. Traditionally, the arrival at the end of the pilgrimage and shrine has been the focus of pilgrimage, but increasingly routes such as El Camino have undergone a metamorphosis in the significance of the route itself as a form of tourist attraction.

Hunter-Jones and Morpeth (1996) in citing the work of Raju (1994) suggest in contrast to other pilgrimage routes staying clear from population centres, El Camino traverses 184 population centres which include Ronscevalles, Pamplona, Estella, Logrono, Burgos, Leon, Astorga, Ponferrada and Villafranca del Bierzo.

Hunter-Jones (1996) cited the work of Raju (1994) to encapsulate the dominant reasons why people set out on a pilgrimage which included a:

- profession of faith;
- form of punishment (i.e. fixed penalty system operational during the Middle Ages);
- means of atonement;
- way of acquiring merit;
- opportunity to venerate sacred relics;
- escape from everyday life;
- professional pilgrims (i.e. those completing the journey for others).

The transmogrification of sacred into secular uses of the route can be traced back into the latter stages of the twentieth century, with people embarking on the journey for a variety of reasons including cultural, sporting and historical interest, as well as for sacred reasons. Hunter-Jones and Morpeth (1996) suggest that the differing motives and characteristics of contemporary pilgrims are recorded on arrival by the Cathedral authorities in Santiago through the maintenance of a pilgrim register.

The data collected for 1992 suggest modern pilgrims to be predominantly male, aged 21–30, of Spanish origin, completing the route on foot, during August and mainly (still) for religious reasons. 'Pilgrims' are mainly independent travellers who make use of the various support services and accommodation, notably in churches, monasteries or *refugios*, i.e. specifically designated accommodation provided by town councils or other such organizations varying in facility provision en route.

In particular, formal recognition of the cultural significance of the Route can be traced back to 1987 when the Council of Europe designated the pilgrimage route to Santiago as the first European Cultural Itinerary because it linked the cultures of many regions and nations. This celebration of the significance of culture and tourism was identified by Richards (1996) who considered the centrality of Europe's cultural heritage to the tourism industry. In his analysis he observed a parallel transformation of tourism, from an elite pursuit to a 'leisure need of the masses' with the 'democratization of culture', opening up 'high culture' for wider consumption.

Further cultural interest in El Camino is noted in the Council of Europes DG XXIII Green Paper (1995) 'The Role of the Union in the Field of Tourism' and through its UNESCO Santiago de Compostela's World Heritage Centre designation.

The European Unions' interest in the cultural aspects of the route mirror the Spanish 'Framework Plan for the Competitiveness of Spanish Tourism, 1992–1995' which sought to encourage diversity in tourism products which maximized social benefits whilst minimizing environmental impacts. As Hunter-Jones and Morpeth (1996) noted, part of this plan involved the regeneration of cultural routes such as the east–west route of El Camino and the north–south Silver Route, focusing upon culture and landscape in 1993. The first of the two parallel projects was the 'revitalization of the Route of Santiago'. Supported by the celebrations of the Holy Compostela Year, 1993, the various autonomous regions crossed by the Route, notably Galicia, invested in resources improvement, infrastructural upgrading and importantly a marketing campaign targeted at pilgrims.

In applying the analysis of Boorstin (1961), MacCannell (1976) and Richards (2001), while it is possible to balance concerns about the dilution of the sacred qualities of pilgrimage, with the enhancement of cultural appreciation, there might nevertheless be concerns that the sacred integrity of religious destinations are being eclipsed by secular utilization. It should be noted that the act of pilgrimage is not exclusively a European phenomenon with the Hajj, the Muslim Pilgrimage to Mecca and the Holy places in Saudi Arabia, an important pilgrimage annually described by Raj within Chapter 10 of this work.

Summary

This chapter in reviewing the 'Lost Art of Travel' (Boorstin, 1961) has considered the implications of increasing demands for the secularization of the Western pilgrim with the anticipated expansion of an 'experience industry'. The example of the El Camino potentially emphasizes both the retention of the sacred qualities of the route and the contemporary multi-uses as a cultural route for tourism. However, arguably this would require empirical insights as to how to manage combinations of sacred and secular pilgrims effectively.

Certainly in this respect, Hunter-Jones and Morpeth (1996) noted how over time there had been a shift in the focus of travel of reaching the religious destination of Santiago de Compestela, to the route itself becoming a cultural and tourist attraction. Furthermore, the traditional act of pilgrimage *a pied*, has been superseded by the use of transport technology, which corresponds to Boorstin's observation that there has been a 'decline of the traveler and the rise of the tourist' (Boorstin, 1961, pp. 84–85).

This chapter has highlighted how there has been a transformation in the contemporary use of the route with sporting, touristic and cultural motivations monitored by cathedral authorities in Santiago who maintain a 'pilgrims register'. It is speculated that the integrity of the pilgrimage function of the route has been maintained, with pilgrims as independent travellers utilizing support services and accommodation which has been established since medieval days in urban centres en route (which includes churches, monasteries or *refugios*, i.e. specifically designated accommodation provided by town councils or other such organizations) infrastructure development over time has stimulated multi-use of the route for secular purposes.

Undoubtedly, the process of 'secularization' has been accelerated by the Council of Europe's (1997) designation of the pilgrimage route to Santiago as the first European Cultural Itinerary, and the Council of Europe's DG XXIII Green Paper (1995) combined with 'The Role of the Union in the Field of Tourism' and the Spanish 'Framework Plan for the Competitiveness of Spanish Tourism, 1992–1995'.

The regenerated El Camino as a cultural route through modifications to route infrastructure, with improvements to signage en route, and a supporting marketing campaign, is targeted at increasing tourist use and diverting tourists from traditional coastal haunts for tourism.

The El Camino despite pressures to create an extended infrastructure for tourism has continued to attract pilgrims engaged in religious worship at the shrine of St James demonstrating the continuing retention of sacred spaces. However, while the act of pilgrimage is a reminder of a slower contemplative form of travel, what remains to be seen is whether secular travellers will dominate pilgrimage routes such as El Camino without consideration to the sacred sensibilities of pious pilgrims in search of an opportunity for sacred veneration. Undoubtedly, it is acknowledged that recognizing the distinctions between sacred and secular forms of tourism requires further empirical investigation (see Smith, 1992).

References

Boorstin, D. (1961) From traveler to tourist: the lost art of travel. In: *The Image: A Guide to Pseudo Events in America*, pp. 77–117.

Eade, J. (1992) Pilgrimage and tourism at Lourdes, France. *The Annals of Tourism Research* 19, 18–32.

Holloway, C. (1989) *The Business of Tourism*. Pitman, London.

Hunter-Jones, P. and Morpeth, N. (1996) Sustaining Spanish culture: El Camino Frances? In: Robinson, M., Evans, N. and Callaghan, P. (eds) *Tourism and Cultural Change*. Business Education Publishers, Sunderland, UK, pp. 109–128.

MacCannell, D. (1976) *The Tourist: A New Theory of the Leisure Class*. Shocklen Books, New York.

Nolan, M. and Nolan, S. (1992) Religious sites as tourism attractions in Europe. *The Annals of Tourism Research* 19, 68–78.

Raju, A. (1994) *The Way of St. James*. Cirecone Press.

Smith, V. (1992) The quest in guest. *The Annals of Tourism Research* 19, 1–17.

Stevenson, R.L. (ND) *Travels with a Donkey*. Routledge and Kegan Paul, in public domain.

Urry, J. (1990) *The Tourist Gaze: Leisure and Travel in Contemporary Society*. Sage, London.

13 Case Study 4: The Symbolic Representation of Religion, Culture and Heritage and their Implications on the Tourism Experience. The Example of the 'Ciudad de Cultura' in Santiago de Compostela

MARTIN SCHEER

Department of Tourism and Event Management, International School of Management, Dortmund, Germany; e-mail: scheer72@gmx.de

Introduction

The transformation of genuine local and regional resources into a tourism product is becoming increasingly a matter of symbolic transformation, and not just merely a matter of material transformation. Symbolic transformation – as well as creation or re-creation of tourism resources – reflects both the rising importance of sensory and visual experience as well as the rising presentation of genuine local and regional cultural and historical distinctiveness and originality.

The search of destinations to differentiate their tourism offer from other providers also becomes a source for symbolic transformation of genuine local and regional resources into tourism–recreation products, and so does the tendency towards strengthening of regional and cultural traditions and identities. Increasingly, an intensive interconnection of these two strands of the symbolic representation of religious, cultural and historical local and regional identities and tourism experiences can be detected. (Dietvorst and Ashworth, 1995)

This chapter focuses on the 'Ciudad de Cultura' in Santiago de Compostela, Galicia, northern Spain, as one of the recent major architectonic projects in Spain, and provides an example where the image and the symbolic presentation of a merely religious–cultural product takes precedence over not only the material, but also the genuine, non-material resource. The religiously–culturally orientated resources of the area primarily represent a symbol for local and regional reality and identity, with a secondary function in promotion of the area for visitors and tourists.

Considering the 'Ciudad de Cultura', the symbolic representation of Galician identity and culture, and of the religious and cultural history and character of the city and region, is as notable as the creation of a new regional landmark for cultural tourism. Together with the subsidiary orientation of the project towards tourism, the symbolic importance of the 'Ciudad de Cultura' for the region – as well as for the tourism experience – will be discussed.

The Symbolic Transformation of Attractions

The symbolic transformation by both producers and consumers of religious- and cultural resources into touristic–recreational attractions represents part of the representation of genuine regional resources for tourism experiences. These thematic–structural changes in the presentation of genuine regional resources, both material and non-material, driven by both local residents and tourists, will be discussed throughout this chapter. The aim, therefore, is to describe and discuss the symbolic transformation of religiously, culturally and historically based local and regional specialities into tourism–recreation products.

The search for destinations to help differentiate their tourist attractions from those of other providers also becomes a source for symbolic transformation of genuine local and regional resources into tourism–recreation products, as much as the tendency to strengthen regional and cultural traditions and identities. Increasingly, there is an intensive interconnection of these two tendencies of symbolic representation of religious, cultural, historical and local and regional identities with tourism experiences.

What makes the chosen example of the 'Ciudad de Cultura' so interesting is the interconnection of two important current tendencies that influence and strengthen each other: (i) increasing interest of Europeans in cultural heritage; and (ii) an apparent shift in the consumption of tourism resources to a more sensitive, visual and sensory experience.

Dietvorst and Ashworth (1995) discuss, in their article on transformation in tourism attractions, the shift from the 'Gutenberg generation' to the 'MTV generation' in order to emphasize this change from an earlier, more reasonable and discursive reception and consumption of scarce tourism resources to a more visually and sensitivity-based reception.

They argue that the visual and aesthetical qualities of the tourism resource become more important for the 'tourist gaze', the tourist experience and consumption. They state that there has been a change from a more intellectually driven motivation, underpinning the experience of tourism resources, to a more sensitive, visual experience. Considering the integration of sensory experiences into religiously, culturally or historically based attractions and resources, one can trace movement from the 'de-intellectualization' of the tourist experience to a more sensory and visual event.

Furthermore, in the course of reinterpreting local culture, two main tendencies and viewpoints are discernible. On the one hand, the integration of regional economies in the world economic system during the process of globalization tends to intensify economic, political and cultural homogenization. On the other, the emergence of locally distinct cultures and the re-strengthening of local and regional distinctiveness is occurring. This has been emphasized by Robbins, who stated that:

> [g]lobalisation is, in fact, also associated with new dynamics of *re*-localisation. It is about the achievement of a new global–local nexus, about new and intricate relations between global space and local space. Globalisation is like putting together a jigsaw puzzle: it is a matter of inserting a multiplicity of localities into the overall picture of a new global system.
>
> (Robbins, 1991, pp. 34–35)

This idea is also reflected in the work of Urry (1995, p. 130), who argued that:

> The effect of globalization is often to increase local distinctiveness for one or more of the following reasons: the increased ability of large companies to subdivide their operations and to locate different activities within different labour markets located in different societies (see discussion in Bagguley *et al.*, 1990); the breaking up of previously relatively coherent regional economies; the competition between local states for jobs, the growth of international differences and the localising of regional policy (see discussion in Harloe *et al.*, 1990); the decreasing tendency for voting patterns to be nationally determined and the increased importance of 'neighbourhood' effects; the enduring significance of symbols of place and location, particularly with the decline in the popularity of the international modern style of architecture and the emergence of local and vernacular styles; and the resurgence of locally oriented culture and politics, especially around campaigns for the conservation of the built and physical environment.

The rising interest in cultural heritage, therefore, becomes increasingly important for regional and local sociocultural resources. This was highlighted by Dietvorst and Ashworth (1995, p. 5), who stated that: 'The sociocultural resources become more and more important, as can be inferred from the tremendous interest of European societies in cultural heritage.'

In interpreting regional effects and changes, the intensive interconnections between these two positions have to be taken into consideration. The consideration of these complex interconnections was emphasized by Urry (1995, p. 152) when referring to his considerations about the reinterpretation of what constitutes the local: 'It is the *interconnections* between [these two tendencies] which account for the particular ways in which an area's local history and culture are made available and transformed into a resource for local economic and social development within a globally evolving economy and society.'

Besides the emphasis on the implications for economic and social development, the importance for all kinds of cultural development or redevelopment must also be considered. Especially in a multicultural society such as Spain, with its long history of cultural hegemony and centricity and the oppression of regional distinctiveness under the regime of Franco, the renewal of local and regional history, culture and identity must be considered as one of the most challenging recent developments for (Spanish) society.

Changes and modifications in sociocultural perception

In order to emphasize the functional changes towards a more 'sensitive' and 'conscious' tourism experience, Butcher (2003) speaks of New Moral Tourism, concentrating on the tourist–host relationship and a sense of personal mission. He posits that tourists should gain a certain deepened personal insight and perception – during their journeys and contact with another culture – in the form of a special guest–host relationship in the material expression of another culture. Moreover, it can be speculated that if the exchange of the tourist with the host becomes more 'sensitive' or 'conscious', there will be more interest in culture, traditions and other cultural expression.

Apart from changes in the main attitudes of perception towards a more sensory and visual experience, tourists increasingly try to gain a certain educational output from their journeys, an individual sociocultural enhancement and, in the view of Dietvorst and Ashworth (1995, p. 8): 'They opt for a cultural return from their travel and use the educational opportunities of cultural tours to experience a mental pilgrimage to the past, which could be the route to Santiago de Compostela or equally the Beatles' cavern in Liverpool or Elvis' Graceland in Memphis.'

Urban space, representation and instrumentality of space

Space, as a symbolic representative of social and cultural flows, is successively gaining importance. There is a focus on the spatial formation of urban identity, the city as a synthesis totality and the loss of coherence or legibility of the city. The first part of this chapter has already addressed the importance and relevance of cultural production and cultural representations of urban space, and this was emphasized by Balshaw and Kennedy (2000, p. 1) when they argued that: 'Space has become an increasingly irrepressible metaphor in contemporary cultural and critical theorising and a point of convergence for the work emerging from the disciplinary meltdown of the humanities and, to a lesser extent, of the social sciences.'

The theoretical contributions concerning themes of the representation of urban and regional reality, of current aspects of social and cultural life, also raise the question of the instrumentality of space and regional cultures. This poses the question of whether 'fact or process' of regional culture is presented in the representation place. There are further questions of the materialization of the identities and the *purpose* of the construction of space, and the different uses and elements it provides. Which social class or group makes decisions on the different contents and uses?

Possible answers to the questions serve as a 'first approximation' in explaining existing relationships of power and their representation in the built environment. Consequently, seeking the purpose of representation of different cultural phenomena, possible answers are directed towards the instrumentality of space. Besides certain purposes of representation, and the instrumental use of what is represented, constructed space also embodies a great variety of signification and meaning.

The built environment and space are always constructed for a certain purpose. One interpretation leads to the assumption that built heritage should primarily legitimate and foster the power and influence of just that social or political class or group that 'introduced its realization'. Choosing the example of representative buildings and the heritage industry in the UK, Hewison (1987, p. 55) speaks of a 'self-perpetuating society' in order to explain the tendencies of legitimization of power by traditional elitist dominance of social stratification. Considering presentation and use of heritage, it is therefore possible to state that '[I]n terms of legitimisation, such heritage could be interpreted as one means of perpetuating elitist control and power, if not always with conscious intent' (Ashworth and Tunbridge, 2000, p. 42).

Symbolic representation of religion, history and heritage: the example of the 'Ciudad de Cultura'

The project of the 'Ciudad de Cultura', near Santiago de Compostela on the Monte de las Gaias in Galicia, forms one of the most ambitious current architectural projects in Spain. With a total surface area of 762,800 m^2, the 'Ciudad de Cultura' comprises sets of different buildings. The main uses comprise a library, a new Museum of Galicia and 'communications museum', a newspaper library and an opera house with auditorium. The surface area of all the public buildings will be approximately 62,800 m^2. Figure 13.1 shows the project site and its location close to Santiago de Compostela on an elevated part of the local landscape.

The most innovative and interesting aspects of the project are its explicit concentration on Galician culture and on the representation of religion, culture and history. Each part of the 'Ciudad de Cultura' provides another representation of Galician cultural identity – from its religious aspects to its cultural and historical evolution and uniqueness.

Fig. 13.1. The future 'Ciudad de Cultura', Compostela (from http://www.cidadedecultura.es).

Within the 'Ciudad de Cultura' in Galicia, the symbolic representation of Galician identity and culture and of the religious and cultural history and character of the city and region are as visible as the creation of a new regional landmark for cultural tourism. Together with the subsidiary orientation of the project towards tourism, the symbolic importance of the 'Ciudad de Cultura' for the region – as well as for the tourism experience – will be discussed in the following parts of this chapter.

The 'Ciudad de Cultura' provides an example where the image and the symbolic presentation of a merely religious–cultural product take precedence over the material and non-material aspects of the resource. The regionally orientated religious–cultural resources represent a powerful symbol for local and regional reality and identity. Figure 13.2 shows a model of the project, in which its conceptual form – a seashell, symbol of Santiago de Compostela and the pilgrims – is evident.

Two questions now arise: (i) in what context does the 'Ciudad de Cultura' represent certain power relationships? and (ii) can it be characterized as a postmodern symbol for the legitimization of Galician cultural independence, cultural identity and historical uniqueness? Furthermore, the project represents the still-rising importance of tourism for the regional economic structure, and helps to intensify the concentration of Galician economy on the service sector, with an emphasis on education, politics, culture and tourism, as well as on the commercialization of Galician culture.

Reflections on relationships of power and the production of space

The interconnections of space and society are one of the major concerns of the work of Manuel Castells, who argues that social characteristics and tendencies

Fig. 13.2. Model of the 'Ciudad de Cultura' in Santiago de Compostela (from http://www.cidadedacultura.es).

in societies will introduce their own special forms and expressions. He stated that:

> Space is not a 'reflection of society', it is society ... Therefore, spatial forms ... will be produced, as all other objects are, by human action. They will express and perform the interests of the dominant class according to a given mode of production and to a specific mode of development. They will express and implement the power relationships of the state in an historically defined society. They will be realised and shaped by the process of gender domination and by state-enforced family life. At the same time, spatial forms will be earmarked by the resistance from exploited classes, from expressed subjects, and from dominated women. And the work of such a contradictory historical process on the space will be accomplished on an already inherited spatial form, the product of former history and the support of new interests, projects, protests, and dreams.
>
> (Castells, 1989, p. 4)

Consistent with this view, Harvey pointed out that: 'Capital represents itself in the form of a physical landscape created in its own image' (Harvey, 1978, p. 124). Considering now the cultural, local and regional capital in the form of history, culture and heritage, what expression of space can be perceived? Is it then possible to say that cultural capital represents itself in the form of a cultural landscape, in the different forms of expressions of regionality in the landscape?

Therefore, it should be possible to connect different local and regional cultures to different forms of expressions in space and in the built environment. This leads to the question of presentation of cultural distinctiveness and uniqueness by new symbols.

Summary

The aim and purpose of this chapter was to explain different forms of the presentation and re-presentation of history and culture in urban environments. The reorientation of regional identity and the increase in importance of regional culture and heritage underline the rising importance of all forms of regional expressions throughout the process of transformation from modernity to postmodernity.

The symbolic composition of the 'Ciudad de Cultura' and its great variety of influences on regional and urban structures raises the question of whether the regional/urban relevance of other projects could be considered in a similar way? The question would be whether or not general guidelines and general paradigms could be found that could to describe symbolical changes in parts of regional realities. Can global changes in geography, economics, society, culture and other areas introduce symbolic changes in regional identity, represented by singular projects of symbolical meaning?

Based on different theoretical findings and conclusions, the abstraction and transformation of the discussed processes into a general and transferable concept would be desirable and very useful in order to describe and evaluate the symbolic changes introduced by different projects. This concept, therefore, should be able to provide a basis for an evaluation of multistructured, multilayered changes in society and the 'materialized, the created, built environment'.

As demonstrated throughout this chapter, in order to evaluate a certain project successfully and profoundly, a multitude of different processes, tendencies and decisions from different social groups have to be considered. This also leads to multilayered, multipurpose analysis, where it is necessary to discuss the intrinsic connections of different processes.

Therefore, a 'concept of symbolic transformation' should be able to describe the multitude of processes and attitudes involved in the symbolic transformation of a site or location by means of certain projects in order to transform regional identity of different aspects, like a reorganization of the economic structure of a region or the socialcultural orientation. Underlying purposes might be legitimization of power relationships, creation of regional USPs or other forms of wide transformation of existing cultural, social, economical and political structures.

Considering the composition, as well as the dimensions, of the project of the 'Ciudad de Cultura' in Galicia, further investigation will be necessary to analyse the contribution of this project, in order to symbolize and strengthen the position and reception of Santiago de Compostela as Galicia's cultural, religious, educational and administrative capital.

References

Agnew, J. and Corbridge, S. (1995) *Mastering Space: Hegemony, Territory and International Political Economy.* Routledge, London.

Allen, J. and Massey, D. (eds) (1998) *Rethinking the Region.* Routledge, London.

Appadurai, A. (1996) *Modernity at Large: Cultural Dimensions of Globalization.* University of Minnesota Press, Minneapolis, Minnesota.

Appadurai, A. (1998) Globale ethnische räume: bemerkungen und fragen zur entwicklung einer transnationalen anthropologie. In: Beck, U. (ed.) *Perspektiven der Weltgesellschaft.* Suhrkamp, Frankfurt am Main, Germany, pp. 11–40.

Ashworth, G.J. and Tunbridge, J.E. (2000) *The Tourist – Historic City: Retrospect an Prospect of Managing the Heritage City.* Pergamon, London.

Bagguley, P., Mark-Lawson, J., Shapiro, D., Urry, J., Walley, S. and Warde, A. (1990) *Restructuring Place, Class and Gender.* Sage, London.

Bahadir, S.A. (1998) *Kultur und Region im Zeichen der Globalisierung.* Arbeitspapiere des Zentralinstituts für Regionalforschung der Universität Erlangen/Nürnberg, Germany.

Balshaw, M. and Kennedy, L. (eds) (2000) *Urban Space and Representation.* Pluto Press, London.

Barrett, M., Corrigan, P., Kuhn, A. and Wolff, J. (eds) (1979) *Ideology and Cultural Production.* Croom Helm, London.

Billington, R. *et al.* (1991) *Culture and Society: a Sociology of Culture.* Macmillan, London.

Butcher, J. (2003) *The Moralisation of Tourism. Sun, Sand … and Saving the World.* Routledge, London.

Castells, M. (1989) *The International City: Information Technology, Economic Restructuring and the Urban Regional Process.* Oxford, UK.

Crang, M. (1998) *Cultural Geography.* Routledge, London/New York.

Duncan, J. and Ley, D. (eds) (1993) *Place/Culture/Representation.* Routledge, London.

Dietvorst, A.G. and Ashworth, G.J. (1995) *Tourism and Spatial Transformation*. CAB International, Wallingford, UK.

Featherstone, M. (ed.) (1990) *Global Culture: Nationalism, Globalization and Modernity*. Sage, London.

Gertler, M.S. (1997) The invention of regional culture. In: Lee, R. and Wills, J. (eds) *Geographies of Economies*. Arnold, London, pp. 47–58.

Gregory, D. (1994) *Geographical Imaginations*. Blackwell, Cambridge, Massachusetts.

Harloe, M., Pickvance, C. and Urry, J. (eds) (1990) *Place, Policy, Politics: do Localities Matter?* Unwin Hyman, London.

Harvey, D. (1978) *The Condition of Postmodernity*. Blackwell, Malden, Massachusetts.

Harvey, D. (1990) *The Condition of Postmodernity. An Enquiry into the Origins of Cultural Change*. Blackwell, Oxford, UK.

Harvey, D. (1993) From space to place and back again. In: Bird, J. *et al.* (eds) *Mapping the Futures: Local Cultures, Global Change*. Routledge, London, pp. 3–29.

Hewison, R. (1987) *The Heritage Industry: Britain in a Climate of Decline*. Methuen, London.

Hobsbawn, E. and Ranger, T. (eds) (1983) *The Invention of Tradition*. Cambridge University Press, Cambridge, UK.

Massey, D. (1994) *Space, Place and Gender*. University of Minnesota Press, Minneapolis, Minnesota.

Münch, R. (1998) *Globale Dynamik, Lokale Lebenswelten*. Suhrkamp, Frankfurt am Main, Germany.

Robbins, K. (1991) Tradition and translation: national culture in its global context. In: Corner, J. and Harvey, S. (eds) *Enterprise and Heritage*. Routledge, London.

Scannell, P., Schlesinger, P. and Sparks, C. (eds) (1993) *Culture and Power: a Media, Culture and Society Reader*. Sage, London.

Soja, E.W. (1989) *Postmodern Geographies. The Reassertion of Space in Critical Social Theory*. Verso, London.

Urry, J. (1995) *Consuming Places*. Routledge, London.

14 Case Study 5: The Importance and the Role of Faith (Religious) Tourism as Alternative Tourism Resources in Turkey

AHMET AKTAS* AND YAKIN EKIN**

*Akdeniz University, Antalya, Turkey; e-mails: *aktas@akdeniz.edu.tr; **yakin@akdeniz.edu.tr*

Introduction

Turkey is a unique country in the sense that it possesses a panoply of historical and cultural resources, with an historical legacy of many different civilizations having lived in harmony in the country, leaving a wealth of heritage to present generations. Due to this rich heritage, the land of Turkey is a place that can be shown as an example of peace and conciliation both for the past and the future.

Moreover, this heritage is of great importance for the development of religion, including that of Christianity. This chapter reviews the characteristics of religious tourism in contemporary Turkish society and explores the policy implications of the development of faith tourism.

Turkey might be considered as the 'open-air museum' of Christianity. However, with its archaeological values, this is its least-known feature in terms of tourist attraction. Turkey is as important as Israel and Greece as regards the significance of Christian religious tourism. However, policies are lacking in the promotion of these sites, because their presentation and promotion tends to portray them as archaeological sites rather than by celebrating their spiritual significance.

The foundations of various ancient civilizations on the lands of Anatolia, the settlement of the disciples during the first quarter of Christianity and that of the Jewish people who had been subjected to the policy of annihilation in their homelands during the Medieval Ages, saw the emergence of synagogues and churches, besides the Islamic works of art belonging to the Turkish nations. The fact that these works of art have been preserved is a testament to the nation's respect and high esteem for a range of religions, arguably providing Turkey with an advantageous position in the promotion of faith tourism in relation to other countries.

Melding the Concepts of Religion and Tourism

Religions, undoubtedly, are main societal components and inform the dynamics of our culture, social structure and humanity. Moreover, they maintain their function in the creation and formation of moral life, social relationships and the 'value judgements' of society. Therefore, social scientists have accepted religious matters as a social phenomenon in dynamic and changing social and cultural conditions and as important topic for research.

Tourism creates a means of social interaction and provides opportunities for encounters in natural, social and cultural environments. However, in order to integrate the concepts of tourism and religion, it is necessary to recognize the significance of commercial, economic, social and cultural factors that underpin the concept of faith tourism.

Faith tourism is regarded as an alternative tourism type, initiated by the visits of people to holy sites in order to show their beliefs and, increasingly, there is scope for an evaluation of the interests of people to visit religious centres through 'faith tours'. The religious tourist is a fixture of both ancient and modern cultures, a constant through the 'Ages', from the 'Exodus' to the present day, when religious tourism has become a mainstay of general tourism.

In this respect, pilgrimage is one of the oldest forms of tourist migration, which is still very much part of the fabric of contemporary society. Religious tourism forms an integral part of the tourism industry. It can be defined from a spiritual point of view as offering to believers a facility to become closer to the saint or God they venerate.

From a sociological point of view, it proposes cultural access to sacred art and artefacts, which exerts some fascination even for atheists, conscious that the roots of their culture 'plunge' into these places. For example, Catholicism seems to have a cognizance that privileges the inner experience and the effective involvement of the subject, for example by a long trek towards a remote place of pilgrimage, e.g. Compostela in Spain, but also from Mont Saint-Michel to Lourdes, from Lourdes to Rome or Fátima or to remote Jerusalem. The Catholic Church encourages these practices today.

Religious tourism is placed at the 'crossroads' of two realities that seem, to a certain extent, irreconcilable: the image of the tourist evokes banality, frivolity and consumption, while that of the pilgrim is related to seriousness, asceticism and engagement.

The challenge for tourism managers is to be able to adapt their product to cater to those who, for example, seek a spiritual retreat, request that a priest accompany a group and evangelize it or simply wish to understand the major significance of a religious building. Other aspects bound up with religious tourism might include the following: (i) testifying to a living church; (ii) inclusion of the religious element in a study trip with broader ambitions (involving other local sites of interest); or (iii) simply providing a guide to the works of art from religious places considered simply as museums.

The professionals have noted this development of a 'spiritual market, animated by the need for demanding knowledge, separate from regulated religious systems'. This also provides a challenge for policy-makers and tourism managers in considering how to adapt the religious tourism product.

A Case Study in Religious Tourism in Turkey

In this case study, the fundamental statistics of Turkish tourism are presented initially and, within this context, it is emphasized that Turkey should pay greater heed to the faith tourism sector, which is developing progressively through the presentation of tourism products relevant to consumer demand. In this respect, it is argued that Turkey should use its resources for tourism more efficiently, not least its resources for faith tourism and, in doing so, become a desired destination in the highly competitive global tourism market.

Before analysing the significance of faith tourism in Turkey, the wider contexts of the growth in tourism in Turkey are highlighted through the following statistics tabulated below. The areas quantified are: (i) numbers of tourists and tourism receipts (Table 14.1); (ii) accommodation availability and type (Tables 14.2, 14.3); (iii) statistical breakdown of visitors to Turkey by area of origin (Table 14.4, 14.5, 14.6, 14.7, 14.8); and (iv) tourists' reasons for visiting Turkey (Table 14.9).

Perhaps it is important to stress, within the wider context of tourism globally, that according to the World Tourism Organisation (WTO) in 2003, there was a foreign trade currency worldwide of US$9 trillion, of which tourism's share was 6%. Moreover, although world commerce has increased by 3% annually, tourism revenues worldwide are increasing by 4% annually. According to the WTO it is anticipated that, by the year 2020, tourism revenues will have reached US$16 trillion.

Tourism as a concept is interpreted as the relations and events resulting from the travels of people to any place other than their normal place of residence, and the classification of different forms of tourism is based on their motives, which are dependent on the prevailing social and economic conditions.

The world of tourism is biased, generally, towards the demand stimulated by 'sea, sand and sun' tourism and, as a consequence, the demand for alternative types of tourism types is increasing. As a form of alternative tourism (forms of tourism beyond the creation of mass tourism) – and certainly from a geographical and historical point of view – the potential of faith tourism in Turkey is unique.

Faith tourism emanates from visits of people to sacred sites in order to express their religious beliefs and, since the very beginning of these religions, visits to sacred sites have meant more than simply the 'personal preferences' of tourists. As a result, sacred sites have, through the ages, hosted millions of people and mass movements have come into being. Nowadays, these movements have become a new, alternative concept, with new forms and insights.

In Turkey, faith tourism presents a sizeable branch of tourism, and potentially possesses an important competitive advantage, with several well-known resources in the Peninsula of Anatolia that house the sites of three main religions (Islam, Judaism and Christianity) – and of other religions, plus hundreds of sects. As with other types of alternative tourism, faith tourism requires the Turkish model to be highly responsive to the changes in (and possible crises in) the fortunes of general tourism in Turkey.

Table 14.1. Annual foreign tourism numbers and spending in Turkey, 1963–2004 (from http://www.tursab.org.tr/).

Year	Visitors ('000)	Annual change (%)	Spending (US$million)	Annual change (%)
1963	198	–	7	–
1964	229	15.7	8	14.3
1965	361	57.6	13	62.5
1966	449	24.4	12	–7.7
1967	574	27.8	13	8.3
1968	602	4.9	24	84.6
1969	694	15.3	36	50.0
1970	724	4.3	51	41.7
1971	926	27.9	62	21.6
1972	1,034	11.7	103	66.1
1973	1,341	29.7	171	66.0
1974	1,110	–17.2	193	12.9
1975	1,540	38.7	200	3.6
1976	1,675	8.8	180	–10.0
1977	1,661	–0.8	204	13.3
1978	1,644	–1.0	230	12.7
1979	1,523	–7.4	280	21.7
1980	1,288	–15.4	326	16.4
1981	1,405	9.1	381	16.9
1982	1,391	–1.0	370	–2.9
1983	1,625	16.8	411	11.1
1984	2,117	30.3	840	104.4
1985	2,614	23.5	1,482	76.4
1986	2,391	–8.5	1,215	–18.0
1987	2,855	19.4	1,721	41.6
1988	4,172	46.1	2,355	36.8
1989	4,459	6.9	2,556	8.5
1990	5,389	20.9	2,705	5.8
1991	5,517	2.4	2,654	–1.9
1992	7,076	28.3	3,639	37.1
1993	6,500	–8.1	3,959	8.8
1994	6,670	2.6	4,321	9.1
1995	7,726	15.8	4,957	14.7
1996	8,614	11.5	5,650	13.9
1997	9,689	13.0	7,008	23.9
1998	9,752	0.6	7,177	2.4
1999	7,464	–23.4	5,193	–27.64
2000	10,412	39.0	7,636	47.0
2001	11,569	11.0	8,090	5.9
2002	13,247	14.5	8,481	4.7
2003	14,030	5.3	9,677	14.1
2004	17,517	24.86	12,125	25.3

Table 14.2. Accommodation in Turkey analysed by those establishments in possession of either/both of the two main Department of Tourism licences, 1966–2003.

Year	Establishments in possession of Licence of Tourism Administration			Establishments in possession of Licence of Tourism Investment		
	Establishments (n)	Rooms (n)	Beds (n)	Establishments (n)	Rooms (n)	Beds (n)
1966	165	–	16,151	291	–	23,807
1967	196	–	18,158	371	–	29,859
1968	225	–	21,643	350	–	26,803
1969	249	–	24,907	340	–	29,048
1970	292	–	28,354	301	–	25,872
1971	337	–	32,114	259	–	25,619
1972	363	–	34,628	157	–	19,874
1973	388	–	38,528	180	–	24,605
1974	400	–	40,895	185	–	25,739
1975	421	23,860	44,957	202	12,846	25,956
1976	439	24,983	47,307	227	12,802	26,068
1977	446	26,496	50,379	261	14,359	28,230
1978	473	27,233	52,385	261	13,127	26,190
1979	494	28,013	53,956	265	12,803	25,727
1980	511	28,992	56,044	267	13,019	26,288
1981	529	30,050	58,242	278	15,159	30,291
1982	569	32,011	62,372	339	18,172	36,332
1983	611	33,694	65,934	376	21,410	43,425
1984	642	34,666	68,266	412	26,372	53,615
1985	689	41,351	85,995	501	34,251	71,521
1986	731	44,342	92,129	638	48,615	101,383
1987	834	51,040	106,214	892	73,537	153,786
1988	957	58,914	122,306	1,268	105,736	218,445
1989	1,102	70,603	146,086	1,662	139,497	288,896
1990	1,260	83,953	173,227	1,921	156,702	325,515
1991	1,404	97,260	200,678	1,987	158,372	331,711
1992	1,498	105,476	219,940	1,938	148,017	309,139
1993	1,581	113,995	235,238	1,788	132,395	276,037
1994	1,729	128,065	265,136	1,578	114,913	240,392
1995	1,793	135,436	286,463	1,334	96,517	202,483
1996	1,866	145,493	301,524	1,309	96,592	202,631
1997	1,933	151,055	313,298	1,402	110,866	236,632
1998	1,954	151,397	314,215	1,365	116,286	249,125
1999	1,907	153,749	319,313	1,311	114,840	245,543
2000	1,824	156,367	325,168	1,300	113,452	243,794
2001	1,980	175,499	364,779	1,240	107,262	230,248
2002	2,124	190,327	396,148	1,138	102,972	222,876
2003	2,240	202,339	420,697	1,130	111,894	242,603

Table 14.3. Western European and Scandinavian visitors to Turkey by country of origin, 1990–2002.

Country of origin	Annual visitors ('000)												
	2002	2001	2000	1999	1998	1997	1996	1995	1994	1993	1992	1991	1990
Western Europe													
UK	1040	844.6	915.3	814.8	996.5	815.3	758.0	734.0	568.0	441.0	314.0	200.0	351.0
Austria	376.9	359.9	320.5	129.4	235.1	307.5	238.0	181.0	138.0	211.0	204.0	102.0	196.0
Belgium	313.4	310.3	256.9	148.6	181.1	155.4	113.0	107.0	75.0	88.0	75.0	33.0	56.0
France	523.8	523.3	449.5	270.2	436.9	333.7	261.0	251.0	233.0	301.0	247.0	117.0	310.0
Germany	3481	2875	2276	1389	2234	2339	2141	1656	994	1118	1165	779	973
Luxembourg	4.2	3.5	2.0	1.1	4.3	1.8	1.7	1.6	1.3	2.0	1.7	1.6	5.4
Netherlands	871.6	632.2	440.0	214.1	328.0	263.3	216.0	203.0	180.0	216.0	204.0	107.0	150.0
Switzerland	143.4	125.3	1.5	38.7	76.8	68.2	70.0	62.0	47.0	82.0	78.0	41.0	76.0
Ireland	53.1	48.4	42.1	37.9	39.9	34.5	24.0	24.0	32.0	26.0	22.0	–	–
Scandinavia													
Denmark	161.2	125.5	100.9	83.4	104.8	148.3	147.0	104.0	76.0	79.0	64.0	32.0	34.0
Finland	80.9	63.6	53.4	39.9	78.0	107.5	124.0	102.0	78.0	96.0	104.0	80.0	104.0
Iceland	1.2	4.1	3.3	5.9	7.0	4.7	4.5	3.6	3.4	2.9	2.4	–	–
Norway	94.8	87.6	67.5	56.6	70.1	112.1	86.0	62.0	50.0	54.0	42.0	24.0	39.0
Sweden	203.8	200.0	148.5	107.4	156.1	199.1	183.0	127.0	93.0	87.0	120.0	69.0	110.0

Table 14.4. Eastern and Southern European visitors to Turkey by country of origin, 1990–2002.

Country of origin	Annual visitors ('000)												
	2002	2001	2000	1999	1998	1997	1996	1995	1994	1993	1992	1991	1990
Eastern Europe													
Bulgaria	833.8	540.2	381.5	259	244.7	219.3	139.0	141.0	170.0	368.0	818.0	943.0	72.0
Czech Republic	63.2	51.8	65.5	40.6	47.1	60.6	40.0	37.0	32.0	75.0	126.0	217.0	66.0
Hungary	51.3	38.2	36.7	25.0	26.2	22.7	15.0	16.0	28.0	98.0	148.0	164.0	172.0
Poland	150.9	150.5	118.1	56.2	80.8	50.8	37.0	33.0	40.0	51.0	111.0	184.0	206.0
Romania	180.2	180.2	265.1	483.1	505.7	398.9	191.0	283.0	414.0	311.0	566.0	503.0	377.0
Russia	1659	1424	1377	1048	1312	1514	1560	1366	1430	1167	1241	731	223
Southern Europe													
Albania	29.2	26.1	29.7	27.3	24.2	31.5	20.0	14.0	16.0	4.6	2.7	–	–
Greece	280.3	196.8	218.6	146.8	158.5	170.4	147.0	154.0	127.0	148.0	147.0	138.0	227.0
Italy	211.1	314.1	218.7	79.0	259.4	207.8	140.0	108.0	105.0	134.0	158.0	64.0	156.0
Portugal	16.6	18.4	13.3	7.6	10.8	9.7	6.5	9.6	10.0	5.8	3.1	6.5	
Spain	88.8	115.2	95.0	35.4	74.6	61.8	47.0	28.0	39.0	63.0	47.0	24.0	62.0
Yugoslavia (former)	367.3	287.3	285.6	213.7	172.3	150.7	104.0	70.0	118.0	169.0	155.0	158.0	325.0
Northern Cyprus	94.2	90.9	103.2	89.2	96.8	96.1	91.0	96.0	71.0	66.0	55.0	45.0	5.0

Table 14.5. North and South American and Middle Eastern visitors to Turkey by country of origin, 1990–2002.

Country of origin	Annual visitors ('000)												
	2002	2001	2000	1999	1998	1997	1996	1995	1994	1993	1992	1991	1990
North America													
Canada	39.0	56.9	56.6	4.9	53.6	46.3	40.0	38.0	34.0	35.0	26.0	17.0	34.0
USA	247.8	423.2	515.0	395.0	438.8	364.7	326.0	290.0	271.0	254.0	182.0	79.0	205.0
South America													
Mexico	11.3	20.9	18.4	9.1	9.6	7.1	5.5	4.2	7.1	7.0	5.0	2.0	6.1
Argentina	2.9	9.4	12.2	10.2	12.7	12.2	10.0	12.0	13.0	8.5	5.1	2.2	2.4
Brazil	8.3	10.4	11.9	6.8	18.2	18.2	16.0	12.0	11.0	8.9	4.8	3.0	5.3
Colombia	2.2	2.5	1.4	1.7	2.7	3.0	3.4	3.0	2.9	2.4	1.8	–	–
Chile	3.3	3.6	4.2	2.7	3.1	4.5	3.3	3.0	2.0	1.9	2.1	0.5	0.6
Venezuela	1.8	2.4	1.2	1.1	1.6	1.5	1.0	1.4	1.1	1.5	1.3	–	–
Middle East													
Israel	271.0	299.9	311.7	201.4	238.2	263.4	254.0	301.0	303.0	100.0	49.0	46.0	40.0
Bahrain	4.6	2.3	0.4	1.9	3.5	3.5	3.9	4.0	5.2	3.2	1.8	1.8	2.4
Iraq	16.6	16.7	20.7	17.5	18.2	17.5	13.0	14.0	16.0	12.0	12.0	3.8	15.4
Jordan	33.1	26.9	22.2	18.0	21.2	22.7	23.0	24.0	28.0	26.0	22.0	15.0	17.0
Kuwait	7.0	5.3	1.3	3.7	8.0	7.7	8.5	7.7	7.7	6.1	7.2	4.9	8.3
Lebanon	31.3	22.3	16.6	14.4	25.2	24.5	23.0	28.0	21.0	19.0	14.0	14.0	14.6
Saudi Arabia	25.7	20.6	15.5	13.8	22.7	22.8	21.0	24.0	27.0	21.0	19.0	15.0	16.4
Syria	126.3	109.5	122.3	102.4	98.6	99.4	91.0	119.0	111.0	120.0	123.0	119.0	112.0
United Arab Emirates	5.0	2.3	1.8	2.0	5.1	4.3	4.4	3.9	4.3	3.8	3.1	1.9	2.9

Table 14.6. Eastern and Southern Asian/Pacific visitors to Turkey by country, 1990–2002.

Country of origin	Annual visitors (1000)												
	2002	2001	2000	1999	1998	1997	1996	1995	1994	1993	1992	1991	1990
Eastern Asia/Pacific													
China	32.0	24.0	21.5	11.0	11.5	12.7	11.0	10.0	8.0	6.9	5.5	–	–
Japan	94.5	87.6	89.4	67.9	81.8	83.8	68.0	66.0	63.0	47.0	36.0	18.0	35.0
South Korea	42.6	29.2	22.2	14.7	10.1	24.2	14.0	11.0	7.0	5.0	3.0	–	–
Australia	51.3	58.4	58.2	46.0	60.6	52.9	46.0	43.0	32.0	30.0	30.0	20.0	37.0
New Zealand	10.8	13.6	13.5	10.2	13.0	11.4	10.0	9.0	8.0	7.0	7.0	6.0	12.0
Philippines	13.0	12.7	16.1	12.4	20.8	9.8	10.0	6.8	6.4	7.3	3.9	–	–
Malaysia	8.2	9.1	8.8	3.8	3.1	4.4	3.9	3.4	3.4	2.9	1.7	–	–
Singapore	5.1	6.0	6.2	5.3	7.4	7.5	6.0	5.5	5.6	2.9	2.2	–	–
Southern Asia													
Bangladesh	0.8	0.7	0.2	0.7	0.4	0.7	0.5	0.4	0.4	0.8	0.5	–	–
India	10.1	8.6	12.4	10.3	10.7	8.7	10.0	9.0	7.0	8.7	4.4	–	–
Iran	432.2	327.0	380.8	351.9	304.9	331.6	351.0	361.0	231.0	119.0	150.0	253.0	253.0
Pakistan	8.4	7.1	7.9	7.3	7.5	8.2	12.0	16.0	15.0	11.0	10.0	9.0	15.0

Table 14.7. North African visitors to Turkey by country, 1990–2002.

Country of origin	Annual visitors ('000)												
	2002	2001	2000	1999	1998	1997	1996	1995	1994	1993	1992	1991	1990
Egypt	21.6	22.2	31.7	26.6	18.7	20.9	19.0	21.0	17.0	12.0	11.0	8.0	11.0
Lybia	30.0	31.4	24.0	9.1	7.6	8.0	5.3	7.2	6.1	9.2	11.5	20.0	22.5
Tunisia	51.3	45.0	39.7	–	–	–	–	–	–	–	–	–	–
Sudan	2.2	2.0	2.0	–	–	–	–	–	–	–	–	–	–
Algeria	41.5	39.9	33.4	–	–	–	–	–	–	–	–	–	–
Morocco	12.7	11.8	11.6	–	–	–	–	–	–	–	–	–	–

Table 14.8. Reasons for visiting Turkey, 1993–2001.

Reason	Annual visitors ('000)				
	2001	1998	1997	1996	1993
Holiday	52.30	49.79	56.12	50.00	60.00
Culture	9.20	9.86	10.45	13.00	9.00
Shopping	8.30	5.73	5.94	4.40	11.00
VFR	7.90	5.91	6.28	4.50	4.00
Convention/conference	2.40	2.17	1.49	1.50	1.00
Health	1.00	0.55	–	–	–
Religion	0.30	0.25	–	–	–
Sport	1.30	1.03	–	–	–
Education	–	1.06	–	–	–
In transit	3.10	0.71	–	–	–
Business/trade	–	8.9	5.51	10.0	6.0
	–	6.1	6.7	4.8	3.5
Fair/event	5.0	–	–	–	–
Government/public business	–	0.40	–	–	–
Employment	–	4.81	3.91	4.3	2.0
On duty	5.0	–	–	–	–
Other	4.3	2.74	–	–	–

Table 14.9. Reasons for visiting Turkey, 2004–2005 (from http://www.rursab.org.tr/).

Reason	Visitors (%)	
	2005	2004
Entertainment	49.59	46.29
Culture	9.56	9.08
Sports	1.80	1.88
Visiting friends and relatives	8.66	7.88
Health	0.95	0.94
Religion	0.84	0.49
Shopping	7.77	8.14
Convention, conference, course, seminar	2.76	3.44
Business	6.17	8.36
Commercial purposes, fair	4.94	6.94
Transit	2.35	1.53
Education	0.71	1.38
Other	3.90	3.67

The Importance and the Role of Religious Tourism in Turkey

It is clear that faith has played a key role in the history of mankind and in the social life of contemporary society. In this respect, Anatolia has 'hosted' almost all of the major religions and is a place where different beliefs have coexisted together peacefully. As such, it is one of the most interesting areas in the world for faith tourism.

Within the peninsula there is evidence of the antiquity of civilizations, from the visits of the Apostles to the Diaspora of the Jews taking refuge from persecution. For this reason, and leaving aside the monuments belonging to Islam, a considerable number of churches, synagogues and other temples – with dedicated schools and foundations giving religious education – are in existence today. Arguably, being the live witness of the history of these foundations and monuments renders Turkey potentially much more competitive than other countries with regard to faith tourism.

The Turkish government, through the Ministry of Tourism, has attempted to implement a 'Faith Tourism Project', with the key aim of diversifying Turkish tourism and, specifically:

- To evaluate its potential.
- To identify those sites considered as 'religious centres' of three main religions (Islam, Judaism, Christianity) by rethinking their restoration, environment, illumination, etc.
- To promote those sites in order to raise visitor numbers and foreign currency income.

According to the 'Foreign Visitors Demand Profile Research' carried out by the Ministry of Tourism, those visits with a religious purpose totalled only 52,000 (0.75%) out of 6 million visits to Turkey in 1993. It is certain that there has been an increase in this figure since 1993, but the numbers measured since than are unreliable. This 1993 research identified that, from the point of view of travel objectives to Turkey, the percentages were as in Fig. 14.8.

What is revealing here is that religious tourism accounts for only 1%, yet Turkey is the second most important place in the development of Christianity after Jerusalem. The challenge for the Turkish Ministry of Tourism is, therefore, to realize the potential of attracting untapped markets to the various religious centres throughout the country.

From a Christian perspective, the triangle of Mardin-Midyat, Antiochia and Cappadocia – apart from the well-known Virgin Mary House and St Nicholas Church – have great potential for tourism. St John is regarded as having been the most important apostle in the early years of Christianity, having played an important role in its spreading. In order to escape the pressure of idolaters, he eventually travelled from Jerusalem to Anatolia. This event is accepted as one of the major events of Christianity.

In addition, the Virgin Mary probably came to Anatolia under the auspices of St John. Considerable archaeological evidence supports this viewpoint, and it is accepted by the Vatican and by a considerable number of Churches.

As for Judaism, the most holy site after Israel is Anatolia, and this community has always had sanctuary in this peninsula, where they lived without fear of cruelty for a considerable period of time. The importance of these events should be stressed, and promoted to current and future generations within the context of religious tourism. This religious aspect could be advanced as an important draw for tourists from Israel.

Faith tours have also been implemented successfully as part of 'Eco-promotion' projects developed by the Ministry of Tourism, with the aim of diversifying Turkish tourism products. The participants in these tours (the foreign press, religious personnel and travel agencies) return home with many images relating to the heritage of religious belief and the wide variety of archaeological evidence to be found within Anatolia from the different civilizations who have left their mark.

Summary

The Peninsula of Anatolia has been the cradle of many civilizations, cultures and religious beliefs for thousands of years. Now, the Turkish Republic, in which this peninsula is situated, is in the position of curator of a considerable multi-religion heritage. However, destinations with less potential in this sphere than Turkey – such as Saudi Arabia – utilize their heritage very efficiently, and demonstrate the potential for faith tourism in Turkey.

In the development and changes seen in the visitor profile of a pilgrimage centre, there are important examples of annual pilgrim flows to such destinations as Lourdes (France), Loreto (Italy) and Fátima (Portugal), which have grown from point zero and developed rapidly.

Furthermore there has been some immigration of workers living in nearby regions, serving pilgrims and the development of the city and its environs economically (Fátima and Lourdes), and sometimes even the economic development of an entire country (Saudi Arabia). Until the end of World War II, when the oil industry was greatly developed, income generated from the pilgrims to Mecca had been the major pillar of the Saudi Arabian economy.

In Turkey, the inventory of faith tourism already started by the Ministry of Tourism should be developed, and a department should be established within the Presidency of Religious Affairs in recognition of the creation of religious tolerance within the community.

Local authorities and partnership organizations have a role to play in the protection and preservation of mosques, synagogues, churches and other religious monuments. The threats of inappropriate construction should be resisted, and necessary restoration and environmental protection should be undertaken.

It is also important that international organizations such as the International Tourist Board (ITB), through conferences and expositions, emphasize the potential of faith tourism in addition to the other tourism resources of Turkey. Events such as the St Nicholas Festival (in Demre) should be supported, and sponsorship should be sought for new events relating to the important religious personalities associated with Turkey, such as the Virgin Mary and St John.

Moreover, these events should possess an international dimension in terms of the advertisement and promotion by religious associations. There are 'personalities' – e.g. Yunus Emre, Pir Sultan Abdal, Hac Bektaş and Mevlana – who are famous not only in Muslim communities but also globally, who could act as key targets for the faith tourism market, with annual ceremonies being promoted to an international audience. In addition, the House of the Virgin

Mary, Seven Churches and St Peter's Church all have importance in the Christian religion, and could be developed, with the help of the Pope, as pilgrimage destinations.

Combined tour programmes might be created by travel agencies, with the aim of diversifying the tourism product (e.g. health tourism, faith tourism, etc.). Universities might support religious associations by instigating academic studies towards the development and protection of faith tourism attraction centres within their region.

Furthermore, incentives such as transportation facilitation and visa exemptions could come into operation, possibly involving mutual agreements with such countries as Israel and Syria.

References

Çeşitli, K. (1996) Türkiye' nin Alternatif Turizm Kaynakları İçinde Dini Turizmin Yeri, Akdeniz Üniversitesi Sosyal Bilimler Enstitüsü, Yayımlanmamış Yüksek Lisans Tezi, Antalya, Turkey.
İpek Yolu Dergisi (1996) Sayı: 10, Cegam Reklamcılık, Ankara, Turkey.
İpek Yolu Dergisi (1997) Sayı: 11, Cegam Reklamcılık, Ankara, Turkey.
Türsab Dergisi (1996) Sayı: 153, Ekin Yazım Merkezi, İstanbul.
Türsab Dergisi (1998) Sayı: 168, Ekin Yazım Merkezi, İstanbul.

Useful Websites

http://www.turizm.gov.tr
http://www.tursab.org

15 Case Study 6: Visiting Sacred Sites in India: Religious Tourism or Pilgrimage?

KIRAN A. SHINDE

Tourism Research Unit, School of Geography and Environmental Science, Monash University, Clayton, Victoria, Australia; e-mail: Kiran.shinde@arts.monash.edu.au

Introduction

Travel provides an opportunity to fulfil one's desire to move away from the routines of life in order to seek changes, such as spiritual, religious or recreational. Such travel, depending on the motivation, the destination and the journey, generally finds expression within the spectrum of two polar types of movements, pilgrimage and tourism.

While the focus in pilgrimage is on the association with some sacred and numinous supernatural power and the ability to go closer to it by means of religious practices, tourism is mainly about 'getting away' to experience a change, and is replete with hedonistic pursuits. There has been a substantial body of literature dominated by discussions on the similarities and differences between the two (MacCannell, 1973; Graburn, 1978; Turner and Turner, 1978; Cohen, 1992; Smith, 1992).

In this fast-changing world, however, these two forms of travel increasingly overlap, because many people travel with the objective of achieving both the recreational and the religious need, and there are immense difficulties in distinguishing between the two. The resulting form of travel does not belong to either of these discrete categories, yet shows characteristics peculiar to them and therefore is described in composite terms such as pilgrimage tourism or religious tourism. Religious tourism implies any visit to a sacred site that is motivated, partly or wholly, by religious motives (Rinschede, 1992).

Traditional pilgrimage in India, the *tirth yatra*, is a religiously motivated journey (*yatra*) to a crossing or river ford (*tirtha*) or, more commonly, a sacred site, where 'crossing over from this world to the other world is easily possible' (Eck, 1982; York, 2002; Singh, 2005) or it is easy to obtain divine help (Tomasi, 2002). More than 1800 such sites are acknowledged as tirthas in popular Hindu religion in India (Bhardwaj, 1973).

In a traditional pilgrimage, pilgrims would arrive at a sacred site from far-flung places on foot, with a strongly religious or spiritual motivation reinforced by a sense of renunciation of worldly matters. Once at the sacred site (temple or sacred objects), they perform the customary rituals in fulfilling the purpose for which such travel is taken. In performing this pilgrimage, they are assisted by pilgrimage priests (or religious functionaries) who specialize in the rituals of pilgrimage (Vidyarthi, 1961). Most importantly, they take *darshana* (the act of seeing and being seen) of the deity and the saints and seek their blessings.

Indian pilgrimages have traditionally been discussed for their spiritual, religious, social and cultural dimensions. In the past, the thrust has been on analysis of pilgrimage by using the classical 'sacred complex' model developed by Vidyarthi (1961), which uses the analytical categories of the sacred geography, the sacred performances and the sacred specialists (Vidyarthi *et al.*, 1979; see Dubey, 1995).

A few studies have attempted to document and report on the sociocultural changes in pilgrimage, especially concerning the sacred specialists directly engaged in the activity of pilgrimage (Van Der Veer, 1988; Fuller, 1992; Parry, 1994; Caplan, 1997). There are still few Indian studies that place pilgrimage within the modern context and allude to the changes in pilgrimage and pilgrims (see Singh and Singh, 1999; Singh, 2002).

The modern expression of pilgrimage travel in India seems to have evolved in a very much more distinct form than the traditional one, even if it has echoes of the former. Along with a substantial increase in the volume of visitors to sacred sites, substantial changes are visible in the very essence and quality of pilgrimage. This modern type of travel indicates more touristic characteristics, including the changing patterns of visits to sacred destinations, limited engagement of visitors with rituals, commercial organization typical of package tours, novel ways of marketing the destinations and the consumerist behaviour of visitors. There has been a substantial shift away from the notion of journeying to that of quick and easy trips, and the focus on the type of journey associated with the traditional pilgrimage has given way to the that on destinations and the ease of reaching them. Short-term trips now constitute a larger proportion of travel to sacred sites than in the past. More people visit sacred sites on weekends from nearby urban centres, usually travelling by car.

This chapter explores the changes that have occurred in the traditional pilgrimage in India and argues that these changes suggest studying the contemporary form of pilgrimage from the aspect of 'religious tourism'. Little recognition, if any, has been given to articulating such modern travel as different from pilgrimage and tourism in the national tourism policy in India. This chapter has two purposes: (i) to uncover the changes that have occurred in the traditional pilgrimage that lean more towards mass tourism; and (ii) to situate the contemporary expression of pilgrimage travels in India within the concept of religious tourism. The chapter derives its findings from observations and personal experience of fieldwork conducted in March 2005 during a pilgrimage to Vrindavan, one of the most popular sacred sites in Northern India.

Pilgrimage, Tourism and Religious Tourism

Many scholars have studied the relations between pilgrimage and tourism within different theoretical constructs (MacCanell, 1976; Cohen, 1992; Smith, 1992; Graburn, 2001). In the most comprehensive of these analyses, Cohen (1992) argues that the similarities between pilgrimage and tourism can be found at the structural level, where both pilgrims and tourists are seeking deeper meanings, and distinctions at the phenomenal level, in the hedonistic pursuits of the tourists. Such distinctions are clearer at the institutional level, where traditional pilgrimage has an explicit, culturally recognized meaning that modern tourism does not possess (but which needs to be revealed); and 'tourism is more "open" than the pilgrimage in terms of obligatoriness, season and itineraries, patterns of demeanour, and relation with co-travellers' (Cohen, 1992, pp. 56–58). Cohen concludes that tourism is 'a modern metamorphosis of both pilgrimage and travel' (Cohen, 1992, p. 59).

Similar ambivalent views have been expressed about pilgrims and tourists whose paths, even though they may seem divergent, frequently cross over (Nolan and Nolan, 1989), and sometimes these paths themselves may become interchangeable lanes (Smith, 1992). However, this does not help us to deal with contemporary forms of pilgrimage, especially with regards to public policy.

Kaelber (2002) notes the difficulty of many observers in distinguishing, analytically and empirically, between pilgrimage, tourism and related types of travel, due to increased blurring of the boundaries resulting from the simultaneous expansion of various forms of travel. Tomasi's (2002) claim that: '[T]he distinction between pilgrimage driven by faith and tourism for cultural and recreational purposes no longer holds, because contemporary pilgrimages involve such huge numbers of people that they can only be organised in the same manner as mass tourism' (Tomasi, 2002, p. 21) seems too far-fetched for the Indian context, because Indian pilgrimages have always involved mass movements. However, Tomasi's argument that such travel should be treated as part of the tourist industry remains valid, as 'Large numbers of pilgrims use the same facilities as tourists do, such as travel agencies, accommodation facilities, catering services, and commercial businesses' (Tomasi, 2002, p. 21).

Many scholars have attempted to articulate such travel that has both religious and recreational purposes within the spectrum of pilgrimage and tourism, corresponding to a continuum of the sacred–profane axis in one form or other. Santos (2003) presents an excellent review of such models suggested by Cohen (1974), Nolan and Nolan (1989), Smith (1992), Stoddard (1996) and Vokunič (1996) (for details refer Santos, 2003).

To describe the in-between situation of contemporary travel, use of different terms such as pilgrimage tourism and religious tourism has become popular. Pilgrimage tourism, according to Tyrakwoski (1994), rests on the realization of the opportunity provided by religious travel for leisure and the subsequent move from traditional pilgrimages towards holiday (vacation) tourism. Observing the Mexican pilgrimage to Tlaxcala, Tyrakwoski (1994) argues that the process of its formation and practices is determined by internal factors such as strong traditions and an inner conscience. Religious tourism is that form of tourism to sacred sites that is motivated, partly or wholly, by religious motives (Rinschede, 1992) and is closely or loosely connected with holidaymaking or with journeys undertaken for social, cultural or political reasons over short or long distances (Tomasi, 2002).

The idea of religious tourism as different from pilgrimage, Santos (2003) observes, arose in Europe in the post-war years, resulting from the decline in religious practice, the growing popularity of trips by car or coach and the secularization of societies (Santos, 2003). Use of this term gained popularity due to its automatic imposition by the market in exploiting a travel segment that combines both spiritual and secular elements in promoting programmes that include visits to religious and non-religious sites (Jackowski, cited in Santos, 2003), and also due to discussions of European Churchpeople regarding the problems and prospects posed by visitors who visit both pilgrimage shrines and religious attractions (Nolan and Nolan, 1989). Many scholars see religious tourism as nested within cultural tourism, because religion is understood as a part of culture (Rinschede, 1992; Santos, 2003; Singh and Sagar, 2004) and, in more practical terms, provides a range of resources including 'religious sites and artefacts' used in the creation of cultural tourism (Nolan and Nolan, 1989; Gettigan, 2003).

Within the Indian context, many scholars maintain that pilgrimage represents the oldest form of tourism, where pilgrimage as a practice of religious tourism 'encouraged local benefits, people's participation, the spiritual and social enhancement of the guests and host, beside respect for the environment' (Singh and Singh, 1999, p. 194). A few studies have shown that commercialization and secularization of pilgrimage has led to the notion that pilgrimage approaches leisure travel (Singh, 2004), and that pilgrimage appears similar to tourism in its impacts (Kaur, 1985; Singh, 2002). Rinschede (1992) observes that religious travel offers the only opportunity of travel for people in developing countries where mass tourism is in its incipient stage. This is clearly evident in India, where more than 100 million Indians embark on pilgrimages each year (*Times of India*, 2001), thereby contributing considerably to the domestic tourism (Richter, 1989). Pilgrimages, in their modern expression, appear to take the form of multipurpose travel, incorporating elements of tourist travel (Singh and Singh, 1999; Singh, 2004), reflecting the changing cultural and economic aspirations of the emerging middle and elite classes in India.

Recent developments in pilgrimage travel published in the popular press indicate its development as an organized tourism activity. Deccan Aviation, India's largest air charter company, has signed up with the state government of Jammu and Kashmir to provide a helicopter shuttle service to the base of the shrine of Vaishno Devi (*Economic Times*, 2002). Though travel company Thomas Cook started its operations in the UK with religious excursions in the 19th century (Rinschede, 1992), it has now entered into the domestic pilgrim travel market of India in association with Indian Railways (*Times of India*, 2001), promising three-star comforts for its clients during their pilgrimages. The National Insurance Company has begun to tailor insurance policies for devotees on annual pilgrimages, and that has boosted the insurance industry's confidence in such travel (*Economic Times*, 2001). Sporadic attempts by the Indian Tourism Ministry to promote pilgrim centres and set up a 'pilgrim tourism development board' to boost domestic traffic (*Financial Express*, 2002) have had limited success in the absence of a clear and defined public policy.

There seem to be sound reasons for believing that the modern expression of pilgrimage in India seems to be emerging along the lines of tourism. Not only has there been a phenomenal increase in the number of people travelling to sacred sites (largely due to improvements in the accessibility and availability of the transport), but also substantial qualitative changes seem to have occurred with regards to motivation, journey and destination of such visits. Though these visits still retain the religious dimension, 'the motivation' and 'the journey' display more touristic features than do traditional pilgrimages. This is illustrated in the following empirical study of Vrindavan, the religious centre at the core of the sacred complex of Braj, in Northern India.

Study Area: Vrindavan

Vrindavan is a popular Hindu pilgrimage centre at the core of the sacred complex of Braj, in Uttar Pradesh, Northern India. Braj represents a cultural region that includes hundreds of sacred sites associated with the mythology of Krishna, the human incarnation of Vishnu (Bajpai, 1954; Entwistle, 1987; Sharma, 1988). Vrindavan is famous as a pilgrimage centre and religious centre in Braj for its mythological importance as the place of Krishna's residence and divine plays (*lilas*) – and more generally as a miniature cosmic representation of Braj, itself (Sharma, 1988).

Vrindavan is also seen as the headquarters of the Vaishnava bhakti movement and has more than 5000 temples dedicated to Krishna. Almost all sects of Vaishnavas have their religious establishments – including temples, ashrams (hermitages) and religious seats – in Vrindavan. Vrindavan is located 150 km south of Delhi (the national capital) and about 50 km north-west of Agra (famous for the Taj Mahal). As such, it falls within the 'Golden Triangle for tourism' in Northern India that has Delhi, Agra and Jaipur as its three most important tourist destinations. By virtue of its location, Vrindavan lends itself to becoming a major centre for tourism. Modern Vrindavan is a municipal town having a geographical area of 24 km^2, with a population of 60,000. It is easily accessible from the Delhi–Agra highway and attracts more than 3.5 million visitors every year.

Pilgrimage in Vrindavan

Vrindavan is a centre for two types of pilgrimages: (i) the long, circuitous journey and pilgrimage to specific sacred sites in Braj (*Braj yatra*); and (ii) the shorter, quicker trip to Braj. Shackley (2001) sees the former journey along the pilgrimage route as a 'longer-term visit' and visit to a site or pilgrimage centre to participate in an event, conference or meeting as a 'short-term visit'.

Braj yatra (literally, journey through Braj) involves circumambulation of the entire Braj region following a route with a perimeter of about 84 *kos* (300 km), covering an area of about 2500 km² around Vrindavan. Braj yatra has received wide attention in Vaishnava literature and from academics alike (see Growse, 1883; Bajpai, 1954; Entwistle, 1987; Haberman, 1994). The contemporary version of the Braj yatra and the changes from its traditional form have been discussed at length by Shinde (2006).

The focus of this chapter is on the pilgrimage to the sacred centre of Vrindavan, involving a brief visit to take *darshana* of Krishna or some religious guru. Such short-term visits now constitute a major proportion of visits to Vrindavan. Following a brief description of the traditional form of pilgrimage, the author compares this with personal experiences of pilgrimage to Vrindavan (in March 2005) and argues that what one sees today does not represent the spiritually focused traditional pilgrimage, but rather modern tourism.

In a typical visit, the pilgrim undertakes a linear journey from home to a particular sacred centre and returns. Commonly known as pilgrimage, such visits have generally been the mainstay of any sacred centre and have helped the pilgrimage industry flourish (Vidyarthi, 1961; Morinis, 1984; Van Der Veer, 1988; Dubey, 1995). Generally, these are short-term and include two types of visit: (i) event-based visits where visitors come for a specific event, such as festival or fair; and (ii) frequent visits, where visitors repeatedly visit the sacred centre whenever they get an opportunity to do so and for different reasons, such as seeing the God and the religious gurus and seeking their blessings. Festivals are a rich resource for tourism (Nolan and Nolan, 1989) and, as such, are promoted as attractions for cultural tourism by the tourism ministry in India. Events such as festivals and fairs are by their nature, a mix of tourism and religious activities (Getz, 1991), and therefore do not demand separate attention. Rather, the frequent, linear, short-term visits constitute a major proportion of visits to the sacred centres of Mathura, Vrindavan and Govardhan in Braj, and are more or less evenly spread out throughout the calendar year.

The main motivation for pilgrims to visit Vrindavan is to derive spiritual experience by seeing and experiencing places where Krishna performed his divine activities. Krishna in Braj (and Vrindavan) is seen in 'human context, free of godly manifestations' and a form that human beings can immediately relate to, 'without having to think of Him as God' (Gelberg, 1983).

It is only when pilgrims immerse themselves in devotion of Krishna, with the emotion of being a companion of Krishna (*sakha bhav*), that they achieve supreme bliss and happiness (Haberman, 1994). This uniquely distinguishes pilgrimage to Vrindavan (and Brig) from other pilgrimages that are generally undertaken for reasons including rites of passage, wish fulfilment and thanksgiving. It follows, however, the typical structure of Indian pilgrimage in which pilgrims are referred to as *tirtha-yatri*, meaning people travelling (*yatra*) on a pilgrimage (*tirtha*) and who, during their pilgrimage, visit specific temples, following a certain pattern of movement and performing certain rituals with the help of religious functionaries (Vidyarthi, 1961; Bhardwaj, 1973; Singh, 1997).

Pilgrims accomplish the traditional pilgrimage with help from religious specialists, commonly known as *pandas*. Typically, the pilgrim stay at a facility provided by the *panda*, be it the *panda*'s own house or an ashram or *dharamshala* (pilgrim lodge), which provide free accommodation. The itinerary includes the taking of a ritual bath (*snana*) in the Yamuna River, visiting different temples, taking *darshan* of the deity, attending specific prayers (*aarti*) and listening to *katha* and religious sermons. The period of stay ranges from 1 day to more than 6 months. The *panda* organized all of this and kept records of the visit and, in return, received his *dakshina* (fees). In essence, visitors belonged to a particular *panda* (*tirth purohit ka yatri*) during the pilgrimage. However, the *pandas* have no role when the purpose is to visit a religious guru. Circumambulation of the sacred centre is an important feature of Indian pilgrimage (Eck, 1982; Saraswati, 1985; Singh, 1997), and Vrindavan is no exception. Pilgrims usually undertake the 21-km *parikrama* (peripheral circumambulation) of Vrinadavan during their pilgrimage. Many visits to Vrindavan coincide with the religiously important occasions or specific calendrical cycles.

Contemporary expression of pilgrimage in Vrindavan

A contemporary pilgrimage to Vrindavan is very different to what has been described in the preceding section. The differences in the 'journey', the composition of visitors, and their motivation and behaviour are obvious, demonstrating more touristic characteristics. In the past, most visits were of longer duration. Staying in a pilgrimage centre for at least one night is deemed necessary for acquiring the benefits of the visit. Today, the majority of regular visits comprise day visits, meaning that visitors (who can be termed day visitors or day-trippers) do not spend more than 1 day at a particular site. In any case, whenever people want to stay overnight, they stay in the purpose-built facilities in modern ashrams. A large proportion of visitors today constitute individual families and young couples from the urban centres of Delhi, Agra and other nearby cities as day visitors or weekend visitors.

The behaviour of the majority of modern visitors defies the notion of pilgrimage as a spiritual pursuit away from worldly concerns. Local people recollect that pilgrims 'used to remove their footwear on entering the boundary of Vrindavan and walk barefoot, sleep in the verandah of a *dharmshala*, cook their own food and defaecate outside the sacred territory of Vrindavan'. In essence, self-regulation and self-discipline were the hallmarks of a pilgrim.

Nowadays, visitors bring with them their urban lifestyle of consumerism and seem to be less sensitive to the sacredness of the place. There is no control over visitors' behaviour and, as a result, the self-discipline associated with a religious site is gone. Such visitors in Vrindavan nowadays are referred to as *yatri* (just plain travellers) rather than *tirth-yatris*. Locals mark the difference: '*Tirthayatri* used to come with *bhav* (devotion), but many *yatris* now come for tourism and entertainment.'

Oblivious to local people, such visitors behave like tourists and are more interested in the eating establishments than in any devotional activity except, perhaps, visiting the temple. They want to stay in bigger rooms with more facilities. One informant summed it up:

> The old form (*svarup*) of Vrindavan has eroded especially since the coming of *Delhiwallahs* in large numbers. They come as if they are on a morning walk and go as if they just finished their evening walk. Today the *yatri* does not come with the vision (*drishti*) of *tirth yatra*, where does he have time now for thinking about what he is seeing or even understanding the form of Vrindavan – he is just a tourist of two hours, unlike the tirth yatri who was never in a hurry. Slow movement of pilgrims is over now, everybody is in a rush and on 'eat and drink party' (*khao-piyo abhiyan*).

The motivation for such travel seems to be the worldly reasons of material well-being typical of urban visitors who seek refuge before the supreme power in the wake of a growing sense of uncertainty and insecurity within the modern world (Guha and Gandhi, 1995; Singh, 1995). Though Krishna, like any other God, is worshipped for material benefits and general welfare, he has never been portrayed as a 'wish-fulfilling' God whose worship needed to be accomplished with certain rituals. But most day visitors come to Vrindavan seeking Krishna's help in solving problems related to their mundane existence. A common discourse among the local *pandas* is that: 'People come for the God and not for Vrindavan, and therefore it is not the place that is important now, it is the God who helps them who is important, that too in a particular temple.' However, a contrary discourse emphasizes that most people come to visit Vrindavan rather than the God, because it provides them with an easily accessible destination to spend their leisure time.

Itineraries for most day visitors include the three popular temples: (i) Banke Bihari temple for its fame as a 'wish-fulfilment deity'; (ii) Rangji temple for its grandeur; and (iii) the Isckon temple for its urban appeal. The last of these is also one of the reasons for the surge in numbers of urban visitors in recent years, because it is devoid of orthodox religious rituals important in Vaishnaism. Many day visitors do not undertake the *parikrama*, but usually go along the Yamuna riverfront and take a boat ride in one of the colourful boats.

The traditional role of the *pandas* has diminished in the light of such travel, which has rendered them largely redundant. Instead, there has been a steady increase in the number of lay guides. A guide, in their limited role, takes visitors on a tour to different temples, tells them about different rituals but does not necessarily perform for the clients. This modern version is more of a 'tourist guide', who is paid for taking the visitor to the main sites and providing visitors with their interpretation and legends.

Along similar lines, the traditional accommodation in *dharamshalas* has given way to more modern types of accommodation facilities, such as purpose-built guesthouses and ashrams. In parallel, the emergence of taxi drivers and tour operators who specialize in tours such as *Braj Darshan* that take visitors to different sacred centres in Braj is evident. However, the behaviour of these taxi drivers, who typify the image of carefree *mastram* (Lynch, 1990) and who are rarely bothered about the emotions of the pilgrims they carry in their vehicles, is very disturbing. Their insensitive and rowdy behaviour raises serious doubts about the 'religious' and the 'sacred' component of the pilgrimage.

Pilgrims intuitively know that the rituals of pilgrimage are aimed at communication (Voye, 2002), but the majority of visitors do not perform (or are not able to perform) rituals due to the size of the crowd in the temples and the need to hurry to make it to the car to visit the next scared spot. Thus, the connection between the ritual and its spiritual meaning has lost its potential for realization. However, there also are visitors – mainly ardent devotees – who religiously perform rituals at every temple and place they stop. They even get down into the water of Yamuna to perform the rituals of bath (*snana*) and sprinkling of water (*acahaman*) (even if the water is seemingly not clear).

The experience of a pilgrim is the central aspect of pilgrimage and is difficult to describe, but generally includes a feeling of exaltation and liminality (Turner and Turner, 1978; Morinis, 1984). This is achieved in Vrindavan by cultivating the appropriate sensibility while viewing the sacred landscape (Entwistle, 1987). The modern pilgrimage, however, does not help in engendering such sensitivity because the mechanical motor car has replaced the physical body of the pilgrim, which was, itself, a vehicle in which to experience pilgrimage. The self-restraint, the endurance, the beautiful pain of journeying, the time to think and to immerse in spirituality – all seems to be fading. One cannot help but wonder whether visitors derive any genuine peace of mind by not realizing the sacredness of the landscape on such short-duration sightseeing tours. But be reminded that, for a firm devotee, however, even such a short visit is overwhelming enough to take him/her into a trance at some point of time during the visit. However, for most, it is a just a visit to another temple of Krishna.

Key observations

The improvements in accessibility and availability of transport have long replaced the traditional and pure form of 'pilgrimage on foot' for the majority of visitors to sacred sites such as Vrindavan. Apart from public transport, such as trains and buses, the private car has become one of the most important modes of travel to sacred sites. With the rise of the Indian middle and upper-middle classes, with their disposable income, travelling by car has become almost a norm and status symbol. Frequent trips that people make to sacred sites in their own vehicles further reinforce such social status. This is visible in the hordes of urban visitors from the nearby regions in Vrindavan (where one may see more than 1000 cars on weekends).

Both pilgrimage and tourism have a 'getting out' character that relates to the abandonment of accustomed social structures and daily routines (Cohen, 1992). However, a modern pattern of 'getting away' to a religious place as a change from the mundane urban life is evident for most visitors, typically on their weekend trips to Vrindavan. The meaning of their visit to Vrindavan, many visitors claim, 'offers them an elevated feeling of spending a holiday in a religious place with their family and a satisfying experience of fulfilling a religious need'.

Such visitors do not engage in elaborate rituals, keep away from *pandas* and spend relatively far less time in the temples. Rather, they wander around, buy some religious trinkets (usually on their first trip only) and spend more time and money on eating and getting there. Visits definitely seem to be more than just religious when one visitor appreciating the kind of food offered in Vrindavan remarked: 'We don't get this kind of *lassi* (sweet buttermilk) in Delhi.'

This supports Cohen's (1992) argument that tourism gives mere pleasure and enjoyment – derived from the novelty and change provided by the destination – while pilgrimage provokes religious 'rupture' or 'exaltation'. The idea that 'free time' and availability of leisure drives such travel puts it within the realm of tourism (Krippendorf, 1987; Smith and Brent, 2001; Tomasi, 2002). Writing about personal visits to many pilgrimage centres in India, one journalist (reporting in *Hinduism Today*) illustrates the point: 'Whenever I have the opportunity, I try to combine my business travel or vacation with pilgrimage. As for most middle-class Indians, it is an essential compromise given the limited resources of time and money' (Malik, 2001).

The meaning of the pilgrimage is related to the experience of travelling itself (Morinis, 1992; Tomasi, 2002). Pilgrimage in Braj is 'sacred sightseeing', where the numinous quality of the landscape is experienced by travelling the land itself and appreciating the legends associated with it (Haberman, 1994; Kinsley, 1998). However, the pilgrim (in relation to the bodily experience) can invoke such an experience only with the right emotion (*bhav*), motivation, self-restraint and sensitive behaviour.

The journey by car, limited to 'driving through the landscape' and seeing 'spots' does not permit the contact of physical body with the landscape, resulting in the loss of its deeper meaning. The religious commitment and intensity of motivation (thanksgiving, vows, spiritual asceticism, etc.) specific to pilgrimage is not easily found in visitors to Vrindavan. The local community in Vrindavan also reiterate such opinions about the visitors and, in common parlance, refer to them as 'religious tourists'; without doubt, they are not 'pilgrims' in the true sense.

From an organizational perspective, Tomasi (2002) argues for the inclusion of contemporary religious tourism as part of the tourist industry because: (i) large-scale movement of pilgrims is comparable to mass tourism; and (ii) pilgrims and tourists alike use the same infrastructure and services. In accordance with changes in visitor patterns and the expansion of pilgrimage travel, many tourism enterprises have emerged in Vrindavan. In the past 5 years, about 50 tour operators have established their agencies and more than 100 eating outlets (and many more informal food vendors) have opened their enterprises in the vicinity of the most popular temples, indicating growing tourism activity. They cater to the consumer pilgrimage, where visitors demand good accommodation and contemporary food. Such services, according to Gladstone (2005), support the 'informal sector domestic tourism' (citing the example of Vrindavan in particular).

The professionalism inherent in tourism enterprise is also now appearing in the pilgrimage industry. It would be prudent here to cite an example that illustrates this point. During the extravagant celebrations of the Holi festival in 2005, one religious guru organized a 'spiritual retreat' for a fortnight on the white island (*shewt-dweep*) in the middle of the Yamuna River in Vrindavan, where participants were charged about INR2000–4000 (approximately €30–60) per night per person for staying in fully furnished 'Swiss tents'. Advertising and marketing of such events within the region and nearby cities has become common practice.

Summary

The study of visits to Vrindavan illustrates the changes that are taking place in contemporary pilgrimage in India. Pilgrimage in its traditional form has not completely disappeared or been replaced, but has been dwarfed by the increasing characteristics of tourism. In its modern expression, pilgrimage seems to be a precursor of tourism as it tends to lean more towards leisure-oriented travel. The focus has shifted from a journey to a trip to the destination that excludes the hardships of the journey and expresses the distinct consumerist behaviour of visitors. It follows the modern trend where: '[T]he journey has been abolished ... there is only the point of departure and that of arrival' (Ferrarotti, cited in Tomasi, 2002). There are good reasons to believe that this has led to the weakening of the spiritual connection between the journey and the experience, unique to pilgrimage.

Tyrakwoski (1994) argues that: 'The aim of real pilgrims is no way a holiday in the sense of leisure tourism; such relaxation is incidental to journey' (Tyrakwoski, 1994, p. 198), but a clear association with holidaymaking is visible in visits to Vrindavan. However, such travel. It finds support in Santos's (2003) observation that 'Most urban visitors are seeking the supernatural in accordance with a way of thinking and acting that is common in contemporary societies' (Santos, 2003, p. 36). It is neither pilgrimage nor tourism, but a mix of the two, tending towards the latter. However, the religious dimension is still very strong and this poses the difficulty of distinguishing it as purely tourism. In order to fulfil the religious needs, people visit such places of religious importance under the guidance of religious functionaries. If the religious element were to be taken out, say from Vrindavan or Braj or from the visit itself, it can only be surmised whether anybody would be interested in seeing the otherwise barren and unappealing landscape of Vrindavan.

The transformation of pilgrimage into a mere 'sightseeing tour' and a 'getaway', with the associated qualitative changes, warrants the need for a new label for such travel. This chapter has argued that this can better be explained by 'religious tourism', because of the presence of both religious and recreational features. Using this term has more neutral connotations and 'fewer theological and traditional implications than the word pilgrimage' (Nolan and Nolan, 1989), and therefore enables us to explore the possibility of its integration into tourism policy.

Empirically, this chapter has also shown that any explanation of religious tourism needs to emphasize the aspects of journey and the behaviour of visitors rather than simply on motivation and destination of the travel – as has been the case with most of the Western literature on religious tourism.

References

Bajpai, K.D. (1954) *Braj ka Itihas* [History of Braj] (in Hindi). Akhil Bhartiya Braj Sahitya Mandal, Mathura, India.

Bhardwaj, S.M. (1973) *Hindu Places of Pilgrimage in India.* University of California Press, Berkeley, California.

Caplan, A. (1997) The role of pilgrimage priests in perpetuating spatial organizations within Hinduism. In: Morinis, A. and Stoddard, R. (eds) *Sacred Places, Sacred Spaces: the Geography of Pilgrimages. Geoscience and Man.* Vol. 34, Louisiana State University Press, Baton Rouge, Louisiana.

Cohen, E. (1974) Who is a tourist? A conceptual clarification. *The Sociological Review* 2 (4), 527–555.

Cohen, E. (1992) Pilgrimage and Tourism: Convergence and Divergence. In: Morinis, A. (ed.) *Sacred Journeys: the Anthropology of Pilgrimage.* Greenwood Press, Westport, Connecticut, pp. 47–61.

Dubey, D.P. (ed.) (1995) *Pilgrimage Studies: Sacred Places, Sacred Traditions.* Society of Pilgrimage Studies, Allahabad, India.

Eck, D. (1982) *Banaras, City of Light.* Knopf (distributed by Random House, New York).

Economic Times (2001) Insurance cover for Devotees. 25 January, Bangalore, India.

Economic Times (2002) Deccan to ferry pilgrims to Vaishnodevi. 27 September, Bangalore, India.

Entwistle, A. (1987) *Braj: Centre of Krishna Pilgrimage.* Egbert Forsten, Groningen, Netherlands.

Financial Express (2002) Tourism ministry to take care of pilgrim facilities. 24 May, Bangalore, India.

Fuller, C.J. (1992) The political and economic position of the Minaksi temple priests in the 1980s. In: Bakker, H. (ed.) *The Sacred Centre as the Focus of Political Interest – Proceedings of the Symposium held on the 375th Anniversary of the University of Groningen,* 5–8 March 1989, Groningen, Netherlands.

Gelberg, S. (ed.) (1983) Interview with Srivatsa Goswami. In: *Hare Krishna, Hare Krishna.* Grove Press, Inc., New York.

Gettigan, F. (2003) An analysis of cultural tourism and its relationship with religious sites. In: Fernandes, C., Mcgettigan, F. and Edwards, J. (eds) *Religious Tourism and Pilgrimage – Conference Proceedings of The 1st Expert Meeting of ATLAS – Religious Tourism And Pilgrimage Research Group,* 23–27 April 2003, Tourism Board of Leiria/Fátima, Portugal.

Getz, D. (1991) *Festivals, Special Events and Tourism.* Van Nostrand Reinhold, New York.

Gladstone, D. (2005) *From Pilgrimage to Package Tour: Travel and Tourism in the Third World.* Routledge, New York.

Graburn, N.H. (1977) Tourism: the sacred journey. In: Smith, V. (ed.) *Hosts and Guests: the Anthropology of Tourism.* University of Pennsylvania Press, Philadelphia, Pennsylvania.

Graburn, N.H. (2001) Secular ritual: a general theory of tourism. In: Smith, V.L. and Brent, M. (eds) *Hosts and Guests Revisited: Tourism Issues of the 21st Century.* Cognizant Communication Corporation, New York.

Growse, F.S. (1883) *Mathura: a District Memoir,* 3rd edn (reprinted in 1978 by The New Order Book Co., Ahmedabad, India).

Guha, S.B. and Gandhi, S. (1995) Evolution and growth of Hindu pilgrimage centres in Greater Bombay. In: Dubey, D.P. (ed.) *Sacred Places, Sacred Traditions.* Society of Pilgrimage Studies, Allahabad, India, pp. 179–189.

Haberman, D. (1994) *Journey through the Twelve Forests: an Encounter with Krishna.* Oxford University Press, New York.

Kaelber, L. (2002) The sociology of medieval pilgrimage: contested views and shifting boundaries. In: Swatos, W.H. Jr and Tomasi, L. (eds) *From Medieval Pilgrimage to Religious Tourism: the Social and Cultural Economics of Piety.* Praeger, Westport, Connecticut.

Kaur, J. (1985) *Himalayan Pilgrimages and New Tourism.* Himalayan Books, New Delhi, India.

Kinsley, D. (1998) Learning the story of the land: reflections on the liberating power of geography and pilgrimage in the Hindu tradition. In: Nelson, L.E. (ed.) *Purifying the Earthly Body of God.* State University of New York Press, Albany, New York.

Krippendorf, J. (1987) *The Holidaymakers: Understanding the Impact of Leisure and Travel* (translated by Vera Andrassy. Ferienmenschen, Butterworth-Heinemann, Oxford, UK).

Lynch, O. (1990) The Mastram: Emotion and person among Mathura's Chaubes. In: Lynch, O. (ed.) *Divine Passions: the Social Construction of Emotion in India.* University of California Press, Berkeley, California.

MacCannell, D. (1976) *The Tourist: a New Theory of the Leisure Class.* Shocklen Books, New York.

Malik, R. (2001) Chances for pilgrimage. *Hinduism Today,* November/December, Hawaii.

Morinis, E.A. (1984) *Pilgrimage in Hindu Tradition: a Case Study of West Bengal.* Oxford University Press, Delhi, India.

Morinis, E.A. (ed.) (1992) *Sacred Journeys: the Anthropology of Pilgrimage.* Greenwood Press, Westport, Connecticut.

Nolan, M.L. and Nolan, S. (1989) *Christian Pilgrimage in Modern Western Europe.* University of North Carolina Press, Chapel Hill, North Carolina and London.

Parry, P.J. (1994) *Death in Banaras.* Cambridge University Press, Cambridge, UK.

Richter, L. (1989) *The Politics of Tourism in Asia.* University of Hawaii Press, Honolulu, Hawaii.

Rinschede, G. (1992) Forms of religious tourism. *Annals of Tourism Research* 19, 51– 67.

Santos, M.D.G.M.P. (2003) Religious tourism: contributions towards a clarification of concepts. In: Fernandes, C., Mcgettigan, F. and Edwards, J. (eds) *Religious Tourism and Pilgrimage – Conference Proceedings of the 1st Expert Meeting of* ATLAS – Religious Tourism and Pilgrimage Research Group, 23–27 April 2003, Tourism Board of Leiria/Fátima, Portugal.

Saraswati, B. (1985) *Tradition of Tirthas in India: the Anthropology of Hindu Pilgrimage.* N.K. Bose Memorial Foundation, Varanasi, India.

Shackley, M. (2001) *Managing Sacred Sites: Service Provision and Visitor Experience.* Continuum, London.

Sharma, G. (1988) Vrindavan ke prachin ullekh aur namakaran. In: Verma, T.P., Sharan, S. and Singh, D.P. (eds) *Yug-yugeen Braj.* Bhartiya Itihas Sankalan Samiti, Vijaygarh House, Varanasi, Uttar Pradesh, India.

Shinde, K. (2006) Religious tourism: intersection of contemporary pilgrimage and tourism in India. In: Robinson, M. and Picard, D. (eds) *Journeys of Expressions V: Tourism and the Roots/Routes of Religious Festivity.* Sheffield Hallam University, Sheffield, UK.

Singh, P.K. (1995) Secular aspects of a pilgrimage: the case of Haridwar. In: Jha, M. (ed.) *Pilgrimage: Concepts, Themes, Issues and Methodology.* Inter-India Publications, New Delhi, India.

Singh, R.P.B. (1997) Sacred space and pilgrimage in Hindu society: the case of Varanasi. In: Morinis, A. and Stoddard, R. (eds) *Sacred Places, Sacred Spaces: the Geography of Pilgrimages. Geoscience and Man.* Vol. 34, Louisiana State University Press, Baton Rouge, Louisiana, pp. 191–207.

Singh, R.P.B. (2005) The geography of Hindu pilgrimage in India: from trend to perspective. In: Jackowski, A. (ed.) *Geography and Sacrum.* Instytut Geografii Gospodarki Przestrzennej, Uniwersytet Jagielloński, Kraków, Poland.

Singh, S. (2002) Managing the impacts of tourist and pilgrim mobility in the Indian Himalayas. *Revue De Geographie Alpine* 90 (1), 25–35.

Singh, S. (2004) Religion, heritage and travel: case references from the Indian Himalayas. *Current Issues in Tourism* 7 (1), 44–65.

Singh, T.V. and Singh, S. (1999) Tourism and the Himalayan tribes: searching for sustainable development options for the Bhotias of the Bhyundar Valley. In: Pearce, D.G. and Butler, R.W. (eds) *Contemporary Issues in Tourism Development*. Routledge, London, pp. 192–210.

Smith, V. (1992) The quest in guest. *Annals of Tourism Research* 19, 1–17.

Smith, V. and Brent, M. (eds) (2001) *Hosts and Guests Revisited: Tourism Issues of the 21st Century*. Cognizant Communication Corporation, New York.

Stoddard, R.H. (1996) Tourism and religious travel: a geographic perspective. *Proceedings of Conference 'Tourism, Religions and Peace'*, Milan, 30 May–2 June, 16 pp.

Times of India (2001) Thomas on the pilgrim trail. 15 May, Mumbai, India.

Tomasi, L. (2002) Homo viator: from pilgrimage to religious tourism via the journey. In: Swatos, W.H. Jr and Tomasi, L. (eds) *From Medieval Pilgrimage to Religious Tourism: the Social and Cultural Economics of Piety*. Praeger, Westport, Connecticut, pp. 1– 24.

Turner, V.W. and Turner, E. (1978) *Image and Pilgrimage in Christian Culture*. Columbia University Press, New York.

Tyrakwoski, K. (1994) Pilgrims to the Mexican Highlands. In: Bhardwaj, S.M., Rinshcede, G. and Seivers, A. (eds) *Pilgrimage in the Old and New World: Geographia Religionum*. Dietrich Reimer Verlag, Berlin.

Van Der Veer, P. (1988) *Gods on Earth: the Management of Religious Experience and Identity in a North Indian Pilgrimage Centre*. The Athlone Press, London.

Vidyarthi, L.P. (1961) *The Sacred Complex in Hindu Gaya*. Asia Publishing House, Bombay, India.

Vidyarthi, L., Jha, M. and Saraswati, B. (1979), *The Sacred Complex of Kashi. A Microcosm of Indian Civilisation*. Concept Publishers, New Delhi, India.

Vokunič, B. (1996) *Tourism and Religion*. Pergamon, Oxford, UK, 208 pp.

Voye, L. (2002) Popular religion and pilgrimages in Western Europe. In: Swatos, W.H. Jr and Tomasi, L. (eds) *From Medieval Pilgrimage to Religious Tourism: the Social and Cultural Economics of Piety*. Praeger, Westport, Connecticut.

York, M. (2002) Contemporary pagan pilgrimages. In: Swatos, W.H. Jr and Tomasi, L. (eds) *From Medieval Pilgrimage to Religious Tourism: the Social and Cultural Economics of Piety*. Praeger, Westport, Connecticut.

16 Case Study 7: Islamic Pilgrimage and the Market Need for Travel Insurance

TAHIR RASHID

Hospitality and Retailing Centre, Leslie Silver International Faculty, Leeds Metropolitan University, Leeds, UK; e-mail: t.rashid@leedsmet.ac.uk

Introduction

The importance of travel insurance is well understood by the Western traveller; however, many Muslim pilgrims travelling to the Islamic holy places do not take out travel insurance as they either believe it is against their religion or are simply unaware of its importance. This chapter discusses these issues.

The chapter begins with an explanation of the most important journey in a Muslim's life, the *hajj*. Possible reasons are explored why Muslims do not take out insurance, and an analysis of Islamic business principles and the Islamic insurance principle of *takaful* is made. A comparison is made between the typical Western form of insurance and Islamic insurance, followed by a case study of the Takaful International Insurance company, based in Bahrain.

The Hajj and the Umra

Muslims have been performing pilgrimages to several holy places and shrines around the world for the last 1400 years as part of their religion. They travel to various religious destinations in Syria, Iran, Iraq, Turkey, Pakistan and other parts of the world. However, the main pilgrimage that Muslims must perform is the one to the holy city of Makkah, Saudi Arabia, known as the *hajj* or *umra* (minor hajj).

For Muslims, the hajj is the fifth and final pillar of Islam. It is the journey that every sane adult Muslim must undertake at least once in their lifetime if they can afford it and are physically able. Every year around 3 million Muslims converge on Makkah. They visit a shrine in the city known as the Ka'aba, built by Ibrahim (Abraham) and Isma'il (Ishmael) at the command of Allah (God). It is a place for all who wish to reaffirm their faith (see also Chapter 10, this volume).

The umra is an extra, optional pilgrimage and can be performed at most times during the year, whereas the hajj has to be performed at a specific time. Although the umra includes some of the rituals of hajj, they are shortened and are fewer in number.

To perform hajj, pilgrims have to go through a number of stages during the 6 days of hajj. The climax of the hajj occurs on the 9th day of the *Dhul-hajjah* (12th month of the Islamic year) until the 13th day of the Dhul-hajjah, the *Arafah*. Pilgrims perform the following duties during the 6 days of the Dhul-hajjah. On the 1st day, pilgrims travel out of Makkah towards Mina, a small uninhabited village east of the city. During the 2nd day (the 9th of Dhul-hajjah) pilgrims leave Mina for the plain of Arafat for the *wuquf* – the standing, the central rite of the hajj.

Muslims travel to Makkah by various means from all parts of the world: by air, sea, car and on foot, to perform this spiritual pilgrimage. Pilgrims feel unanimous in the view that nothing can quite prepare them for the sheer beauty of the experience and the overwhelming feeling of humbleness that overcomes them during the pilgrimage of hajj. One pilgrim, called Aysha, reflected:

> I hope if it's not closeness to God I hope I've learned how I can become closer, how I can become more sincere with myself. I think that's most important because you have to be very honest with yourself about who you are and where you want to be and how you want to be. And I think it's only then you can get close to anyone else. In terms of spirituality you need to really know your soul to be able to know how you can get closer to Allah.
>
> (http://www.bbc.co.uk/religion/religions/islam/customs/hajj/ hajj2005_12.shtml; 2006)

This is never an easy journey: the hajj and umra carry enormous risks for the pilgrim. The hajj, in particular, is fraught with hardship, risk and danger from beginning to end. The sheer number of people gathering in a small place for a short period of time presents enormous challenges for the organizers and the pilgrims. As Muslims arrive from all over the world, there is the risk of missed flights, trains, etc., loss of baggage and valuables, illness, injury and even death on this journey. In fact, every year several hundred Muslims die from incidents ranging from stampede, sickness and transport accidents to fire. In the 2006 hajj, over 345 pilgrims died as a result from a stampede, while several hundred were injured in the incident (http://www.cnn.com/2006/WORLD/meast/ 01/12/hajj.stampede/index.html; 2006).

With so much risk and danger involved, it would be common sense to take out travel insurance for the purpose of this journey. However, few take out the insurance, and those are mainly Muslims from Western countries.

The Question of Insurance for Muslims

Why do Muslims not take out travel insurance?

Insurance generally does not play a big part in Muslim culture. Everything, according to common belief, is in the hands of God, and He alone is the sustainer and protector of all creatures. In fact, this somewhat resigned view does not contradict basic Islamic beliefs; but these also emphasize the exertion of human effort which helps to create a good standard of living without going against God's will.

Moreover, in the past there was only the Western model of insurance available, and this effectively did not meet the needs of Muslims without violating their beliefs. Therefore, most Muslims were unwilling to enter into such transactions – except for car insurance, which was considered unavoidable as it was strictly imposed by the power of law.

In contrast, non-Islamic types of insurance have targeted those sections of society in the Muslim world who are interested in insurance, regardless of its incompatibility with the *Shari'ah* principles. This section represents a minority in most Muslim countries, and advertising campaigns are targeted at these people only. This can be seen in the advertising language, which is usually in English, though the language of the Muslim world is mainly Arabic. Therefore there is a need for Islamic insurance and the market potential for it can be grasped from the size of the Muslim population around the world. Furthermore, in order to understand Islamic insurance, we need to examine Islamic business principles.

The Muslim population around the world

Islam is a global phenomenon and its influence on society and the economy is ubiquitous. In Africa, Islam is the second most dominant religion after Christianity, with over 40% of the population Muslim. In Asia, where Islam is again the second most popular religion after Hinduism, over 20% of the population abide by Islamic principles. Muslims also comprise approximately 7% of the European population. In the USA, the number of Muslims has grown from a mere 10,000 in 1900 to over 6.62 million in 1997. It is noteworthy that, in 2005, 1.56 billion Muslims were living in 184 different countries, comprising about 23.52% of the world population. The Muslim population is currently growing by more than 2% per year (http://www.islamicpopulation.com).

Islamic business principles

Many Muslim countries have increasingly persuaded companies to operate their businesses under the stringent guidelines of Islamic principles that emphasize equality in wealth distribution and shared responsibility among the participants in business transactions. According to Muslim laws, businesses are discouraged from engaging in business activities that have uncertain outcomes, and they can expect predetermined gains from financial transactions like interest on deposits or loans. Under Islamic law, interest cannot be charged to individuals or companies taking out loans in that country. It is obvious that these principles of operation are totally at variance with those prevailing in Western society.

Those unfamiliar with these principles may falsely conclude that Islam does not promote profit-oriented business transactions. In fact, Islamic principles do encourage people to engage in business transactions as long as they do not expect a predetermined return, even when the outcomes of such transactions are uncertain.

This encouragement became even stronger with the rapid developments in industrial infrastructure in Islamic countries from the early 1970s. As a result, numerous financial organizations were incorporated locally in those countries, and currently conduct business both at home and abroad. A number of Western financial players have already entered, or plan to enter, the Islamic market (e.g. Citibank, Credit Swiss Bank, HSBC Bank, etc.).

Islamic insurance

Takaful, an Arabic word meaning 'guaranteeing each other' denotes insurance, is approved specifically under Islamic jurisprudence or Shari'ah guidelines. It represents the concept of insurance based on mutual cooperation and the solidarity of those participating in a takaful scheme.

There was a need to develop a marketing strategy for takaful (insurance), because traditional insurance had certain features that contradicted some of the essential values of an Islamic financial contract. Muslims are directed by their faith to follow a path of righteousness in pursuing the activities of their daily lives; for example, gambling and exploitation are strictly forbidden.

In Islam, what is called *riba* or usury is considered an extreme form of exploitation. In addition, charging interest may not in itself be exploitative but it can certainly lead to forms of exploitation, and hence is strictly prohibited. Moreover, a genuine sense of fair play is fundamental in an Islamic financial arrangement. A lender who lends purely for profit by charging interest is exploiting his position as owner of the principal amount, without sharing in the risks associated with the use of that principal in the activities of the borrower.

The traditional Western contracts of insurance are built on such features. First, investments and operations are based on debt and equity, debt being interest-based. Also, where a loan is granted on a traditional insurance contract, interest iss charged. This is not permitted in Islamic contract. Secondly, the situation is liable to exploitation, where even though the contracts are priced at marketable level, the profit from insurance operations accrued from policyholders' money is owned by the shareholders. This point is also seen in Islamic eyes as policyholders gambling away the policy-holders' hard-earned savings for no return where there is no claim. In contrast, in a takaful contract, a 'no claim' scenario always leads to a refund of some of the policy-holder's money.

The difference between takaful insurance and 'classic insurance' is outlined in Table 16.1. The classical insurance business, which deals with the uncertainties of loss and does not conform well to Islamic principles, has therefore long been discouraged, if not prohibited, in Islamic society. In recent decades, however, many Islamic countries have found that insurance plays a crucial role in furthering their economic development and, even in some of those countries, Western (non-Islamic) insurers are allowed to underwrite risks. A few

Table 16.1. Differences between takaful (Islamic) insurance and 'classic' (Western) insurance (from Ajmal, 2000).

	Takaful insurance	'Classic' insurance
Shari'ah Supervisory Council	Shari'ah Supervisory Council, whose function is to monitor marketed products and fund investment	Not available
Contract	Mutual help/helping each other; participants own the insurance funds managed by the company; participants give up individual right to gain collective rights over contributions and benefits	Trading insurance is a buy–sell contract; policies are sold and buyers are policy-holders
Fund investment	Fund investment based on Shari'ah with sharing system Mudaraba, which means investment returns must not be driven by interest or by unethical commercial activities	Fund investment based on interest
Fund ownership	Common fund from participants (premiums) is owned by the participants; the company is only a mandatory holder, and manages it for a fee	Collecting fund from participants (premiums) is owned by the company, which is free to decide on its investments
Company	Company acts as a trustee and entrepreneur	Relationship between the company and the policy-holders is on a one-to-one basis
Payment of claims	From the participant's tabarru account (Goodness Fund); from the beginning, it has been planned that participants help each other in the event of an accident	From company's funds
Guarantees	No contractual guarantees are given by the company; joint indemnity between participants is a prerequisite of participation in a takaful scheme	The company guarantees benefits, especially in the case of death benefits
Sales distribution	A sale through salaried staff is normally preferred	Sales on basis of salary + commission
Regulation	(i) Statutory; (ii) Islamic principles through Shari'ah committee	Statutory only
Profit	Shared between participants and company (according to sharing principle, Mudaraba) and paid from defined funds under joint indemnity by participants	All profits to insurance company

local insurance companies were also incorporated in selected countries. None the less, it seemed a somewhat remote idea that Muslim communities would broadly accept the Western concept of insurance, for the reasons given above.

These communities have developed, instead, a new concept of insurance that complies with Islamic principles, called takaful insurance, discussed above.

This is a type of joint guarantee insurance mechanism based on 'the law of large numbers', in which a group of societal members pool their financial resources against particular loss exposures. Takaful insurance is now popular in many, although not all, Islamic countries, e.g. Indonesia, Malaysia, Saudi Arabia, Bahrain and United Arab Emirates. It is also practiced in some other countries with a significant Muslim population, e.g. Luxembourg and Switzerland and, recently, in the USA, the UK and Australia (Directory of Islamic Insurance, 2000).

Islamic socio-economic principles and insurance

In Islam, everything that happens in this world is through the will of Allah, and all activities of Muslims must conform to the Qur'an, the Muslim Holy Book. The Qur'an exhorts Muslims to accept all misfortunes as predestined, but in order not to passively endure them they must take necessary steps to minimize losses from unfortunate events. Muslims are also taught to abide by the Shari'ah – the code of social conduct that Islamic scholars have built based on the Qur'an.

For example, the Shari'ah applies the concept of *zakat*, under which all members of society should share equally in the benefits afforded by that society and all are united in helping others who suffer misfortune. It exhorts that all resources must be put to optimum use and that no individual has the right to wantonly squander his or her resources. Of course, neither an individual nor a state should gain from the misfortune of others.

The Shari'ah classifies all matters into either *halal* (those permitted) or *haram* (those prohibited). For example, it permits takaful (shared responsibility) and strongly encourages this practice among Muslims. It also permits zakat, which obliges the rich to help the destitute and weaker members of society. Also, the Shari'ah prohibits exploitation and risky investments because Muslim jurists generally consider that these activities are *ghara* (contracts in which results are unknown, hidden or speculative in nature) (Ismail, 1997), and the market must be a place for the exchange of products and services where all parties to each contract explicitly know the prices. *Riba* (charging of predetermined interest) is also forbidden in Islam regardless of the purpose for which such a loan is made and the rates at which interest is charged. As a result, Islamic financial transactions are, at least in principle, interest-free.

Ariff (1988) explained that the prohibition of riba does not mean that capital costs are less; however, Islam permits the making of a predetermined claim on the surplus derived from the use of capital for production. Therefore, a profit-sharing arrangement where the profit-sharing ratio – but not the rate of return – is predetermined is allowed in Islam. This arrangement can technically replace its Western counterpart, the interest rate, and allow capital to flow into this arrangement that offers the highest profit-sharing ratio to investors. The Shari'ah also permits share-holding, as Islam encourages movements of capital for the benefit of individuals and society as a whole.

The idea of cooperation in Islamic insurance

According to the prophet Muhammed in *Hadith*, he states:

> A Muslim is the brother of a fellow-Muslim. He should neither oppress him nor ruin him; and whoever meets the needs of a brother, Allah will meet his needs and he who relieves his brother of hardship, Allah will relieve him of the hardships to which he could be subject on the Day of Resurrection.

Therefore, it is permitted (or even encouraged) to gain benefits from, because this does not involve interest (*riba*).

A consultant in Islamic religion, Qaradawi (1986), stated that Islamic insurance may exist in a condition where each participant contributes to a fund used for mutual support. Islam aims at establishing a social order under universal brotherhood and the underlying concept is that of mutual cooperation and help. The prophet Muhammed stressed:

> In mutual compassion, love and kindness you will find the faithful like a body, so that if one part feels pain, the whole body responds with wakefulness and fever. A Muslim is the brother of another Muslim; he neither wrongs him, nor leaves him without help, nor humiliates him.

(Hadith)

There are other references to takaful in the Qur'an, for example: '[Allah] who prepares nourishment to prevent the fear of hunger and saves/puts at peace those who fear' (Qur'an, 106, p. 4).

Concepts of protection in Islam

A takaful contract must be based on principles of cooperation, protection and mutual responsibility and must avoid acts of interest (*riba*), gambling (*maisir*) and uncertainty (*gharar*).

A takaful company conducts all its affairs in a manner compatible with Islamic Shari'ah tradition, whether in investing its funds, in carrying out its business in all classes of insurance or in any other related financial field. The company's (Islamic insurance) Memorandum and Articles of Association underlines this approach (Qaradawi, 1988).

The company normally has a committee of prominent Shari'ah scholars. Their direct guidance and advice is essential at all stages of takaful operations, from the point of sale activities to payment of benefits, from accounting to investment of funds, from public dealing to serving the community through insurance and non-insurance activities such as the support of charitable work, etc. All operations and contracts are set up to ensure that any element of speculation, uncertainty and gambling are eliminated or minimized. This is essential for maintaining the 'caring and cooperative' principles of takaful.

Recent changes

On examining recent trends in the Muslim world, it is evident that people have not taken up insurance products – including travel insurance – in the same way as in most non-Muslim countries. However, most Muslim countries have the potential to at least double their insurance volumes (Qaradawi, 1986).

One of the main reasons for the low penetration of insurance in these countries is that it remains underdeveloped, and a decade of misunderstanding has created a mindset amongst Muslims. Yet travel insurance is essential in providing vital protection for oneself and one's family. The premium of the insurance industry globally amounted to a total of US$2.3 trillion in 1999 (up by 7.3% on 1998).

Al-Zarqa (1995, p. 80) is optimistic about the opportunities for growth of the Islamic insurance industry: 'The takaful industry has the opportunity to unlock this potential with life insurance and non-life insurance.' In fact, Islamic finance and banking has now firmly established itself, with a total US$7 trillion of capital, more than US$4.1 trillion of assets and more than US$120 billion of deposits. Takaful insurance is expected to grow over the next decade in line with the rapid development of Islamic investment and banking systems. Total premiums written by takaful insurers are expected to reach US$2.1 billion by 2010, or approximately 9% of global insurance market shares (Ajmal, 2000).

> In the first World Takaful Conference held in Dubai in 2006, Dr Habib Al Mullah, chairman of the Dubai Financial Services Authority (DFSA), in a speech to inaugurate the conference, stated that Islamic insurance companies must adopt an innovative approach to their products and regional governments need to open the insurance market. The chairman continued that: 'Insurance remains an important tool to reduce risk, and it is as important to emerging markets as it is to developed economies. Regulators must recognize that the modern takaful industry is still in its formative stages and many issues need to be resolved'.
>
> (http://www.tradarabia.com)

Case Study: Takaful International

Takaful International (TI), formerly known as the Bahrain Islamic Insurance Company (BIIC), was incorporated in 1989. As one of the early players in the Islamic financial field, BIIC offered insurance products and services that were designed to meet the increasing demand for such products. With only a handful of employees, BIIC evolved into what is today (TI), a thriving corporation with a staff of 68 dedicated and experienced professionals.

In 1998, the current name was adopted to underline the unique system offered by the company, based on fairness and in complete harmony with Muslim social and cultural values. The new name also reflects the planned expansion of operations outside of Bahrain into other selected markets, where TI's products have the potential to appeal to a wide audience of prospective customers.

The company was restructured in 2000 to meet the challenges of the new millennium. TI then focused its efforts on making the company the preferred choice in the region in terms of new Shari'ah-compliant products.

Mission statement and business mission

The mission of TI is to be the insurance company of choice, based on caring and cooperative principles and committed to people, performance and growth. In terms of its business mission, it intends to be the leading provider of takaful products and services by creating awareness and maximizing the potential for takaful, and to spearhead the development and marketing of innovative products that conform to Shari'ah principles and provide services that build and uphold their corporate values.

Takaful product

TI offers a range of insurance products, including motor, fire, marine, engineering, liability, general accidents and family medical and healthcare. Under its general accident cover it offers travel insurance and, under the umbrella of family medical and health care, the company offers hajj and umra insurance.

The travel insurance product provides the client with the financial protection needed in case of sudden illness or an accident while on a business trip or a vacation abroad, by settling all related medical expenses. Other services under the plan include travel assistance, legal assistance, lost luggage assistance, emergency medical evacuation, repatriation of mortal remains, medical translation services, delivery of essential medicine, arrangements of compassionate visits, convalescence expenses and others.

The hajj and umra insurance provides the pilgrim with suitable protection during the holy trip by covering injuries and accidents (including death and disability) sustained during such holy trips, providing health care and medical treatment when needed, free of charge. The company was also able to play a major role in serving the national economy and lay down the principles for application of Shari'ah in insurance transactions.

The company continues to pursue its ambitious investment and underwriting policies and to cooperate with other Islamic financial institutions that comply with the principles of Shari'ah in all its business and investment dealings. Its successful strategy has focused mainly on three key areas: underwriting policy, investment policy and customer services. As a result, the company was able to achieve outstanding results that reflected the success of such a strategy and the establishment of a wider customer base.

The company's financial results during the year were characterized by the achievement of profit in all insurance departments, an indication of the success of its underwriting policy. Insurance premiums increased, in total, to BD5.19 million (Bahrain Dinars) and net profits were realized from the shareholders' and policyholders' portfolios totalling BD1.01 million – an increase of 265% over the previous year, representing the highest profit level ever realized by the company. Return on the paid-up capital was 13.8%, which was a significant return by any standards, enabling the company to pay dividends to the shareholders at the rate of 10% of paid-up capital.

There has been an announcement concerning a change in the company's logo, revealing a new face of Islamic insurance, in addition to the participation of all associates in the investors' group, thereby standardizing the group's overall identity. This will help to promote its strategy for global expansion and imbue its various activities with new values and principles, deriving their roots from Arab and Islamic culture.

Mr Jamal (General Manager) added the palm frond in the new logo as a symbol of the elements of life and growth, and this is a reflection of the care and security provided by TI for its customers. Moreover, the palm frond enjoys a special status in Arab culture and traditions, demonstrating the company's continuing philosophy and ambition for expanding its operations worldwide, supported by local knowledge.

In addition, investment in staff training and development was a vital requirement for ensuring the launch of the company's products within the framework of a proper strategy. The company believes that investment of human resources and having the right amount of capital are basic ingredients for the success of any business.

Concluding, Mr Jamal has highlighted the fact that the company is currently seeking to expand its insurance business throughout the Gulf region and the overall Arab world, given its long experience in the takaful business. The company is the first ever takaful company in the Kingdom of Bahrain and is one of the early leaders of takaful insurance at both regional and international levels.

Summary

This chapter has discussed the fundamentals of Islamic insurance and the market needs of the Muslim population. Muslims have been travelling and performing pilgrimages to several holy places and shrines around the world for the past 1400 years as part of their religious belief. They have been travelling to religious destinations such as Syria, Iran, Iraq, Turkey, Pakistan and several other parts of the world.

Muslims travel to Makkah by various means from all parts of the world: by air, sea, car and on foot, to perform this spiritual pilgrimage. But this is not an easy journey: the hajj and umra carry enormous risks for the pilgrim. In fact, every year several hundred Muslims die from incidents ranging from stampede, sickness and transportation accidents to fire. With so much risk and danger involved, it would be common sense to take out travel insurance for the purpose of this journey. However, few people take out insurance, and these are mainly Muslims from Western countries.

It is important to develop a marketing strategy for takaful (insurance), because traditional insurance has certain features that contradict some of the essential values of an Islamic financial contract. Muslims are directed by their faith to follow a path of righteousness in pursuing the activities of their daily lives: for example, gambling and exploitation are strictly forbidden.

The prohibition of riba (predetermined interest) does not mean that capital costs less; however, Islam permits the making of a predetermined claim on the surplus derived from the use of capital for production. A profit-sharing arrangement, where the profit-sharing ratio – but not the rate of return – is predetermined, is allowed in Islam. This arrangement can technically replace its Western counterpart, the interest rate, and allow capital to flow into the arrangement that offers the highest profit-sharing ratio to investors.

It is evident that the Muslim population around the world is growing. And with this increasing population, improved education standards and the increasing trends in global travel mean that there will be greater opportunity and demand for travel insurance from the Muslim world.

Insurance companies will need to identify and better understand the needs of the Muslims by offering innovative takaful insurance products and marketing them in an appropriate and effective way. This is particularly needed in Muslim countries, where there is a huge potential for the development of insurance products and the need to dispel, through education, the mythology surrounding insurance. Furthermore, the Saudi authorities, in order to reduce risk factors, could make travel insurance a necessary requirement for pilgrims travelling for hajj or umra.

Glossary

Fatwah

Decisions made based on the guidelines in the Qur'an and Hadith. These decrees are problems or matters that are vaguely mentioned in the Shari'ah. There are rules regarding who can issue a fatwah. This is needed for insurance, for although commerce was common in the time of the prophet, insurance *per se* was not, and thus there are few clear references to insurance in either the Qur'an or Hadith.

Fiqh

Discussion on religious deeds (*ibadah*).

Gharar

Sale of what is not present. This is not permitted in Islam, and there are grades of acceptability. Gharar basically means 'uncertainty'. The definition of uncertainty is 'lack of information about a certain product or agreement (object); the existence of uncertainty in the presence of that object and the lack in quantity and conciseness of information about the object'. Ibn Taimiyah, who is of the Islamic school of thought, states that gharar means: 'When a party obtains his rights and the other party does not get what is rightfully his.'

Hadith

Sayings and actions of the prophet Muhammad. These were collected and organized during and shortly after the prophet's death.

Halal

Permissible in Islam.

Haram

Not permissible in Islam.

Hibba

A gift.

Ijtihad

Opinion on a religious matter by individuals. This is one level down from fatwah.

Maisir

Gambling. This is not allowed in Islam. Insurance is mistakenly thought of as gambling by some people.

Mudarib

The operator in a Mudaraba transaction, i.e. the banker or insurer.

Mudaraba

A type of business transaction involving profit-sharing. This is used extensively with takaful insurance, and sometimes modified to include sharing of surplus as well, termed modified Mudaraba.

Nasiah

Paying more, either in terms of money or exchange of goods, when taking out a loan due to the condition of the loan. The excess payment is *riba*.

Qard Al-Hassan

An interest-free loan. This is used when there is a deficit in the insurance fund of a takaful company.

Riba

The simplest explanation of this term is interest.

Shari'ah Law

Islamic laws written in the Qur'an or narrated in Hadith, concerning what is permitted or not permitted for a Muslim.

Takaful

Insurance designed for Muslims.

Wakalah

A type of business transaction involving an agency or representative. This is used in takaful when the operator does not share in any surplus, but is acting as a representative of the policy-holders.

Zakat

Alms, obligations upon charities that provide for a certain group of people stated in Shari'ah and for the development of the Islamic Community.

References

Ajmal, M. (2000) Insurance and takaful. *New Horizon* 1, 11.
Alzarqa, M. (1995) *The Boom for Islamic Insurance in the 21st Century.* Dar Al-Marafa, Jordan.
Ariff, M. (1988) Islamic banking. *Asia Pacific Economic Literature* 2, 46–62.
Directory of Islamic Insurance (2000) *Takaful.* Institute of Islamic Banking Insurance, London.
Ismail, A. (1997) Insurance and Shari'ah: Part I. *The Call of Islam Journal* 19, 22–23.
Qaradawi, Y. (1986) *The Islamic Economics Rolling in Terms of Attitude and Ethics.* Dar Al-Eamman, Lebanon.
Qaradawi, Y. (1988) *The Ethical and Islamic Insurance Business.* Dar Al-Eamman, Lebanon.

Websites

http://www.bbc.co.uk/religion/religions/islam/customs/hajj/hajj2005_12.shtml (acccessed 3 May 2006).
http://www.cnn.com/2006/WORLD/meast/01/12/hajj.stampede/index.htm (accessed 4 May 2006).
http://www.islamicpopulation.com (accessed 3 May 2006).
http://www.tradarabia.com (accessed 4 May 2006).

17 Case Study 8: Fátima – the Religious Tourism Altar

MARIA I.R.B. DE PINHO* AND ISABEL M.R.T. DE PINHO**

*Departamento de Artes e Motricidade Humana da ESE, Instituto Politécnico do Porto, Porto, Portugal; e-mails: *inespinho@ese.ipp.pt; **i.r.t.p@mail.pt*

Introduction

Fátima, a very popular name among the Arab peoples (due to the fact that it was the name of the prophet's favourite daughter), is also the name of a small village in Portugal that is well known all over the world nowadays. According to the legend, a young Muslim named Fátima converted for the love of a Christian, and after being baptised, she adopted the name Oriana. The name Ourém, the current regional administrative centre, is derived from this new Christian name.

In a contemporay context, religious, cultural and leisure tourism in its many aspects (nature, environment, heritage, history of Portugal, the cult of Our Lady of Fátima, pilgrimage) constitutes the increasing internationalization and creation of the successful brand of Fátima. This chapter analyses the basis of pilgrimage to Fátima and its branding, and speculates on its future direction, using a range of bibliographic references and research insights.

Geographical location

Fátima is situated in the central coastal region of Portugal, belonging to Santarém district and not to Leiria District – which is nearer, although it is part of this latter diocese. Geologically, it is part of the Orla Lusitana, bordering Maciço Central, with sedimentary soils of limestone, sands and marl that constitute this huge Maciço Central Estremenho, the largest in the country, which runs to the coast in steep slopes among lakes and capes.

Off the coast, a small group of unique islands (The Berlengas, currently a protected landscape due to their flora) forms a marine outcrop of the same rock mass. The type of soil here, very fragmented because of tectonic movements and subterranean tunnels that have resulted in the dissolution of the limestone, is rendered very permeable but very resistant to erosion – physically and by water.

The mountains around Fátima (Serra de Aire and Candeeiros, part of a National Park) also have a geological characteristic of their own due to the many natural caves (Minde, Alvados and Santo António) full of stalactites and stalagmites created by the mechanical and chemical actions of water. One can take a 1-day guided tour in this area, an excellent way of studying the geological features. The low-growing vegetation covering the slopes hides dozens of gullies, which provide natural access to these geological features.

This kind of soil has also recorded the imprints of dinosaurs' feet, engraved in Pedreira de Galinhas (Serra d'Aire), the most famous footprints in Portugal. They are on permanent display in the open air and cover a wide area; explanatory notices featuring geological and paleontological concepts guide the visitor. The limestone legacy of this region can also be found in the great monasteries, such as Alcobaça, Batalha and Santa Cruz in Coimbra, Jerónimos in Lisbon and, more recently, in the architecture of Fátima's sanctuary.

The way of life in Portugal before, during and after Fátima's apparitions

Modern Portugal has endured a long and painful path in its development. The 19th century had been steeped in social, religious and economic conflict, which had all contributed to the absence of progress for the country, and Portugal entered the 20th century beset by the same vices and lack of horizons. The rhetoric of politicians remained the same, privileges and commodities remained untouchable in spite of the change in regime in the first decade of the 20th century ('Long live the Republic').

The new constitution promised new things to an impoverished and illiterate population. However, the Portuguese people were mistrustful of 'old gentlemen in new clothes'. Despite increasing urbanization, which saw the emergence of compulsory education, the introduction of women's rights and divorce, etc., the stranglehold of the secular church still dominated society, stifling any improvements in material gain. The rural population, oblivious to any political problems, suffered the consequences of bad government, and children soon learned that the only goal was survival.

During the 16 years of the First Republic (1910–1926), the country saw 50 changes in government and eight presidents. Life was uncertain, with chaos reigning for the most part in Lisbon, the setting for all political developments. *Coups d'état* were frequent, as well as bombing by anarchists, and by the end of 1917 social unrest had became intense. Although Portugal was a peripheral country, it retained colonial links with large tracts of territory globally, and in that year had become engaged in the Great War (The First World War).

In Cova da Iria, a small hamlet near Fátima, life meant survival, like everywhere else in the country. Though geographically distant, the war was present in everyone's mind, thinking of those who were fighting on the Western Front and of the hardships of daily life. All children were adults in miniature, contributing to the family budget with their labours. The three seers of the apparitions (see below) (Jacinta, the youngest, Francisco and Lúcia, the oldest) were cousins and therefore close; together, they searched for the best pastures for their families' sheep. In addition, periodically, groups of people migrated in search of work in order to increase their meagre earnings, travelling to the south and west of Portugal to harvest cereals, pick olives or gather grapes.

In 1917, Cova da Iria was a desolate place and started to expand only in the mid-1920s (it was considered the newest in mainland Portugal), developing gradually as a result of the apparitions (in 1959 it was still embryonic). Very few houses were made of stone and tile: the majority were wooden. This way of life changed almost completely with the fame brought by the 'apparitions' phenomenon. Therefore, the primary sector gave way to a strong tertiary sector essentially structured on tourism and associated services. Those who go to Fátima cannot imagine what the place looked like in even relatively recent times (< 100 years ago), demonstrating the development redolent of an agrarian society.

The Marian Cult of Fátima

The cult of Mary is not new, the first apparitions having been witnessed by monks, nuns or hermits as early as the first century AD. It was similar to a spiritual experience and therefore intimate, and important to note that public worship was not well regarded at that time. It was only with the Edict of Milan in AD 313 that Constantine acknowledged Christianity as the religion of the empire and ordered the reconstruction of Jerusalem and excavations in search of any holy traces, paving the way for the first pilgrimages, with the Church using pilgrimage as a form of penance.

It was in the Middle Ages that this form of punishment was at its peak, due to the ever-present spectre of death. Shrines began to multiply, especially those based on the relics of saints' and the great pilgrimages became ever more common until the 16th century, when they started to decline in popularity. Although the Reformation questioned Mary's status, the cult of the Virgin was kept alive and was strengthened in the Council of Trent.[1] The political upheaval in France since the French Revolution, and afterwards throughout the 19th century, was unable to destroy people's faith in their belief in several apparitions of the Virgin in France (Pontmain, 1817; Rue de Bac, Paris, 1830; Lourdes, 1858).

Pilgrims normally undertake pilgrimage either in search of relief or to seek something, but in Fátima things are different: along with those who believe they can be healed in body or soul, the pilgrim who walks long distances (even from abroad) comes to 'pay' their due, to fulfil a promise for grace already received.

Besides the sacrifice of long treks, possibly lasting weeks and in all weathers (May in Portugal is quite unpredictable), many other hardships were encountered: only bread and water for sustenance, walking in total silence and

---

[1] The Council of Trent was the 19th ecumenical council of the Roman Catholic Church (1545–1563); it contained sweeping decrees on self-reform and dogmatic definitions that clarified virtually every doctrine contested by Protestants; thus was the Catholic Church revitalized in many parts of Europe.

carrying a heavy cross across the shoulders (very common during the conflict involving Portugal and its former African colonies).

Instances of miraculous healing are another reason that led people to the Marian shrines, and Fátima is no exception. Though not so imposing as Lourdes, year in, year out, Fátima's sanctuary receives all those who ask for Mary's intervention in its hospitals. The Church is cautious in their assessment. Most importantly, the patient must have a well-structured process prior to the 'healing' and this must be spontaneous, without gradual recovery, without convalescence and the person must remain healthy for a minimum of 5 years thereafter. It is stipulated that a team of doctors should accompany and examine the patient. Spiritual healings are the most numerous, less noticeable and harder to evaluate.

There are many Marian altars all over the world, but only a few have been confirmed by Pontiffs. Fátima seems to have been one of the favourites among the Popes of the second half of the 20th century: Cardinal Roncalli, Patriarch of Venice and future John XXIII presided over the International Pilgrimage in 1956; Paul VI presided over the 50th anniversary of Fátima in 1967.

John Paul II, a true devotee to the Virgin, was in Fátima in 1982 to thank 'Her' for having survived an attempt on his life in Rome the previous year (the third secret of Fátima). He brought with him the bullet, which was then placed on the Virgin's crown. In 1984, the image travelled to Rome and to Saint Peter's Square, before John Paul II for an act of consecratation to the Immaculate Heart of Mary. In 1991 this Pope, a pilgrim himself, came to Fátima for a second time to preside over the International Pilgrimage. In 2000, the year of the public revelation of the third secret, John Paul II returned for the last time in order to announce the beatification of the young seers, Jacinta and Francisco. That year in Rome he consecrated the third millennium of the world to the Virgin of Fátima.

The devotion to Our Lady of the Rosary of Fátima was taken to South America by Portuguese immigrants: to Argentina (the diocese of Mendoza has had a Marian sanctuary since 1952), Venezuela (the dioceses of Barquisimeto – a chapel since 1963 and Bahia Blanca – a church since 1954) and Brazil, where native cults have truly meshed with the cult of Our Lady of Fátima – often confused with Yemanjá, the goddess of the waters.

Other parts of the world have also been touched by the Marian spirit: Korea (Tae Jeon since 1966), India (Kumbakonam since 1956 – here there are many institutions providing social support dedicated to Fátima). The Virgin is a pilgrim as well and 'She' has travelled throughout the world to visit Her children.

This is not, however, the image that is in the Apparitions Chapel (once a target when someone attempted to destroy it – nowadays it is protected by a bullet-proof glass box). This image has left only for short trips: in 1942, 1946, 1947, 1948 (to Madrid), 1951 (to Leiria) and in 1959 to Lisbon, for the opening of the monument to Cristo Rei which, from the south bank of the River Tagus, blesses the Portuguese capital. The image was in Rome in 1984 and was requested again for the funereal ceremonies of Pope John Paul II in 2005, but logistical reasons prevented this.

It was present, however, in Lisbon at the end of that year to preside over the closing of the International Congress of the New Evangelization that took place in November. In the cold and rain, 200,000 people joined the candlelit procession, accompanying 'Her' during that short stay. The Pilgrim Virgin is another image that started 'Her' travelling in 1947, and which lasted until 1982. As a result of 'Her' stay in the Western Islands in 1950 a new church was build in Clery, Catries, the capital of Santa Lucia, which was enlarged in 1965. But the Virgin started travelling again throughout the world after 'Her' return to the sanctuary in 1982.

The religious phenomenon of Fátima

The young seers, Lúcia de Jesus, Francisco Marto and Jacinta Marto, were born in Aljustrel, a place under the administrative jurisdiction of Fátima, in 1907, 1908 and 1910, respectively. In 1916, three apparitions of an angel that introduced himself as the Angel of Portugal preceded the ones of the Virgin the following year (Lúcia told of this only in her memoirs, published in 1937).

The apparitions of the Lady took place from May to October 1917, each time on the 13th of the month, as 'She' had announced – except in August, when it occurred on the 19th and at a place called Valinhos. The local administrator had held up the children until the fifteenth and the persecutions came not only from the republican civil power, but also from the masonry.

The Church, which had been associated with the recently fallen monarchy, tried to distance itself from the apparitions phenomenon, fearing the reprisal of the new anti-clerical political regime. The separation between the Church and the State had been decreed, as well as the suppression of religious teaching in schools and the nationalization of Church property. In spite of this radical republican position, conservative movements coexisted, these becoming decisive in the establishment of Fátima's phenomenon: António de Oliveira Salazar, future head of the government for the following 50 years, and Cardinal Cerejeira, jointly responsible for the centralization of Portuguese Catholicism in Fátima.

In those troubled times, however, the shadow of suspicion of deceit hung over the three seers, and even their family denied any complicity. Despite the threats, imprisonment, the multiple, painful questionings of both lay and religious (including the bishop and the local priest) authorities, the insults and the physical abuse, the three children remained unshakable: they maintained that they had seen a flash of lightning, and then a woman appeared on top of a small oak tree, dressed in white with a golden skirt and a shawl on 'Her' head saying that 'She' had come from heaven. It was said that 'She' had asked them to recite the rosary daily so that the war would end and promised to take them to heaven (Jacinta and Francisco would die shortly afterwards in an influenza pandemic – within 12 months of each other).

There were six apparitions – the same number of months spanning the period of May to October. The third apparition (a secret divided into three parts, two of which were revealed immediately) concerned the condemnation of sinners and the threat of a new conflict if mankind did not mend their ways. The conversion of Russia was also a promise of the Lady that called Herself the Immaculate Heart, and 'She' also asked for the consecration of Russia (this happened in 1952, under Pope Pius XII). The dogma of the Immaculate Heart had already been confirmed by Pope Pius IX in 1854 following the appearance of the apparitions – in the Rue de Bac, Paris – to a woman named Catherine; she was subsequently canonized in 1947.

The Virgin of Fátima also announced that an aurora borealis would be the presage of misery, hunger, persecution and war. John Paul's representative revealed the last part of the secret on 13 May 2000, during Lúcia's lifetime (she died in 2005 at the age of 97). The number of people that had started to watch the apparitions grew steadily, and on the 4th celestial visit scheduled for 13 August, 10,000 people were present. For the above-mentioned reasons (the arrest of the children until 15 August) the apparition took place on 19 August; 30,000 people witnessed the fifth on 13 September.

It is said that only the three little shepherds were able to see the Lady, and that only Lúcia talked to 'Her'; then they were told that everyone present would see a great miracle on 13 October, and the news was subsequently spread by the press, attracting more than 50,000 people to Fátima on the designated day, providing everyone with the opportunity to watch the 'Miracle of the Sun'.

This was the last public apparition of the Lady who said 'Her' name was also the Lady of the Rosary, asking people to recite the rosary (the origin of this devotion lay with the Dominicans in the 13th century, was later spread by the Carthusians in the 15th century and was a favourite of Leon XIII, who published nine encyclicals on it). Apparently, 'She' also asked that a small chapel be built there and announced the end of the war. After the apparition, many witnesses told of what had happened, for example: 'a vertiginous movement of the sun rotation that has all the colours of the rainbow, casting its light in every direction on the people and then a movement of the translation of the sun earthwise in three successive movements' (Alonso, 1995, p. 536, cited in Pereira, 1995, p. 68).

In 1925, Lúcia entered a convent of the Sisters of St Dorothy in Spain, first in Pontevedra and later in Tuy, where she took her vows. Legend has it that between 1925 and 1929 she was visited by the Virgin Mary, who asked for her prayers and sacrifices for the world and for Russia.

She returned to Portugal and entered the Carmelite Convent in Coimbra, where she remained, leaving it only for special occasions and communicating only with Rome. She wrote her memoirs in the solitude of the convent between 1935 and 1941, but they were published only in 1996/97. The Vatican took hold of the third part of the secret in 1957. The interpretation was perfect when the assassination attempt on John Paul II took place: he, himself was a devotee of Mary, born in an entirely Marian country where the Czestokowa shrine – which worships the Black Virgin – reigned.

The 1920s were controversial in Portugal; with a state of flux between politics and religion. Caught in the middle, Fátima appeared to emerge from of it stronger, despite the constant attacks upon it. The masonry tried in every way possible to discredit the phenomenon, persecuting and abusing the believers. They even dynamited the little chapel that had been built in 1922. The outcome was the opposite of what they had expected: the nation became angry and the crowds of pilgrims swelled.

Meanwhile the Church, stung by the extent of people's faith, nominated a commission to study the apparitions. Still, the number of pilgrims arriving in Fátima grew larger and larger, regardless of approval by the laity or clergy. Eventually, along came commercialization, first flimsy and seasonal and very haphazard. Fátima became a huge fair, with merry-go-rounds and other such amusements on the 13th of each month. Pilgrims and onlookers alike congregated in the fields without any facilities.

This drew the attention of the central government and the patriarchy in Lisbon – represented by Salazar and Cardinal Cerejeira. It had become necessary to give a new public façade to this religious centre that was drawing people from both home and abroad. First, appeared the basilica, designed by the Dutchman, Gerardus van Kricken, a classical structure started in 1928 (13 May); it has a 70-metre-high tower, bordered by large colonnades and connected to two hospitals (Nossa Senhora das Dores and Nossa Senhora do Carmo).

It is constructed from local limestone, and the colonnades are decorated with polychrome ceramic panels, representing the Via Sacra. The suite of buildings occupies an area of about 86,400 m² (twice as large as St Peter's Square in Rome), including the chapel of the apparitions (rebuilt), the oak tree upon which the Virgin descended and, in the middle a narrow column, a monument to the Sacred Heart of Jesus, erected over a water fountain found after the apparitions.

Only in 1930 was the cult in Fátima confirmed by the Pastoral as 'The Divine Providence' (many years after the phenomenon, considering that in Lourdes the commission created to study the subject was nominated in the same year that the apparitions took place, and it took only 5 years between the apparitions and the confirmation of the cult in La Salette); and, therefore, the children's visions were then declared believable and the cult of the Lady of Fátima was ratified.

In 1929, a preliminary urban plan engineered by Luís Cristino da Silva and Ernesto Korrodi was presented; this had bold proportions, following fashionable French models. It was too ambitious for the time and place, as it anticipated a car park and a railway station. Other projects followed, while provision of visitor accommodation was being devised. After approval of the Marian cult, the first religious congregations settled there. In 1944, Cotinelli Telmo's urban project confirmed the vocation of the religious pilgrimage of the site.

In 1946, the Church obtained autonomy from the government: a nominated rector would be in charge of all administrative and judicial matters and, in that year, the Virgin was adorned with a golden crown, offered by Portuguese women. In 1948, a law decreed a protection zone, allowing the expropriation of land to enlarge and reform the entire area. The Holy Year Jubilee took place in Fátima in 1951, attracting thousands of people and, in the following year, Pope Pius XII consecrated Russia to the Sacred Heart of Mary.

Many foreign pilgrims are attracted to Fátima, and so the construction of seminaries, convents, schools and pastoral houses has occurred. The ancient, dilapidated architecture in the old northern area of the village was soon replaced by new building – partly for local housing, but mostly for accommodation and dining facilities, although vernacular designs have been retained. In the 1980s, the Paul VI Congress Centre was built, with associated shops selling religious items and local and national handicrafts.

Fátima: Place of Pilgrimage and Religious Tourism

Sites of religion and tourism

Life in Fátima has changed with the apparitions. The local population cannot cultivate the land near Cova da Iria, and they saw the selling of religious items and other articles (from wooden huts) as the only way to improve their financial situation. In 1943, there were a total of 18 huts; in January 1951, the sanctuary had the huts demolished and 90 shops built as an alternative (the first 45 shops were built and opened in 1950 on the northern side of the sanctuary, known as Praceta S. José; the remaining 45 were opened in 1961 on the southern side, known as Praceta de S. António).

The phenomenon of faith that Fátima inspires attracts many religious institutes and congregations. Today, all the amenities expected by the tourist are well catered for. Tiredness caused by the long distances travelled and the desire to watch evening ceremonies – especially the candlelit procession – has made the provision of adequate accommodation a priority; some locals have even constructed huts on their property for tourist accommodation.

In 1928, the first hotel was built near to the main road; a wooden building with eight rooms, a kitchen, two bathrooms and a dining room. Four years later the first Fátima Hotel Society was established, the 'Sociedade Iniciativas de Fátima', with construction of a large economy-level hotel, sleeping dormitories and a dining room. However, this society was to be dissolved a few years later.

Other significant events were:

- The coronation of Our Lady's Image on 13 May 1946.
- The closing celebration of the Holy Year Jubilee on 13 October 1951.
- The celebration when Fátima became a village and no longer a simple hamlet (13 August 1977); and later, when it became a small town (1997).
- Papal visits: John XXIII (1956), Paul VI (1967) and John Paul II (13 May 1982, 1991 and 2000) – facilitated by the construction of new hotels and restaurants.

By 1989 Fátima could boast: 14 hotels, one inn, 12 guest houses, 18 boarding houses, 44 restaurants, coffee shops and snack bars, five confectionery shops, three travel agencies, six banks and one monetary exchange office (Oliveira, 1990, p. 111). By 2002, the town' facilities included eight banks/monetary exchange offices, two supermarkets, seven travel agencies, 15 hotels, one inn, 14 boarding houses, 65 restaurants, 57 religious houses (42 female, 15 male), five museums, four grottos, one bus station, one taxi rank, one fire department, two police stations, two medical centres, four bookshops, four florists and no less than 72 religious memorabilia shops (Região de Turismo

Leiria-Fátima, 2002, pp. 87–113). Incrementally the 'cult areas' stimulated a local micro-economy that kept pace with the pilgrimage movements and the proliferation of a religious tourism phenomenon.

The Sanctuary of Cova da Iria

According to the priest who currently runs Fátima's sanctuary (Luciano Guerra), the sanctuary can have three meanings:

- Everything that is holy in the presence of God and, therefore, can be applied to religious objects.
- The high places of faith, i.e. those where the experience of the divine takes place at its higher level.
- The heart of Man, i.e. the place where they record their religious experiences.

Summary

In general terms, Fátima is no different to any other pilgrimage centre that has appeared in a lowly populated area and to which the apparitions phenomenon has brought unprecedented development. Since immemorial times, man has gone on pilgrimage and has travelled across the land. The pilgrim was the 'foreigner', and that 'foreigner' has started to identify him/herself with a religious objective since the 11th century. First, Jerusalem, then Rome and, in the Middle Ages, Santiago de Compostela, were the first great pilgrimages.

Nowadays, the most famous are the Muslim pilgrimage to Mecca – the one that a believer must do at least once in a lifetime, and one of the pillars of Islam. Pilgrims do not need to go on foot: today, people go on pilgrimage by the most varied means of transport. But many still walk long distances to express their faith. Fátima is one of those destinations and it has plenty to offer regarding accommodation, eating facilities, health centres, etc.

If, in October 1917, 70,000 people visited Fátima and nowadays 6 million people from all over the world make the pilgrimage, one can see that it has become a major pilgrimage centre. Therefore, the above-mentioned issues must be considered as a form of developing religious tourism and in a sustainable way. Besides, when the sanctuary was designed, only the physical area/space was planned, with no thought given to the remainder of the town.

The idea of sustainable tourism continues, through the elaboration of three plans that are considering the urbanization of the town itself and its surroundings. Simultaneously, one must achieve economic development through the diversification of activities and the development of activities compatible with the town-sanctuary and the creation of complementary activities in the surroundings. The commitment to environmental quality and the establishment of partnerships between the state and private sectors will be the guarantee of a new concept in religious tourism: 'Fátima – the world altar.'

In terms of the expectations concerning religious tourism in Fátima in the 21st century, one can speculate that tourism will increase in importance as long as the quality of the tourist service in the area continues to expand. The local town council, the clergy and society in general should cooperate to promote the sustainability of this concept; the former communist countries will be the greatest drivers of this increase, because the willingness to travel will be associated with the willingness to go on a pilgrimage.

Fátima will be a favoured destination for those former communist countries, due to the third secret concerning the conversion of Russia. The opening up to Asian countries, both in economic and cultural aspects, together with the standpoints taken by the late Pope John Paul II, will lead to a greater interchange between regions and, as a result, an inflow of pilgrims to the sanctuaries. Former African colonies, eager to resume a good relationship with their former European colonizers, will try to strengthen religious interchange, so far achieved only through missionary travel.

Projects like COESIMA must be supported, not only to develop the research network between sanctuaries, but also to find ways to predict, quantify and qualify and motivations of pilgrims. The sustainability of religious tourism must not merely be preoccupied with the economic impacts for destinations, but thought should be given to the type of religious tourist and the features of religious tourism, otherwise Mammon may ultimately triumph over God.

References

Abumanssur, E.S., 2003, Turismo Religioso, Ensaios antropológicos sobre Religião e Turismo, Papirus editora, S. Paulo.

Fátima 50, Ano I, n.º 6, 13 de Outubro de 1967.

Fátima 50, Ano I, n.º 7, 13 de Novembro de 1967.

Fernandes, C. *et al.*, 2003, Religious Tourism and Pilgrimage, 23–27 April, ATLAS, Special Interest Group, 1st expert Meeting, Fátima, Portugal.

Fernandes, J.L.J, 2000, O Homem, o Espaço e o tempo no Maciço calvário Estremenho, o olhar de um geógrafo, edições colibri, Faculdade de Letras da Universidade de Coimbra.

Fialho, J. et Larcher, B.F., 2002, Guia de Fátima, Paulinas, Lisboa.

Guerra, Padre Dr. Luciano, O Turismo religioso no Mundo de amanhã, 1988, Tourism Education for the early 21st Century, VIII World Congress of WAPTT (16th–19th November), Instituto das Novas profissões.

Guerra, Padre Dr. Luciano, Santuário Nossa Senhora de Fátima, 1992, 75º aniversário das Aparições, Expansão Urbanística de Fátima, Análise ao aglomerado Urbano que se foi formando após as aparições de 1917, ExpoFat, 1917–1985, Serviço de Ambiente e Construções, SEAC.

Martins, J.A.N., 2001, Fátima profunda, Esboço Etnográfico, Casa do povo de Fátima, 1ª Ed.

Medeiros, C.A., 2005, Geografia de Portugal, O ambiente Físico, Círculo de Leitores, Lisboa.

Neves, J.M., 2005, A Fátima dos inícios do século XX, A freguesia de Fátima 1900–1917, Edição Rotary Clube de Fátima.

Oliveira, F.P. de, 1990, Fátima como Nasceu e Cresceu, Ourém Estudos e Documentos, Volume V, Câmara Municipal de Ourém.

Pereira, P., 2003, Peregrinos um estudo antropológico das peregrinações a pé a Fátima, crença e , As peregrinações ao longo do tempo e do espaço, Instituto Piaget, Lisboa.

Região de Turismo Leiria Fátima, 2002, Guia de Fátima, Paulinas.

Região de Turismo Leiria/Fátima, 2004, Relatório de Gestão.

Rodrigues, M.F.S., Fátima Problemas Geográficos de um centro de peregrinação, 1974, Chrorographia, colecção de estudos de Geografia Humana e Regonal, Instituto de Alta Cultura, Centro de Estudos Geográficos da universidade de Lisboa, Lisboa.

Rosa, I., Procissão Fátima em Lisboa, 17 de Novembro de 2005, Revista Visão, pp. 36.

Torgal, L.F., 2002, As aparições de Fátima – Imagens e Representações, A Fundação da "Lourdes Portuguesa", Editora Temas e Debates, Lisboa.

Vukoni, B., 1996, Tourism and Religion, University of Zagreb, Elsevier, Croatia 2º seminário Transnacional (COESIMA) – 27 de Outubro de 2005–Material de Apoio.

Websites

http://weekly.ahram.org.eg/2000/469/tr2.htm
http://portal.rt-leiriafatima.pt/destaques.php?idreg=103
http://www.turismoreligioso.org/
http://www.fatimashop.pt/cgi-bin/fsvg.cgi/?page=f_ini
http://www.venezuelatuya.com/articulos/turismo0106.htm
http://www.lxjovem.pt/?id_tema=241

Index

aborigines, Australian 36
Abraham 13, 131, 132, 133
abstinence, fasting and 21
advertising 60
Afghanistan 68
allocentrics 5
Anatolia 180–182
animals, sacrifice of 134–135
animism 3
Arafat, plain of 132–133
architecture, Buddhist 107
Arthur Rank Centre, Warwickshire, UK 73
attractions
    definitions 65
    purpose-built 37, 69
    symbolic transformation 161–183
austerity 21, 38–39

Bahrain Islamic Insurance Company 205
Ballylanders, County Limerick 27
Banneux, Belgium
    development 143–144, 145, 146(fig)
        150(fig) 151
    origin as sanctuary town 140–141
basilicas: in sanctuary towns 143–144
Beco, Mariette 140
belief: not essential to religious tourism 37–38
'Black Madonnas' 55
Black Stone 132
Braj, Uttar Pradesh *see* Vrindavan, India

Buddhism 17, 99–100, 103–106, 106–107,
    108
business: Islamic principles 200–201
Butler, Richard 147–149

Canterbury Tales, The 18–19, 41
Caribbean 114–118
    paradise imagery 122–124
    Turks and Caicos Islands 118–121
Caribbean Tourism Organization 120
carnival 115–117
Castells, Manuel 166–167
cathedrals *see* churches and cathedrals
CEE countries 49–50, 56–57
'centre of the world' 52
China
    Buddhism 99–100, 103–104, 106–110
    Christianity 106–107
    Confucius 104
    destinations of religious tourism 103–104,
        105
    economic benefits of religious
        tourism 108
    environmental issues 108–109
    interest in religion 105–106
    Islam 104, 106–107
    reform and religious tourism 104
    religious art 107–108
    Taoism 105, 106–107
    Temple Fairs 99

Christianity
  in China 106–107
  significance of Turkey 181
  see also Church of England; Roman
    Catholicism
Church of England
  evangelization 68, 74–75
  problems of rural communities 70
churches and cathedrals
  basilicas in sanctuary towns 143–144
  cathedral visitor numbers 67
  problems and issues 69–70, 71
  promotion of visits 67–68
  UK case study 70–73
Ciudad de Cultura project, Santiago de
    Compostela 165–166
commodification 8
communism, pilgrimages under 56–57
communitas 52
Como Shambhala Spa, Parrot Cay 120–121
Confucius 104
conversion *see* evangelization and conversion
Cornwall 71–72
Council of Europe 158
Croagh Patrick, County Mayo 23–24
Croatia
  Marija Bistrica *see* Marija Bistrica, Croatia
  role of Catholic Church 50
culture
  importance to tourism 5
  and reconstructed ethnicity 117
  restoration of cultural identity 118–120

day trips: definition 64–65
developing countries: paradise imagery
    122–123
Druidry 66–67
Durkheim, Emil 51

ecotravellers 93
Edison, Thomas 17
El Camino Frances: secularization 157–159
Eliade, Mircea 51, 52
environment: and religious tourism 108–109
Epworth, Lincolnshire, UK 66
ethnicity, reconstructed 117
Europe and cultural heritage 163
European Cultural Itineraries 158
evangelization and conversion (Christian) 68,
    74–75, 78
expectancy theory 43–44

factors, hygiene and motivating 42
Faith Tourism Project, Turkey 181
fasting and abstinence 21
Fátima, Portugal
  development 144, 146, 147(fig), 150(fig)
    152, 217–218
  history of tourism 218–219
  location 211–212
  Marian cult 213–215
  nature of apparitions 215–216
  origin as sanctuary town 141
  political hostility 216–217
  Portuguese way of life 212–213
Fleming, Ian 123
fords: objects of Indian pilgrimage 184
Freud, Sigmund 17

gaze
  mystic 90, 91, 92
  tourist 155
globalization 16–17, 163
  and Irish pilgrimage 29–31
'glocalization' 29
Grand Tour 154
gypsies, Irish 27–28

Hadith 128–129, 204, 209
hajj *see under* Islam
Hardy, Dixon 20–21
Herzberg's two-factor theory of motivation
    42–43
Hidden Britain initiative 73–74
Hinduism *see under* India
Holy Island, East Clare, Ireland 20–21
hygiene factors 42–43

Ihram 129
Inca trail 93–95
Incas 91
India
  development of organized religious travel
    187–188
  pilgrimage
    case study *see* Vrindavan, India
    characteristics 38–39
    modern variant 185
    traditional pilgrimage 184–185

information *see* media: for communication and
    promotion
insurance
  for pilgrimages in India 187–188
  Islamic *see under* Islam
Ireland *see also* Knock, Ireland
  Catholic pilgrimage rituals 20–21, 23–24
  early church and pilgrimage 20
  holy wells 25–28
  inbound pilgrimage 31
  overseas pilgrimage 28–29
  pilgrimage and globalization 29–31
  sites of pilgrimage 21–25
  visitor statistics 22(fig) 23
Irish Pilgrimage Trust 28
Islam
  business principles 200–201
  in China 104, 106–107
  glossary 208–210
  hajj: obligatory pilgrimage to Mecca
      (Makkah)
    edicts in Hadith 128–129
    entry into Ihram 129
    historical basis 130
    the Ka'aba 131–132, 135
    obligation 8, 17, 127–128, 130
    personal experiences 135–137
    risks 199
    route 132–133
    rules of animal sacrifice 134–135
    types of pilgrimage 129–130
    versus Western view of pilgrimage
        137–138
  insurance
    case study: Takafal International 205–207
    concept of protection 204
    idea of cooperation 204
    Islamic *(takaful)* versus classic insurance
        201–203
    reasons for not having 199–200
    recent trends 205
  Muslim population around the world 200
  socio-economic principles 203
  umra: optional pilgrimage to Mecca
      (Makkah) 199

Jerusalem 102
Joe Walsh Tours, Ireland 28, 29
Judaism 17, 181
Jung, C.G. 117

Ka'aba 131–132, 135
Knock, Ireland 24–25
  development 144, 145–146, 150(fig) 151
  origin as sanctuary town 141–142
Krishna 188, 189, 191

lakes, sacred 103–104
Lent 116
Lincoln Cathedral 67
Lonely Planet Guide 123
Lough Derg, County Donegal 21–23
Lourdes, France
  commercialization 156
  development 144, 146–147, 148(fig)
        150(fig) 152
  Irish pilgrims 29
  origin as sanctuary town 142
  typical image of pilgrimage 66

MacCannell, Dean 137, 154–155
Machu Picchu
  methods of access 93–95
  role in New Age tourism 89, 90–92
Makkah *see under* Islam
Malcolm X 135–136
management: of pilgrimage sites
  products and services 58–59
  promotion and communication 60–61
  target groups 57–58, 59
Marija Bistrica, Croatia
  basis of local Marian cult 55–56
  promotion and communication 60–61
  services and products 58–59
  site characteristics 59–60
  social context of pilgrimage 56–57
  target groups 57–58, 59
Marley, Bob 123
Mary, cult of 24, 27, 28–29
  see also Banneux, Belgium; Fátima, Portugal;
        Knock, Ireland; Lourdes, France;
        Marija Bistrica, Croatia
Mashhad, Iran 68
Maslow's hierarchy of needs 40–41
mass tourism 5, 154
  conflict of interests with spirituality 68
Mecca *see under* Islam
media: for communication and promotion 60
  UK rural churches 72–74
meditation 91

Medjugorje 29
mementos 55
Mina 133
miracles 59
missionaries: from Ireland 20
models: development of tourist destination
        147–152
motivations
    content theories 40–43
    effect on behaviour 39
    for pilgrimages *see under* pilgrimages
    process theories 43–44
    of visitors to village churches 68
motivators 42
Mould, Pochin 15
mountains, sacred 103–104, 105, 107, 108,
        110
Muhammad 128, 130
'mystic gaze' 90, 91, 92

nature, culture of 95–96
needs: Maslow's hierarchy 40–41
Nepal 36
New Age
    and Machu Picchu 89, 90–93
    retreats 120–121
    search for visions 92–93
    use of the body 91–92
New Moral Tourism 120, 164

offerings, votive 26–27
ownership, spiritual: of heritage sites 67

package tours 61
Padre Pio: canonization 28
paganism 66–67
pandas (Hindu) 189–190, 191
Papal Council for the Pastoral of the Migrants
        and Itinerants 78, 79, 80
Parrot Cay, Turks and Caicos Islands 120–121
Pattern Festival, Ballylanders, County Limerick
        27
pilgrimages
    academic perceptions 80–82
    approaches to study 51–52
    and austerity 21, 38–39
    definitions and characteristics 16, 37, 38,
        64, 79, 81–82

distinction from tourism: implications
        39–40
    economic impacts 66
    historical patterns 56–57
    important in all major religions 17–18
    in India *see under* India
    linear versus circular direction 38
    to Mecca *see under* Islam
    motivations 18–20, 45–46, 80–81, 158,
        191
        backlash against science 49
        family holidays 56, 192–193
        other non-religious 53–54
        penance 20
        spiritual 50–53, 78–80
    origin of tourism 99
    pilgrimage site management *see under*
        management
    pilgrims' experiences 81–82, 192
    secularization of pilgrimage routes 156,
        157–159, 190–192
    souvenirs 55
    theoretical approaches 51–53
    versus tourism 9, 31, 45–46, 53–54,
        82–86, 184, 186–187
        implications of the difference 39–40
Pope John Paul II 28
Portugal *see* Fátima, Portugal
postmodernism 3

Qur'an 128, 131, 139, 203
qurbani 134–135

religion
    believer statistics 99(tab)
    categorization 3–4
    definitions 1, 2, 17, 64
    function 117
    non-institutional alternatives 2
    secular 'religion' 38
    versus science 48–49
retreats 118–120
rituals 39
    during hajj 129, 132–135
    Hindu 190, 192
    Irish Catholics 20–21, 23–24
    sightseeing as ritual 7, 83, 154–155
    'softer' alternatives 22
rivers: objects of Indian pilgrimage 184

Roman Catholicism
  evangelization 78
  pilgrimage rituals 20–21, 23–24
  role in CEE countries 49–50
  sanctuary towns
    consecration of seers 143
    development process 143–147
    origins 140–143
    prospective analysis 147–152
  view of pilgrimage 78–80
    contrasted with tourism 84
running 95
Ruskin, John 154

sacrifice, animal 134–135
safety, personal 36
Santiago de Compostela, Spain 157
  Ciudad de Cultura project 165–166
Saudi Arabia 68
Schumacher, E.F. 109
science versus religion 48–49, 80
Sea of Galilee Theme Park 69
Shari'ah 200, 201, 203, 206, 210
Shinto 17
shrines
  definition and characteristics 37, 51
  Mashhad, Iran 68
  meaning and role 79–80
  as political arenas 50
'sight sacrilization' 137, 154
sightseeing
  as ritual 7, 154–155
Sites and Monuments Record, Ireland 26
Soubirous, Bernadette 142
souvenirs 55
spaces
  enclavic versus heterogenous 7
  interconnections with society 166–167
  religious: definition 8
  and urban identity 164–165
Spain
  contemporary tourism 156–157
  secularization of El Camino Frances
        157–159
  see also Santiago de Compostela,
        Spainspectacles, creation of 7
spirituality
  conflict of interests with mass tourism 68
  in a secular society 66–67
  New Age *see* New Age
St Bernadette 142

St Brigit's well, Liscannor, County Clare 26
St Helens Church, Darley Dale, UK 71
Stonehenge 67
superstition 28
sustainability 5–6

Takafal International 205–207
takaful (Islamic insurance) *see under* Islam
Taliban 68
Taoism 105, 106–107
  role of environment 108
Tawaf 132(fig) 135
Temple Fairs, China 99
theme parks 69
Thomas Cook (travel agency) 154
Tibet 103–104
tourism
  definitions 2–3, 36–38, 54, 64–65, 100,
        101
  development and growth 4–5, 100
    impact of cultural backgrounds 101–102
  economic impact 66, 67, 108, 172
  interactions of religious tourism with other
        types 65–66
  lay tourists and religious tourism 100–101
  mass tourism *see* mass tourism
  modes of experience 54
  New Moral Tourism 120, 164
  origins and definitions 4
  as postmodern pilgrimage 123
  psychographic typology of tourists 5
  versus pilgrimage *see under* pilgrimages
tourist gaze 155
trails: historical significance 155–156
travel: historical changes 153–154
travellers, Irish 27–28
Trsat, Croatia 56
Turin Shroud 69
Turkey
  future prospects and strategies for religious
        tourism 182–183
  reasons for visiting 180(tab)
  significance of religious tourism 180–182
  tourist accommodation 174(tab)
  tourist numbers and spending 173(tab)
    visitors from Asia and Australasia
        178(tab)
    visitors from Eastern and Southern Europe
        176(tab)
    visitors from North Africa 179(tab)

visitors from North and South America
and Middle East 177(tab)
visitors from Western Europe and
Scandinavia 175(tab)
Turks and Caicos Islands
restoration of cultural identity 118–120
spiritual retreats 120–121
Turner, Victor and Edith 51, 52–53
two-factor theory of motivation 42–43

umra 199
UNESCO 158
statistics on religions 99(tab)
United Kingdom
churches and cathedrals
cathedral visit statistics 67
income streams from visitors 72(tab)
information provision 72–74
problems and issues 69–70, 71
promotion of vists 67–68
significance of rural churches 70–71
economic impact of tourism 66, 67, 72
Hidden Britain initiative 73–74
paganism 66–67

Vaishnava bhakti movement 188
valence 44

vigils, prayer 21
visions and apparitions 24
Vrindavan, India
commercialization 193–194
loss of 'sacred sightseeing' 193
motivation for pilgrimage 191, 192–193
pilgrims' experience 192
rituals 190, 192
secularization of modern pilgrimage
190–192
significance and location of Braj and
Vrindavan 188
traditional pilgrimage 189–190
transport 191–192
types of pilgrimage 188–189

wells, holy 25–28
Wesley, John 66
extent of travel 8–9
World Tourism Organization 172
World Youth Day 28
Wuqoof of Arafat 133

York Minster 67

zakat 203, 210

DH

203.
51
REL